The Rationality of Perception

The Rationality of Perception

Susanna Siegel

OXFORD
UNIVERSITY PRESS

OXFORD
UNIVERSITY PRESS

Great Clarendon Street, Oxford, OX2 6DP,
United Kingdom

Oxford University Press is a department of the University of Oxford.
It furthers the University's objective of excellence in research, scholarship,
and education by publishing worldwide. Oxford is a registered trade mark of
Oxford University Press in the UK and in certain other countries

First Edition published in 2017

Impression: 1

Published in the United States of America by Oxford University Press
198 Madison Avenue, New York, NY 10016, United States of America

British Library Cataloguing in Publication Data
Data available

Library of Congress Control Number: 2016949363

ISBN 978-0-19-879708-1

Printed in Great Britain by
Clays Ltd, St Ives plc

for Zoe O. Siegelnickel

Contents

Part III. Applications

Introduction to Part III

List of Tables

Preface

In 2007, I went on vacation to Tulum, México with my mother and my two-year old daughter. I was finishing my first book, *The Contents of Visual Experience*, which I wrote because I wanted to understand which properties we can be presented with in conscious visual perception. In that book I argued that in conscious visual perception, which I called "visual experience," we're presented with all sorts of complex properties—not just color, shape, luminance, and motion, but also kind properties (such as being a tree, or a bicycle, or a dog), causal properties (such as the property a cat can have of being supported by a hammock, or the property a knife can have of slicing through a piece of bread), and even personal identity (such as the property of being John Malkovich). I had set aside the epistemological question about visual experience that had shaped much of the discussion of perception in analytic philosophy during the twentieth century: whether, and how, perception can provide justification for everyday beliefs about ordinary things, such as the belief that there's mustard in your fridge. Like many philosophers, including many who wrote long before there was such a thing as analytic philosophy, I found this question irresistible to think about. But the answer seemed to depend on what kind of mental phenomenon visual experience was. Did experiences even purport to tell us about ordinary things, like bicycles and mustard jars? If so, what could it purport to tell us about these things? Perception is indispensable to every type of inquiry, from the curiosity-driven (are any birds at the feeder?) to the practical (is the mustard in the fridge? who just stepped in to the elevator?) and the scientific (what color does sulfur burn?). The role of perception in justifying external-world beliefs will depend heavily on what perception tells us about the external world. Settling on an answer to that question makes it clearer what one is asking, when one asks what role perceptual experience plays in justifying beliefs.

My analysis in *The Contents of Visual Experience* drew on the claim that being able to visually recognize things such as your own neighborhood, pine trees, or John Malkovich can influence how those things look to you when you see them. I took it for granted that these influences on perceptual experience are possible. It still seems plain to me that they are. My vacation did what vacations should do: it brought my mind away from the book I was writing, but also helped me see its cornerstones more clearly. And by the sea, an epistemic question about the phenomenon I was writing about began to bother me. If your ability to recognize John Malkovich, your neighborhood, or pine trees could change the way these things look to you when you see them, then couldn't beliefs, desires, or fears do the same? And if your prior beliefs could influence your experiences, how could your experience go on to strengthen those very beliefs? Reminded daily of the marvel of birth by my young child's existence, I thought of the story (probably apocryphal) about the seventeenth-century Dutch preformationists, who triumphantly claimed to see embryos in sperm cells.[1] At the time, microscopes had only recently been invented. Imagine looking into the hitherto invisible structure of the physical world! What a thrill to look behind the appearances, and find evidence for what you suspected was true all along: that humans reproduce by sowing a seed that contains miniature, pre-formed humans. From these fictional preformationists' point of view, what they saw using the new scientific instruments gave them evidence for preformationism.

Anyone narrating this fiction could feel its absurdity. It was almost a comedy. A moment of seemingly scientific discovery with its gleeful "I knew it!" turns out to be nothing more than the machinations of the inquirer's own mind. What should a person in such a situation believe? I was gripped by the fact that for this realistically complex fictional hero, as for many others, the concepts of blame and responsibility seemed to have no clear application. Could you blame the fictional preformationist for strengthening his belief after looking in the microscope, when you considered how things looked from his point of view? Not really. Yet since the problem originates in his own mind, what else besides his mind is there to blame? The epistemic situation seemed to call for normative notions that allowed us to consider the preformationist's situation by viewing it from outside their point of view. The normative notion that mattered, it seemed to me, had to allow that the kind of epistemic support our preformationist hero failed to get from his experience was

---

[1] For a book-length study of seventeenth- and eighteenth-century preformationism that traces the life of this story, see Pinto-Correia (1997).

also a kind that he could have gotten, if his experience had come about in a different way. The fact that his experience failed him seemed independent of whether he could be blamed for believing his eyes.

The more I turned this epistemic problem around in my mind, the more of its complexities came into view. I initially favored a simple approach to the epistemic role of perceptual experience. Normally, merely by seeing an ordinary scene, such as the inside of one's refrigerator, one gets excellent reason to believe that things are the way they appear. I was drawn to this simple approach because it gave a lot of weight to perceptual experience, and in countless everyday cases, perceptual experience carries this weight easily. If it looks to you as if there's mustard in the fridge, then unless you have good reason to think things aren't as they appear, you get good reason to believe that there's mustard in the fridge. And even if the property of being mustard in the fridge is too complex a property for perceptual experience alone to attribute, perceptual experience makes it reasonable for you to believe that what you see has less complex properties, such as color and shape, and helps make it reasonable to believe that the fridge contains mustard.

The preformationist's situation seemed to complicate this simple approach. It made me think that the weight that experience could carry in justifying belief was sensitive to the route by which the experience came to occur in the subject's mind. If experience could be an artifact of a prior belief, suspicion, or preference for preformation, then it seemed susceptible to something like confirmation bias. In Tulum, I began to write "Cognitive Penetrability and Perceptual Justification" in an effort to identify the most basic constraints that the preformationist case placed on perceptual justification, and the theories of perceptual justification that could meet them. That paper, which the journal *Nous* accepted in 2009, was my first attempt to understand the contours of the epistemological problem. It seemed to me that the constraints placed by the problem could be met by many theories of justification, but not by the most straightforward one, known as phenomenal conservatism. According to this position, merely having a perceptual experience suffices to provide prima-facie justification for believing suitably related contents. Such extraordinary power belongs to perceptual experience, on this view, thanks to its *phenomenal character*: the subjective aspects of experience that characterize how the world looks to the subject, in having the experience. Phenomenal conservatism appeals strongly to many philosophers, and

I felt the appeal myself. It answers a basic question in a way that simply rings true: When you look in the fridge, why is it reasonable for you to believe that mustard is on the shelf?—Because it looks that way. And its looking that way partly constitutes your perceptual experience. Yet this appealing approach seemed unable to respect the complexities of cases like the preformationist's. The role of experiences in justifying beliefs might be saved, but that role could not be supported purely by phenomenal character.

I found this conclusion disturbing. It opened more questions for me than it settled. This book grew out of my attempts to answer them. The pressures that shaped my answers came from three corners: epistemology, psychology, and politics. Here is how they combined to produce this book.

From epistemology, I felt pressure to understand the implications of possible cases like the preformationist's on our knowledge of the world. If such cases were pervasive, would they obstruct the route from perception to reasonable belief? To make progress with this question, I felt I had to identify what, if anything, saps the preformationist's experience of its power to justify his belief that the sperm cell contains an embryo. What was the epistemic culprit? I had convinced myself in "Cognitive Penetrability and Epistemic Justification" that there were bad-making features in the preformation case and others like it, including cases in which perception is influenced in ways that fall outside the narrowly defined category of cognitive penetration. But I didn't know what the bad-making features were. And not knowing what they were made it hard to assess the extent to which they preclude gaining reasonable belief about the external world from perception. The mere fact that an experience is influenced by one's prior outlook is often innocuous. Sometimes it is even beneficial, as when expertise allows one to see a tumor in an X-ray. What made the difference between epistemically good influences on perceptual experiences from within one's mind, and epistemically bad ones?

From psychology, an obvious pressing question was whether cases like these really are pervasive, and indeed whether they occur at all. I set out to learn more about the kinds of influences a mind could harbor between perception and one's other mental states. Are perceptual experiences ever actually influenced in the ways depicted by the preformationist scenario? I knew the long-standing controversy surrounding cognitive penetration. At the level of theoretical psychology, the controversy plays out in debates over the role of stored information and past experience in perceptual processing. At the level of experimental work, there are many paradigms that purport to show these kinds of influence on perception. These experiments come from the labs of psychologists aiming to revive the questions posed by New Look psychologists of the 1970s.[2] Other experiments come from researchers working at the intersection of vision science and social psychology—two fields that for a long time had little to do with one another.[3] There is also a host of spirited attempts to rebut individual experiments at the level of their specific methods.[4]

It is not hard to find evidence that judgments and other behavior are influenced by prior beliefs and presumptions—that conclusion is hardly news. But which of these effects, if any, are effects on perceptual experience? Which are effects on properly perceptual processing, whether that processing culminates in experience or in unconscious perception? These questions are the ones with controversial answers. Many experiments leave open the possibility that influences on behavior and judgment operate through influence on perceptual experience: gray bananas are categorized as more yellowish than gray patches; a face is matched to a darker or lighter patch depending on the racial label placed under it; faces in a continuum are seen to shift from pleased to angry at a lower threshold by physically abused children compared to children who have not been abused; a mild human collision is seen as aggressive or playful depending on the race of the shover; a boy in a photograph said to be accused of a felony is estimated to be older when the child is black than when he is white or latino.[5]

I eventually came to think that the epistemological questions didn't depend on how these controversies got resolved. Perception in the narrowest senses allowed by psychology is a category at one extreme, and perception in the broad sense encompassing judgments about a

[2] Bruner (1973). One group of researchers collaborate with Dennis Proffitt (Bhalla and Proffitt (1999), Proffitt et al. (2003), Schnall et al. (2008), Witt and Proffitt (2005), Witt et al. (2005)). For a review of other work, see Collins and Olson (2014).

[3] The papers in Adams et al. (2010) attempt to bring these fields together.

[4] A small sample includes Fodor (1984) and (1988), Durgin et al. (2009), Russell and Durgin (2008), Firestone and Scholl (2015).

[5] Bananas: Witzel et al. (2011) and Olkkonen et al. (2008), Hansen et al. (2006), Goldstone (1995); Faces: Levin and Banaji (2006), Anger: Pollak and Sinha (2002); Shoving: Duncan (1976), Sagar and Schofield (1980); Age: Goff et al. (2014).

situation is a category at the other extreme. Between the two extremes, perceptual experiences are the conscious dimensions of perception that subjects respond to in forming judgments. As a phenomenological category, perceptual experience—the conscious dimension of the sensory modalities (vision, touch, audition, taste, smell), and of their interaction—seems well-defined, even if it is an open question which processes in the mind actually give rise to it.[6] Some opponents of the cognitive penetration of perception, such as Zenon Pylyshyn, work with a category of perception distinct from perceptual experience. When Pylyshyn claims there are no "top-down"-influences on perception, he is talking about early vision.[7] But there is more to visual experience than the products of early vision, and there is more to perceptual experience than purely visual experience, due to the other sensory modalities and their interaction.

More importantly, even for scientists who were talking about perceptual experience, or who claimed to be, the epistemological questions seemed indifferent to whether such influences actually occurred. We want to know, in epistemology, what epistemic powers perceptual experiences have, and we think we can find this out by considering non-actual situations. Just as experimental scientists use controls to rule out confounds, philosophers use hypothetical situations to isolate some factors and screen out others. We isolate factors in this way to help us understand what difference they may make to a subject's epistemic situation. As a piece of history, the preformationist story would probably be fraudulent. And to categorize its fiction as psychologically realistic might turn out to be overreaching. But with all their artificiality, fictional cases play as important a role in epistemology as controlled experiments play in science. I use fictional cases to discuss my basic epistemological question: what epistemic impact on perceptual experience can beliefs, fears, desires, or other psychological precursors to it have?

I knew I could make the question more exact by specifying the kind of influences at issue. Here bloomed another set of complications. Consider the many parameters along which routes from psychological states to experience can vary: experiences could arise through "cognitive"

---

[6] For more discussion of the category of perceptual experience, see Siegel (2016) and (2010) ch. 1.

[7] Pylyshyn (1999).

influences of expertise, fear, preferences, or through perceptual learning (processes internal to perceptual systems); through Bayesian inferences (either within or across the boundaries between perception and cognition), or inferences of other kinds, or non-inferential processes. And the differences multiply when one factors in differences in the format and structure of the influencing states alone—such as whether those states are associations, belief-like representations, desire-like motivations, pure affect, fears, or some combination; what kind of representation, if any, they involve; and so on. Which of those psychological differences make a difference to the epistemic impact on perceptual experience? And why? These questions are not answerable by experimental methods. But they are nonetheless related to psychology in a different way. The questions let us formulate hypotheses about different routes to experience. Each of these routes involve different potential psychological mechanisms.

I gradually came to think that the distinctions that mattered in psychology mattered much less in epistemology. I wanted to know what kinds of relationships between experiences and their psychological precursors had an epistemic impact on those experiences, and I didn't see any reason to assume at the outset that there was a psychological configuration, or set of them, that aligned exactly with those epistemic relationships. Moreover, in all of the examples that seemed to pose the kind of epistemic problem illustrated by the preformationist, the types of influencing states had something in common: they formed an antecedent *outlook* of the subject on the world. So I thought it would be best to try and identify what the epistemological relationships were between antecedent outlooks and perceptual experience.

At this point, the central idea of this book came into focus. Perceptual experiences themselves—or more exactly, the state of a subject's having the experience, or the event of their undergoing it—could manifest an epistemic status in the same way beliefs do. Experiences could thereby enter the calculus that determines in the most general way how rational or how irrational a subject is. And like the epistemic status of beliefs as justified or anti-justified, the epistemic status of experiences could be affected by how they are formed.[8] Just as beliefs could be formed

---

[8] Since "un-justified" is ambiguous between having negative justificatory status and lacking either positive or negative justificatory status altogether, I use "anti-justified" here to denote the state of having negative justificatory status. The terms "rational" and

epistemically badly, for instance if they resulted from wishful thinking, or if they were unduly influenced by fears, the same could happen to experiences. Locating experiences on the same dimensions of epistemic evaluation as beliefs provided an answer to the epistemic questions that had been hanging over me ever since I began thinking about the pre-formationists. What was the epistemic culprit in the preformationist case? Wishful seeing. Why didn't cognitive penetration per se always have epistemically bad effects? Because it is not always an irrational route to belief.

The approach to perception in these answers provided a framework for describing the ways in which what seems commonsensical can be deeply shaped by cultural forces. Perception is the underside of common sense. When something seems obvious, you seem to be able to just see it. And in many situations, you can. When you peer into the fridge looking for mustard, it can be obvious that a jar of mustard is there. But in other types of perceptual situations, what seems commonsensical and even obvious in perception is shaped directly by highly specific cultural forces. The psychologist J. J. Gibson appreciated this point. He used the concept of affordances to suggest that social configurations, despite their cultural contingency, are perceivable as plainly as any other information conveyed by vision. In his discussion of affordances, he wrote:

What other persons afford, for man, comprise the whole realm of social significance. We pay the closest attention to the optical information that specifies what the other person is, what he invites, what he threatens, and what he does. For each of these kinds of affordance the question we must ask is, how is it perceived?[9]

The realm of social significance includes the realm of social value. Think of the experience of feeling summed up at a glance, for better or worse. When this happens, of all the human interactions that are possible in a situation, it is as if some of those possibilities are foregrounded, and others pushed into the background, and still others are off the radar. One's sense of this modal profile can be more accurate or less accurate, since there is no doubt that in every interaction, some possibilities of

---

"irrational" have many uses in philosophy, psychology, and elsewhere. In Chapter 2, section 2.1, I explain the meaning they have in this book. Until then, a specific definition won't be needed.

[9] Gibson (1977).

interactions really are closer and others farther away. In the hypothesis that we can have perceptual experiences of affordances, I found a way to describe how social hierarchies that are culturally contingent can nevertheless make themselves felt as normal, and even, for some people, as part of common sense.

This idea unlocked the political dimensions of the phenomenon illustrated by the preformationist. These dimensions provided the third set of pressures that shaped this book. Since political phenomena are best illustrated with examples from specific times and places, I decided to focus on a phenomenon close to (my) home and central to US history. The annals of American history are replete with narratives in which racialized identities of being white or black are taken for granted. In some such narratives, which take place in public spaces—elevators, sidewalks, parks, schoolrooms, or retail stores, for example—a white perceiver instantly perceives a black perceiver as dangerous, threatening, or out of place. Sometimes the results are quietly insulting, as when white perceivers feel they must cross the street or clutch their belongings to maintain their sense of security. Other times, the white perceiver's fear, disdain, or discomfiture results in aggression or violence, rather than silent aversion. Narratives like these can be found in political science, psychology, criminology, legal scholarship, American history, and myriad art forms—memoir, fiction, poetry, music, film, television series—where these dynamics are discussed, depicted, or re-enacted.[10]

One can't read off the contents of anyone's perceptual experience from the narratives that depict this well-documented dimension of American public life. That's because the distinction between perceptual experience and judgment matters mainly in the context of discussing philosophical problems about perception and epistemology. And though the range of contexts in which these familiar narratives occur is very wide, it has not typically included academic discussions of epistemic problems about perception. What we can infer from the phenomenon behind the familiar narrative is that purely as a function of someone's outlook, a minimal

---

[10] The occurrences of this narrative would be too numerous to list, and even cursory familiarity with American culture from outside observers is likely to encompass them. For a contemporary analysis and discussion of this dimension of social meaning in America by political scientists, see Lerman and Weaver (2014), ch. 5, and for a popular depiction of it in the form of memoir, see Coates (2015).

social situation consisting simply of perception can on the one hand become a social trading of racialized fears, or an exchange of fear for incredulity or resentment, or on other hand it can be a humdrum moment in a stretch of uneventful neutrality, undeserving of study or artistic re-enactment. The familiarity of this pervasive narrative warrants a metaphorical attribution, to a cultural milieu, of the presumption that black men are dangerous—as if a milieu were the kind of thing that can make presumptions. Why black *men* in particular? In the interests of specificity, I decided to focus on only one of the explicitly gendered forms of this presumption—the one most commonly articulated.[11]

Thinking through the political dimension of perception using the example of the narrative I've described has shaped this inquiry in two ways.

First, it convinced me that perceptual experiences themselves can be epistemically weakened by their psychological precursors. Cases like the preformationist's had brought the problem into focus for me, which meant that they left me feeling the force of both sides of the problem: the side from which the preformatist's experience of sperm cells in the embryo seemed *just as powerful* as it could be, without being influenced by favoring preformationism; and the side from which the experience seemed to be *made less powerful* by this influence. In contrast, the political examples seem to be ones in which the second of these two sides was more compelling than the first. The political cases showed me which way to tip the balance in cases like the preformationist.

Second, the political example raised a scaled-up version of the epistemic question with which I began. The scaled-up question concerned the epistemic relationship between a person's cultural context and the marks it leaves on their mind. I was most interested in a special case of this relationship: the case in which a person's mind recapitulates a culturally entrenched presumption. My question was this: if the culturally entrenched presumption was epistemically ill-founded, and someone whose social position allowed them to absorb the presumption with ease

---

[11] Arguably, the presumptions that rationalize white aversion to sharing public spaces and institutions with blacks in the US have long been gendered (Cooper 1872). Some of the ways in which they affect black girls and women is discussed in a contemporary context by Crenshaw (2015) and Morris (2016). I thank Lauren Woomer for discussion of this point.

made it their own, would the recapitulation of the presumption in that individual's mind be ill-founded as well?

In considering this epistemic question, I encountered a problem isomorphic to the problem concerning the preformationist. Whereas that the preformationist's problem concerns a relationship within an individual's mind, this problem concerns the interface between individual minds and cultural milieu. Like the intra-personal epistemic problem, this epistemic problem consists of two conflicting ideas.

The first idea was that even if the presumption in what I decided to call "the mind of world" is ill-founded, the result of an individual's absorbing it need not be.[12] Here I was reminded of how elusive the notions of blame and responsibility proved to be, in the case of the preformationist. One could not obviously be individually blamed on the usual grounds for absorbing a culturally pervasive outlook. Nor was one responsible, initially, for such absorption, at least not in the usual ways. And these facts could seem to suggest that alongside the moral obtuseness and political oblivion of an individual—most realistically, a white individual whose ordinary life tends not to be shared with black relatives or friends—there might be nothing epistemically wrong with this individual's presumption that black men are dangerous.

But on the other hand, the second idea, at odds with the first, was that there did seem to be epistemic shortcomings of the individual who absorbs this outlook from his cultural milieu. The observations about blamelessness seemed orthogonal to the epistemic standing of the outlook that some people absorb. If the source of the individual's presumption is an ill-founded presumption in the mind of the world, why shouldn't the individual inherit the ill-foundedness?

This problem seemed to me to admit of the same kind of solution as the intrapersonal problem illustrated by the preformationist. From the point of view of the person whose social position allows them to absorb the socially normal presumption with ease, the presumption seemed commonsensical. The idea that it could nonetheless be epistemically unsupported fit together with my core idea that perceptual experiences

---

[12] I unpack the metaphor of the mind of the world in Chapter 10, and argue that it earns its explanatory keep. The *world* in the metaphor is a cultural world, and minds of worlds are as numerous as cultural milieu.

could be irrational, even if they are experienced by the perceiver as the ground of common sense.

I could anticipate many responses to my use of the political example, including this one: perhaps it was impolitic or disturbing to say so, but wasn't the presumption in the United States that black men (or a subset of black men) are dangerous in some sense reasonable? I imagined and encountered several versions of this response. My answers to them are in Chapter 10. It seemed that I had to solve the scaled-up problem, because it arose from the political example that led me to my confidence in the Rationality of Perception, and it played that dialectical role most powerfully on the assumption that the racial attitude—the attitude that hijacked perception—was ill-founded.

My idea was that just as beliefs can inherit the rational standing of their psychological precursors, such as a racial attitude, so can experiences. If such an attitude led a perceiver to jump to the conclusion that a man they saw as racially black was also dangerous, that route to the conclusion would be at least as epistemically poor as the presumption itself. In drawing this conclusion, the perceiver would be irrational. My core idea was that the same would be true of a perceiver whose perceptual experience itself was shaped by the presumption. In having the perceptual experience of the person as dangerous, the perceiver was irrational, because that perceptual experience arose from an unreasonable presumption.

At first, my core idea seemed like overkill. Wouldn't it be enough to account for the preformationism case, the political example, and others like them, if experiences simply lost their power to support subsequent beliefs? Why not stop short of the idea that perceptual experiences can be rational or irrational, and settle instead for the traditional position that takes perceptual experiences to be beyond reproach? The more cautious position seemed to account for the central epistemic phenomenon, but left intact the picture that had grown entrenched in epistemology: perceptual experiences can provide justification, but cannot be justified or anti-justified in themselves. In contrast, the fuller position accounts for the phenomena in a way that overturns the entrenched assumption that perceptual experience stops at the threshold of the house of reason.

Both positions have similar motivations. It seemed to me worth exploring the fullest version of the idea, rather than stopping at the highly circumscribed, less disruptive one. In philosophical situations like these, it is often illuminating to anchor a discussion to a more extreme position, especially when it is simpler, and then see what, if anything, forces one away from it. If one keeps the more extreme position out of view, it can be harder to assess whether it really is less plausible than its more measured cousin. Both positions, I found, have a lot of explaining to do. And the more I explored considerations against the idea that experiences can manifest an epistemic status like justification, the less powerful those considerations seemed. This discovery made me view my initial instinct to favor the measured position as a habitual rehearsal of philosophical caution, rather than a stopping point demanded by intellectual rigor.[13]

The less measured, more extreme view offers a cleaner account of the epistemic situation than the moderate view. Once it is granted that absorbing an outlook can make one less reasonable, it seems to pull the punch to deny that perceptual experiences shaped by the outlook do the same. *The Rationality of Perception* is an attempt to see what the epistemology of perception looks like if perceptual experiences can be rational or irrational. To see what it looks like, what's needed is an account of what exactly it would mean for perceptual experiences to be rational or irrational, how it could be that perceptual experiences could be formed rationally or irrationally, and what epistemic roles perceptual experiences would then play. Such an account can be provided only by describing these roles in detail, and clarifying the concepts used to describe them. And that is what this book does. What better register for probing these topics than analytic philosophy, with its ear for new questions, its respect for complexity, its caution with common sense, and its patience with the realm of the possible?

---

[13] My initial instinct framed the discussion in Siegel (2013a).

PART I

The Problem and Its Solution

1

The Problem of Hijacked Experience

Vivek is a vain performer. To him, the faces in the audience range in their expression from neutral to pleased. Remarkably, no one ever looks disapproving. In the past, Vivek was under-confident. In those days, to him, the faces in the audience ranged in their expression from neutral to displeased. But remarkably, no one ever looked approving. Vivek's vanity or diffidence influenced the character of his perception. Depending on his self-conception, how a scene looked to him differed, even when all other conditions stayed the same.

Vanity of Vivek's sort is just one among many potential examples of irrational perception. Influences on perception could come from beliefs, hypotheses, knowledge, desires, traits, and moods.[1] They could also come from evaluative states that psychologists call "attitudes." Attitudes encode attributions of value or disvalue to situations, objects, companies, individual people, or groups.[2]

Attitudes and the other mental states just listed all belong to a subject's outlook on the world. When someone's outlook influences what she perceives on a given occasion, her perception is shaped by the outlook she had prior to perceiving on that occasion.

Let's look more closely at what kind of perceptual state can bear the marks of a prior outlook. We can distinguish between perceptual

---

[1] R. W. Emerson (1844) makes vivid an extreme idea: that all life experiences, and so all perceptual experiences, are colored by mood: "Life is a train of moods like a string of beads, and as we pass through them they prove to be many colored lenses, which paint the world their own hue, and each shows us only what lies in its own focus."

[2] In contrast to the use of "attitude" prevalent in Psychology, analytic philosophers typically use "attitudes" to denote the mental states that they take to consist in relations to propositions, and the paradigms of these mental states are beliefs and desires.

judgment and perceptual experience. Perceptual judgment is a form of belief in which perceivers respond to the way things appear. For instance, Vivek might form the belief that the audience is pleased, by jumping to conclusions: the facial expressions in the audience are neutral, and they look neutral to Vivek, but he comes away thinking they're pleased.

Alternatively, Vivek's vanity might reach all the way to the appearances themselves. Vivek's perceptual experience is the conscious part of perception that Vivek is responding to, when he forms his judgment. If his vanity influences his perceptual experience, then there's no need for him to jump to conclusions from the visual appearances. If he just believes his eyes, he'll end up believing that the people are pleased. That's how their faces look to him. If you saw the faces, in contrast, you'd most likely think they were just neutral. Unless you admire Vivek as much as he admires himself, you're not motivated to see the faces as approving.

The distinction between perceptual experience and judgment gives us at least two broad kinds of potential effects on perception. Whether the effects are actual is a question for Psychology. First, vanity might leave perceptual experience untouched, and influence only the interface between experience and subsequent judgment or behavior. A variant of this kind of effect leaves both experience and judgment untouched, but neutralizes their role in guiding behavior: one behaves in ways congruent with vanity, and not with one's experience or judgment. In the second broad kind of effect, vanity influences the perceptual experiences in response to which those judgments are made.

Whether it affects perception at the level of experience or not, an outlook can sustain itself through creating the appearances that the world is the way the outlook suggests it is. From the subject's point of view, her fear or suspicion is confirmed, or her desire satisfied, but this is a self-generated illusion. It's a frightening illusion for someone fear-ridden, and a happy illusion for Vivek. But it's an illusion all the same. In some cases, the illusion takes on political dimensions: what's perpetuated is an illusion of inequality between people who share a society—illusions that could easily make a perceiver internally conflicted, morally obtuse, or both.

A self-generated illusion of this kind is an epistemic problem. In theatrical terms, the problem is that perception becomes a farce, and the joke is on the perceiver. Perception seems to open the perceiver's mind to the things around us, but for some important things, it doesn't. It purports to tell the perceiver what the world is like, but in crucial cases, it won't. Perceivers seem to be able to use perception to check our prior beliefs, fears, and suspicions against reality, but for some of the purposes that matter most, we can't. We seem to use perception to guide our actions—but in the task at hand, we don't. And the reason for these limitations comes not from the tricks of light, sleights of hand, or an inbuilt structural mismatch between our minds and reality, but from our own individual prior outlooks. Just as in a theater showing a farcical comedy, spectators can see the sorry situation from the outside and grasp the perversity that eludes the characters in the play, a philosophical analysis can illuminate the epistemic situations of subjects like Vivek, whose perception and outlooks are, unwittingly, mutually sustaining.

When perceptual judgments or perceptual experiences arise from processes that give prior outlooks too much weight and fail to give proper weight to perceptual inputs (if there are any such inputs), we can say that the outlook *hijacks* the perceptual state. In whatever mode it may occur, the notion of hijacked perception rests on two background assumptions. It assumes that there's such a thing as distinctively perceptual input to the mind. And it assumes that a principled distinction can be drawn between giving perceptual inputs proper weight and not giving them proper weight in behavior, in belief, and in perceptual experience itself.

What if one or both of these background assumptions is false? Then no principled distinction between hijacked and un-hijacked perception can be drawn, and the problem of hijacked experiences dissolves, as does the motivation to solve it. For now, I'll take these background assumptions for granted.

Perceptual hijacking can be seen as steering gone awry. It is a bad version of something that can be okay. Perception goes well, either as experience or judgment, when perceptual inputs are given proper weight. And perception goes badly, when perceptual judgment or experience is hijacked by one's prior outlook. It is also possible for a prior outlook to properly steer the processing that leads to perceptual experience or judgment. It is properly steered when the prior outlook and perceptual inputs are both given their proper weight. For instance, constructivism about visual processing is the theory that information stored by the visual system is used to interpret retinal data and in producing visual experiences. Constructivism does not entail that all visual perception is hijacked perception.

Clear examples of perceptual hijacking can be found in wishful, fearful, and prejudiced thinking. Before seeing Jack, Jill fears that Jack is angry at her. When she sees him, her fear causes her to perceive Jack as angry, and this perception strengthens her fear. If Jill's fear affects only her perception only at the level of perceptual belief, leaving her perceptual experience untouched, there is little temptation to say that the resulting judgment is formed epistemically well. Fearful thinking, like wishful thinking or prejudiced thinking, are paradigms of irrational routes to belief.

But if Jill's fear makes her perceptual experience congruent with the fear, then the situation is epistemically more complicated. When we look more closely at hijacked perception that reaches all the way to a visual experience, we find a distinctive philosophical problem. I'm going to call this problem *the problem of hijacked experience*.

Like many philosophical problems, the problem of hijacked experience consists in a pair of opposing pressures: the pressure to say that it is rational for Jill, Vivek, or the preformationist to believe their eyes, and the pressure to say that it isn't.

On the one hand, if Jack really does look angry to Jill when she sees him, and she has no indication that the experience is misleading, then what else could Jill reasonably believe about his emotional state, other than that he is angry? Isn't Jill just doing her best with the evidence about Jack that perception gives her? How could we fault her for that?

On the other hand, if perceptual experiences retain their usual epistemic powers in those cases, then they would rationally support the fearful suspicion that leads to Jill's hijacked perception.

On the face of it, this result seems wrong. Suppose Jill takes her experience to confirm her suspicion that Jack is angry with her ("just look at his face!" she tells herself). She seems to have moved illicitly from her starting suspicion to a strengthening of it, via her experience. From Jill's point of view, she seems to be gaining additional evidence from this experience for her belief that Jack is angry at her, elevating the epistemic status of that belief. Is it that easy to confirm a suspicion?

The examples can be multiplied. In the early days of microscope use, no theory of mammalian reproduction was well-confirmed. Many of the first users of microscopes favored preformationism. Some preformationists claimed to see embryos in sperm cells that they examined using a microscope.[3] If the sperm cells they examined really did contain embryos within, an excellent explanation of this fact would be that preformationism is true. So if the embryo-experiences retained their epistemic powers, those experiences should provide incremental confirmation of preformationism, and the preformationists who started out believing preformationism without adequate grounds would end up having better grounds for their belief, via their experiences. But it is not that easy to confirm preformationism. And yet, if the microscope-users seemed to see an embryo when they looked at the slide, what else are they supposed to conclude?

We can find the same two pressures in other cases. Consider experiences that are influenced by expertise in ways that mimic reasonable inferences. Suppose a gray banana looks yellowish, due to learning about the color of bananas from exposure to them over a lifetime. Is the resulting experience as epistemically powerful as an experience that accurately represented the color of the perceived banana, and that was due to that particular banana's color? As before, we can ask about the epistemic power of experience to support the generalizations that gave rise to it. Do the generalizations (that bananas are yellow, or that banana-shaped things are yellow) gain the usual amount of support from experiences of yellowish bananas, when those experiences arise in large part from those very generalizations? On the one hand, there's pressure to say No: the path from the generalization to the experience and on to a strengthened generalization looks suspiciously like badly circular reasoning. On the other hand, there's pressure to say Yes: given your experience, and no inkling that it was influenced by your expertise, it seems reasonable to believe that the banana is the way it looks, and it looks yellow. The power of experience is not comfortably denied.

Finally, the same opposing pressures arise when background beliefs, fears, preferences, or prejudice control patterns of attention, whether the attention is strictly perceptual or not. It is well known that hiring committees respond differently to applications from socially stigmatized and socially dominant groups in ways that perpetuate these patterns of

---

[3] As noted in the Preface, a discussion of the historical origins of this amusing narrative can be found in Pinto-Correia (1997).

inequality.[4] This phenomenon could arise from a range of different psychological mechanisms. But suppose it arises in this way: the features that detract from the stigmatized applicants' candidacy are selected for further processing, while features that support it are excluded from such processing. They are, in other words, anti-selected. A fuller picture of the candidate would reveal counterbalancing strengths, but the strengths in the application are simply not registered to begin with. From the evaluator's point of view, the stigmatized applicants simply have little or nothing to recommend them, and so the seemingly reasonable (if regrettable) conclusion to draw is that they are poorly qualified.

Here we find our conflicting pressures again. On the one hand, it seems wrong to allow that the evaluators' prejudice could become incrementally more reasonable, on the basis of selectively generated impressions that are truly congruent with it. If the dismissive conclusion about the stigmatized applicant were reasonable, it would seem to provide incremental support for the generalization that lies implicitly behind the differential response—roughly, that the socially stigmatized candidates (for whatever reason) are poorly qualified. Strengthening prejudice in this way may be a good sociological explanation of how prejudice perpetuates itself, but that explanation does not make the strengthening epistemically appropriate. On the other hand, if the anti-selection of evidence occurs under the radar, then what else could it be reasonable to conclude? Why rate an application highly if it seems mediocre?

The hiring case thus hands us the same pressures as the ones we met in the case of Jack and Jill, preformationism, Vivek's vanity, and the yellow-looking gray banana. In all of the cases, the challenge is to assess whether the ultimate conclusions are epistemically appropriate (the stigmatized applicant is under-qualified, Jack is angry, the sperm cell contains an embryo, the audience is pleased, the banana is yellow), and to either explain away the appearance of an epistemic flaw in the conclusion, if there isn't one, or else identify the epistemic flaw, if there is one.

[4] Steinpreis et al (1999), Goldin and Rouse (2000), Dovidio and Gaertner (2000). More recently, Ceci and Williams (2011) report that when extraordinarily highly qualified women apply for jobs in fields related to science, technology, engineering, and math, then with the exception of economics, hiring committees in those fields prefer to hire them, rather than preferring equally highly qualified men. There were no controls for race in this study.

The problem of hijacked experience differs from standard visual illusions or the philosophers' fictional hallucinations that are used to generate skeptical scenarios, which have long fueled discussions in perceptual epistemology.[5] Unlike standard illusions, such as the Müller-Lyer lines or the straight stick that looks bent when immersed in water, perceptual hijacking lets us focus on the psychological relations among a subject's own mental states. These relations figure in the route to hijacked experiences. They can bring to light the most intimate ways that presumptions can permeate everyday life.

In philosophy, most discussion of hijacked perception has focused on cognitive penetration of perceptual experience. But this form is just one among many. Consider the following experiment, which was designed to test the influence of racial attitudes on perception.

> *Weapon categorization*: Participants in an experiment are shown an object quickly and asked to press a button designated for "gun" if it is a gun, and a different button if it is a hand tool—pliers, wrench, or a drill. Before they see the object, they are quickly shown a man's face. The man is either black or white. Participants frequently indicate "gun" when shown a tool, but more frequently make this error following a black prime, compared with a white prime. (Payne 2001)

When participants in Payne's experiment misclassify a pair of pliers as a gun, there are many possible ways in which they might, in principle, arrive at their misclassification.

- *Disbelief*: The pliers look to the subject exactly like pliers. But the subjects disbelieve their perceptual experience, and misclassify the object as a gun.
- *Bypass*: The pliers look to the subject exactly like pliers. Subjects do not respond in any way to the experience—not even by disbelieving it. The state activated by the black prime controls their classification error directly, bypassing their experience.
- *Cognitive penetration* (hijacked experience): The pliers look to the subject exactly like a gun, due to a cognitive state activated by the black prime.

---

[5] Price (1932), Ayer (1940), Austin (1962).

- *Attention* (hijacked experience): The pliers look somewhat like a gun, because the state activated by the black prime directs the subjects attention to features of the pliers that are congruent with being a gun (metallic), and away from features incongruent with being a gun (shape).
- *Introspective error*: The pliers look to the subject exactly like pliers. But subjects make an introspective error in which they take themselves to experience a gun. The introspective error makes them misclassify the object as a gun.
- *Haste*: The pliers look to the subject somewhat like pliers and somewhat like a gun. Before perceiving enough detail to decide the matter on the basis of what they see, subjects judge that the object is a gun, due to the state activated by the black prime.
- *Disowned behavior*: The pliers look to the subject exactly like pliers. But the state activated by the black prime guides the behavior of pushing the button that subjects use to indicate their classification verdict. Subjects immediately afterward will regard their answer as mistaken.[6]

These options differ from one another along several dimensions. Some options impact the content of a judgment, rather than the content of perceptual experience (Disbelief, Bypass, Introspective error). Other options impact the content of experience, either by influencing it directly (Cognitive penetration), by selecting which features will be attended (Attention), or by controlling the extent of perceptual processing (Haste). A different dimension of influence concerns the role of the experience in making a judgment (Bypass, Haste), or in producing behavior (Disowned behavior). This ultimate option (Disowned behavior), like the Bypass option, illustrates the possibility that perception could have less impact on behavior than we might have supposed—even when we are engaged explicitly in a classification task that we would normally use perception to accomplish. Perception's usual role in guiding behavior is neutralized.

---

[6] The results of Payne's experiment are probably best explained by this option, given a follow-up experiment allowing participants to correct their responses. Stokes and Payne (2010).

Many standard epistemologies of experience would classify these cases differently, according to such factors as the subject's awareness of the effects or the level of processing that was influenced. But if a racist outlook leads to misclassification, there's a strong sense that the resulting judgment in all of these cases should be ill-founded. In all of the cases, due to the outlook of the perceiver, perceptual inputs are not given proper weight in determining perceptual experience, perceptual belief, or both. They are all cases of perceptual hijacking. When one focuses on the outcome of these misclassifications in belief, behavior, interpersonal relations, or social impact, treating all of them as epistemically on a par can seem natural. A theory that predicts that some of these judgments are ill-founded but others are not seems blind to an important epistemic continuity.

Some approaches to the mind might seem to exacerbate the problem of perceptual hijacking, by making it pervasive. Suppose Immanuel Kant is right that we bring our own construals of space, time, and causation to bear on whatever information we take in. If perception is a way of reasoning from information we have already, then there is nothing epistemically special about cases where the mind is insulated from reality by its own assumptions. This situation will pervade every case of perception. The resulting insulation of the mind seems to extend the farcical nature of hijacked perception as far it could possibly go: to every perceptual experience.

In a similar way, some Bayesian approaches to the mind seem to make this kind of perceptual farce pervasive. These approaches start from the hypothesis that all of our perceptual processing relies heavily on stored information. They apply Bayesian models globally, rather than limiting it to isolated computations.[7] According to this approach, perceptual experience reflects perceivers' best guesses about what's in their immediate environment. This picture of perception differs starkly from the picture of perception as a system of gathering input from the world, where guessing what is behind a curtain is fundamentally different from opening the curtain to see what's behind it. Andy Clark and Jakob

---

[7] For instance, as Hohwy (2013) advertises his view of the mind, it posits "a single type of mechanism, reiterated throughout the brain [that] manages everything," and is thus "a very ambitious unificatory project" (pp. 2–3). By contrast, there are many Bayesian analyses of local computations that take no stand on whether the global approach is correct. For discussion of some local applications, see Rescorla (2015).

Hohwy, proponents of global Bayesianism, both suggest the contrast is not so stark after all.[8]

My solution to the problem of perceptual hijacking, outlined in Chapter 2, takes as a fixed point that some perceptual judgments truly deserve their status as common sense. We can discover that a fear of running out of mustard is unfounded, by opening the fridge and seeing a jar of mustard there. If common sense is right in this instance, it won't matter whether the mustard jar is what Immanuel Kant would call a "thing in itself," or whether it is instead merely a part of "empirical reality"—reality structured by our conceptual apparatus. And it is possible to discover that one's fear is unfounded, even if perceptual experiences are constructed from Bayesian computations. Either way, according to common sense, perception can provide baseline rational support for beliefs about things like mustard jars.

We ordinarily assume that we can know if the fridge contains mustard (by looking inside the fridge), which way is downhill (by looking out the window), and whether people are coming down the stairs (by hearing voices and footsteps). Powerful philosophical arguments have been made for why these commonsense assumptions are untenable. In metaphysics, idealists, including idealists in the style of George Berkeley and constructivists in the style of Martin Heidegger, argue that there is nothing external to our ideas or our social practices relative to which our perceptions are veridical or falsidical. In epistemology, skeptics about the external world hold that even if there is an external world, we can't have reason from perception for our ordinary beliefs about it. One could try to use cases of perceptual hijacking as skeptical scenarios from which to mount a skeptical argument. But on the face of it, there is no reason to expect these arguments to be any more powerful for using perceptual hijacking as a skeptical scenario. So in this book, I'm assuming that we can know by looking in the fridge that the fridge contains mustard, where mustard is not an idea. Both external-world skeptics and idealists

---

[8] In describing his Bayesian model of the brain, Clark (2013) writes: "[the predictive coding model] makes the lines between perception and cognition fuzzy, perhaps even vanishing. In place of any real distinction between perception and belief we now get variable differences in the mixture of top-down and bottom-up influence, and differences of temporal and spatial scale in the internal models that are making the predictions." For discussion of the distinction between perception and belief in global Bayesian models, see Farennikova (ms) and Macpherson (2016).

would deny this assumption. But by starting here, we can more clearly see what the epistemological contours of perception would be, if some of these kinds of commonsense assumptions are true.

Part I of this book hones the epistemic problem that the rest of the book tries to answer, and introduces the centerpiece of my solution to it. Part II describes the core epistemic roles of perceptual experience, and introduces the notion of inference that helps define these roles. Part III applies the account beyond the core case of influences on experience by belief, and argues that the epistemic impact on perceptual experience of fears and preferences, selection effects, and social forms of consciousness can all be treated using the same analytic tools.

The rest of Part I sketches the solution to the problem of hijacked experiences, and explains the concepts that are central to it: the rationality of perception, and epistemic charge.

2

The Solution Sketched

The problem of hijacked experiences consists in a pair of opposing pressures: the pressure to say that it is rational for Jill, Vivek, or the preformationist to believe their eyes when they have their hijacked experiences, and the pressure to say that it isn't. Since the problem has this structure, a solution to it can take the form of finding that one of these pressures is the correct one to follow, while the other one is not.

My solution is that it is not rational in these cases for the subjects of hijacked experiences to believe their eyes. It is not rational because in each case, the subject's having the perceptual experiences detracts from his or her rational standing, and it does that because the experience came about through an irrational process. These subjects are not in a position to know, on their own, what the reasonable reaction to their experiences is.

If their faulty experiences are the main source of information about the subject-matter of those experiences, then although they're not in a position (all by themselves) to know it, the reasonable response is to suspend judgment on whether Jack is angry, the audience is pleased, or the sperm cell contains an embryo.[1]

---

[1] With enough distinctions, the verdict that Vivek's experience is irrational because it is formed irrationally might seem compatible with the idea that Vivek is at the same time rationally required to believe his eyes, given that he has the experience and no reason to discount it. Jackson (2011) comes to this conclusion, using different vocabulary: someone like Vivek would be rationally required to form a belief that is nonetheless unjustified, because of its relationship to the experience it is based on, together with the relations of that experience to its psychological precursors. On this picture, Vivek should have neither the vanity-constituting beliefs, nor the perceptual experience they give rise to; but given that he has the experience and no reason to discount it, he should believe his eyes. The putative rational requirement is the kind discussed by Broome (1999) under the heading of "wide-scope" rational requirements (sometimes also called "coherence requirements").

Arguably, the pressure to say that Vivek and others in situations like his would be reasonable to believe their eyes need not be explained by something as strong as a requirement of rationality. Nothing in this book makes this case fully. McGrath (2013a)

This solution to the problem of hijacked experiences contains two ideas. First, it is possible in principle to arrive at a perceptual experience by rational or irrational means. Second, perceptual experiences themselves can be rational or irrational. Applied to Vivek's case: his visual experience of the pleased audience is irrational, and it is irrational because of the influence of his vanity.

Taken together, these two ideas formulate the thesis at the heart of the book.

The Rationality of Perception: Both perceptual experiences and the processes by which they arise can be rational or irrational.

This chapter explains what each part of the Rationality of Perception means.

2.1 "Rational" and "Reasonable"

The terms "rational" and "irrational" are used widely in many areas of philosophy. These uses vary greatly. They help describe ways in which people, mental states, actions, social arrangements, or combinations or patterns of these things can be appropriate or inappropriate, relative to certain types of norms—norms of rationality.

In epistemology, beliefs, modes of inquiry, and transitions into or out of inquiry are taken to be evaluable as rational or irrational. There are many dimensions of epistemic appropriateness that "rationality" is used to label. Here are just a few putative epistemic norms, such that a person would be rational to the extent that she follows these norms, and is less rational, to the extent that she departs from them:

- What one should believe, disbelieve, or suspend judgment on is wholly determined by one's total evidence.
- What transitions one should make from one's overall doxastic state (where this includes what one suspends judgment on) are wholly determined by one's total evidence.
- What one believes should accord with one's reasons.

gives reason to doubt that there is any wide-scope or coherence requirement to believe one's eyes. If there isn't any such requirement, then the Rationality of Perception can't be supplemented with it. At most, coherence requirements would supplement the Rationality of perception, not challenge it.

- One should not simultaneously believe: P, If P then Q, and ~Q.
- If one believes that P, one should believe all of P's logical consequences.
- One should form beliefs in a way that maximizes true beliefs and minimizes false ones.
- One's credal states should conform to the axioms of probability.

These norms govern various kinds of things: synchronic states, transitions between them, credal states (which are gradable), binary states (which are not), belief, disbelief, and suspended judgment. Some of the norms that govern the same things (such as beliefs) are conceptually distinct, so that whether they exert exactly the same pressures in every circumstance is a substantive issue. And the norms differ as to whether the fact that one is falling short of the norm can be within one's ken. Taken together, these examples of epistemic norms exhibit only some of the many putative ways of being rational.

If we abstract from the differences between the norms listed above, we can see that they have something in common. They all assume that the phenomena they govern are epistemically appraisable. They are norms that purport to describe how a specific aspect of a properly rational subject's mental life would be. The kind of rationality that figures in the Rationality of Perception hypothesis is located at this high level of abstraction. The Rationality of Perception articulates the assumption of appraisability that underlies the specific norms of rationality described above, and applies that assumption to perceptual experiences. It says that they can be rational, in this most abstract sense of being epistemically appraisable, which I'll occasionally use "reasonable" to denote as well. For instance, in the case of Jill, the problem of hijacked experience consists in whether it is rational or irrational, or equivalently, reasonable or unreasonable, for her to believe on the basis of her hijacked experience that Jack is angry.

The assumption of epistemic appraisability applies to perceptual experience in two ways. First, merely having a perceptual experience can benefit or detract from the subject's rational standing, and in that manner redound on the subject. Second, how the perceptual experience so redounds can depend on how the experience was formed. The Rationality of Perception is neutral on which norms govern perceptual experience in these ways. Later on (Chapters 6 and 7), I identify norms governing inference, and show how they apply to experiences that result from rationally evaluable inferences.

2.2 Perceptual Experiences Can Be Formed Rationally or Irrationally

What does it mean to say that perceptual experiences can be formed rationally or irrationally? Let us begin with some comparisons.

Vivek believes that people like him. He believes that, because he's vain. He expects approval, and approval is what he thinks he gets.

Vivek is not the type to offer justifications for his self-assurance. He just takes it for granted. But in taking it for granted, he arrives at his presumption by irrational means. Even though Vivek didn't announce to anyone (or to himself) his explicit reasons for thinking that people like him, we'd have a clue that he is, silently, *reasoning*, if he presumes that people like him because he has some other beliefs that constitute his vanity (beliefs about himself and other people), and if the unreasonableness of his presumption stems from how unreasonable those other beliefs are. Vivek draws an inference covertly, silently, and unreflectively. He infers that people like him, from other things he believes.

The Rationality of Perception says that perceptual experience can arise through covert, silent, unreflective inference of the sort illustrated by Vivek, when he reasons to his presumption that people like him. It is a commonplace that we sometimes reason in this way to form beliefs, or to strengthen pre-existing ones. The Rationality of Perception says that it is possible for us to reason in this way to form perceptual experiences.

It might sound strange to you to call any process of forming perceptual experience "reasoning," if you take that term to denote only explicit deliberation, or conscious rehearsals of one's reasons to others (or to oneself), or awareness of revising or adjusting one's conclusions in light of reflection on other things that one believes. If at first, you can't hear "reasoning" as describing a process that could potentially culminate in a perceptual experience, the idea that such a thing could happen might become audible if you focus first on cases of unreflective reasoning to beliefs like Vivek's. When Vivek unreflectively figures (from their behavior) that people like him, his unreflective reasoning modulates the epistemic status of his conclusions.

That kind of epistemological modulation would make a route to perceptual experience rational or irrational. Reasoning one's way to a perceptual experience would make that experience rational, if the elements and process of the reasoning are good—or irrational, if the elements or process of the reasoning are bad. In the end, it isn't important whether or not any process leading to perceptual experience can be a case of reasoning in any specialized sense that goes beyond the minimal idea that the route to perceptual experience is rationally appraisable. What's important is that a perceptual experience can be rational or irrational, and so can transitions leading up to them.

Perceptual experiences that arose from this kind of reasoning would be rational, in a broader sense that encompasses both good and bad outcomes: they are evaluable as rationally better or worse. Any perceptual experiences that have an epistemic status that can be modulated by reasoning of this sort belong to what Donald Davidson once called "the house of reason," rather than being relegated to those parts of the mind that are beyond epistemic reproach.[2]

It is standard to call a belief "well-founded" if it has been formed and maintained epistemically well, and "ill-founded" if it has been formed or maintained epistemically badly. I follow standard usage, and tie it to my abstract uses of "rational" and "irrational" in the following way: a belief is ill-founded if it is formed or maintained irrationally, well-founded if it is formed and maintained rationally.[3] These notions are also gradable. One belief can be more ill-founded (or well-founded) than another.

Descending from the height of abstraction at which I've been using "rational," "reasonable," and now "reasoning," we can see that Vivek's unreflective route to belief is a kind of inference. When one arrives at a conclusion by inference, the conclusion's epistemic power to support subsequent beliefs, as well as its own epistemic standing, can be modulated by the inputs to the inference. Inference is an example—perhaps it

---

[2] Davidson (1982).

[3] Conee and Feldman (1985/2004) initially define "well-founded" in terms of justification and evidence, but then abstract from evidence and claim that reliabilists, when they deny that evidence has to play the role in the well-foundedness that Feldman and Conee describe, are disagreeing with them about the nature of well-foundedness, and therefore are subscribing to the same pre-theoretical notion. The same move is made more explicitly by Feldman (an evidentialist) in the Afterword to "The Generality Problem for Reliabilism" (1998/2004), and by Bergmann (an anti-evidentialist) in his 2006, ch. 1.

is the prime example—of a process that can issue in beliefs and that can be rational or irrational. If perceptual experiences can arise from inference, then the Rationality of Perception is true.

2.3 Significance

Most discussions of perceptual epistemology focus on the route *from* perceptual experience to belief. The Rationality of Perception focuses on the route *to* perceptual experience from other psychological states of the perceiver. It extends the domain of rationality to transitions and states that were previously assumed to be entirely a-rational. It expands the house of reason.

The Rationality of Perception pushes against traditional ways of thinking about perception and perceptual experience. It is at odds with a sharp division in the mind between perception and reasoning, and with the idea that the route to perception is "passive" as compared with the mental activity found in reasoning. And it opens the possibility that epistemic evaluation could begin upstream of belief and knowledge, contrary to the traditional view that perceptual experiences are immune from any epistemic effects of psychological precursors. If epistemic evaluation can begin already at perception, then epistemology expands beyond its traditional domain of knowledge and inquiry.

In addition to introducing the useful metaphor of the house of reason, Davidson also claimed that only beliefs can justify other beliefs—perception could at most play a merely causal role in influencing which beliefs we end up with. This view exiled perception from the house of reason. In opposition to Davidson, many philosophers have held that experiences could at least make it to the threshold: they have the power to support certain beliefs—in the way that Jill's experience of Jack as angry would normally make it reasonable for her to believe that he's angry. But even these philosophers assumed that perceptual experiences, and the perceptual processes leading up to them, were not epistemically appraisable. Ernest Sosa notes the status of this idea as an entrenched presumption:

[W]hen [perceptual] experiences help explain the rational standing of some other state or action, they do not thereby problematize their own rational standing. Being so passive, they have no such standing.[4]

---

[4] Sosa (2007), p. 46. Sosa ultimately disowns this picture.

The Rationality of Perception is widely presumed to be false. Why? There are substantial principled objections to the idea that experiences could redound well or badly to the subject's rational standing. Think of Jill. She can (let's suppose) articulate a reason for her belief that Jack is angry. Her reason for this belief is one she might express by saying "because he looks angry"—a reason that points back to her experience. Jill can also, perhaps, articulate reasons for a different belief: her belief that Jack *looks* angry. Here she might point to the contortions of his face. But in giving reasons for these beliefs, she does not thereby give reasons for the experience in which Jack looks to her the way he does. Some philosophers would say that if she can't articulate reasons for her experiences, then her experience can't redound on her well or badly.

Another principled objection starts from the observation that Jill can't rationally control her perceptual experience that presents Jack as angry. Compare her belief that Jack is angry. Jill can in principle modify this belief in response to new information or evidence. But she can't modify her experience in response to such factors. At best, she may come to see Jack differently if she learned that he isn't really angry after all. But whether that happens is not merely a matter of her assimilating new information. Some philosophers take these facts to show that Jill is not in any way accountable for her experience, and therefore could not speak to how rational she is.

These objections both invoke what we might call upper-echelon rational capacities, which include the capacities to deliberate about what to believe, to formulate one's reasons for what one believes or decides, to revise or adjust one's conclusions in light of reflection, including reflection on other things one believes, and on one's reasons for holding one's beliefs. If one presumed that the only exercises of rational capacities were the upper-echelon kind, then the Rationality of Perception would be off the radar.

The flipside of this observation is that since there are ways to exercise rational capacities in forming beliefs that are not upper-echelon capacities, we can ask whether those more relaxed capacities could produce perceptual experiences.[5]

---

[5] Vivek's belief that the people in the audience like him is formed without using upper-echelon capacities. Several other examples of beliefs formed in this way are given in Chapter 5, section 5.5.

If a perceptual experience could be the conclusion of an inference, the inference would modulate its epistemic status—just as an inference modulates the epistemic status of a belief that is a conclusion of the inference.

Since the Rationality of Perception does not specify the kinds of routes to perceptual experiences that can be rational or irrational, it does not entail that perceptual experiences can be conclusions of inference.[6] But if experiences can be conclusions of inferences, the Rationality of Perception is true. In discussing the Rationality of Perception, it is useful to have a label for the epistemic status it says experiences can have, and a label that enables us to describe how that status can be affected by inference. My label for this property is "epistemic charge." I choose this label to highlight the similarities between epistemic charge and electricity. The similarities are discussed in Chapter 3, section 3.3.

The Rationality of Perception is entailed by two theses about epistemic charge, which are the focus of the rest of this book:

The Epistemic Charge thesis: Experiences can be epistemically charged.

Inferential Modulation thesis: Experiences can be formed by inferences that can modulate their epistemic charge.

In the guise of these two theses about epistemic charge, the Rationality of Perception provides a solution to the problem of hijacked experiences.

2.4 Solving the Problem of Hijacked Experience

The solution to the problem is that it is not rational for Jill, Vivek, or the preformationist to believe their eyes. It is not rational, because their hijacked experiences are irrational. They are irrational because they are epistemically sensitive to their psychological precursors, in the same way that conclusions of inference epistemically depend on inferential inputs. It is no more rational for these subjects to believe that the world is the way their hijacked experiences present it as being, than it is for them to

---

[6] I discuss potential cases of rational or irrational experiences without inference in Part III.

believe something on the basis of assumptions that are themselves irrational.

This solution to the problem of hijacked experiences uses both parts of the Rationality of Perception. First, it is possible in principle to arrive at a perception by rational or irrational means. Just as Vivek can arrive at his belief that the audience likes him by rational or irrational means, he could arrive at a perceptual experience that the audience likes him by rational or irrational means. Second, perceptual experience itself can be rational or irrational, and its rational standing can be modulated by the rationality or irrationality of the route by which it was formed. Vivek's perceptual experience of the pleased audience can be irrational, and it can be irrational because of the way it is influenced by his vanity.

This solution to the problem can make sense of the idea that Vivek's experience can be irrationally influenced by his exaggerated opinion of himself. It can make sense of the idea that Jill's experience is irrationally influenced by her fear, and that the preformationists' experience is irrationally influenced by the prior commitment to preformationism. It can explain why it is not rational for subjects in these cases to believe their eyes—even though, to them, they are simply taking in what comes their way, even when they are not in a position to understand what the epistemically best option is.

In contrast, the traditional approaches to the epistemic role of perceptual experience predict that when Jill, Vivek, and the preformationist have their hijacked experiences, those experiences can provide just as much epistemic support for believing that Jack is angry, that the audience is pleased, and that there is an embryo in the sperm cell as non-hijacked experiences could. And even if a racial stereotype was entrenched in a culture because it rationalizes a pattern of undeserved burdens and benefits, if that stereotype happened to operate at the level of perceptual experiences, the traditional view would predict that those experiences can rationally vindicate the stereotype.

2.4.1 Why not settle for less?

My defense of the Rationality of Perception argues that Jill's hijacked experience does indeed lose epistemic power to support beliefs formed on the basis of those experiences, and it offers a systematic theory of what makes those experience susceptible to losing epistemic power. I don't claim to defend this theory from the ground up. Like any detailed theory, it is likely to contain mistakes. But since hijacked experiences have been overlooked in the construction of the most enduring theories of perception and its epistemic role, putting this phenomenon into focus provides a valuable opportunity to consider in detail what epistemic properties of perception could plausibly lie behind it.

Other possible solutions to the problem of hijacked experience are more minimal, and don't allow that perceptual experiences can be irrational. Perhaps the most minimal solution locates the epistemic problem at the level of the epistemic power of the experience to support beliefs.[7] If Jill goes ahead and believes her eyes anyway, then her belief is not as well-founded as it could be, because it is formed on the basis of an experience that lacks the baseline amount of epistemic power that the same experience could have, if it weren't influenced by fear. Her experience is merely *downgraded*, meaning its epistemic power is reduced below the baseline.

The most minimal solution stays entirely silent on what causes Jill's experience to be downgraded, and is therefore neutral on this question. If one stops short of the Rationality of Perception at the minimal solution, one does not identify what kind of influence on experience by fear makes experience lose its power, nor does one explain which influences have that effect and which do not. For all the minimal solution says, Jill's fear may be incidental to explaining downgrade. The most minimal solution on its own does not look under the hood.

A differently minimal solution looks under the hood, claims to find at a minimum a causal relationship between the downgraded experience and a psychological precursor, but does not further illuminate the nature of that relationship, and so does not explain any further why epistemic downgrade occurs. Like a copper wire puncturing a balloon, the psychological precursors (Vivek's vanity, Jill's fear, etc.) deflate the epistemic powers of the experiences they influence. Presumably only some causal relations will have this effect—just as causation is only part of the story when it comes to the basing relation in epistemology.[8]

---

[7] A differently minimal proposal allows that the epistemic powers of the experience to provide justification remain intact, but its powers to support knowledge do not. I argue in Chapter 4 that this approach leaves most of the problem unaddressed.

[8] For a critical review of several approaches to the basing relation, see Korcz (1997) and (2015) and Evans (2013). Macpherson's (2012) and (2015) discussion of potential relations of cognitive penetration makes the analogous observation about cognitive penetration: causation can be only part of the story.

So just what kind of relationship between precursor and experience causes the deflation remains to be explained.

Despite being more minimal than the Rationality of Perception and keeping the house of reason its traditional size, the minimal solutions are in an important way more complex than the Rationality of Perception. Consider their application to judgments of reasonableness in the law. In US law and elsewhere, some forms of aggression, including lethal ones, are licensed both for citizens and for police, only if the defender reasonably believes that he or she is in imminent danger. Jurors are supposed to assess the reasonableness of the defendants' actions, in part by assessing the reasonableness of their beliefs. And to determine whether the belief is reasonable, they're supposed to consider what a reasonable person in the defendants' circumstances would believe about the imminence and the severity of the threat that they face. They are supposed to ask what would be reasonable to believe about those things, in those circumstances.

Consider a defendant who attacks a man he believes is holding a gun. The man was holding something, and it looked to the defendant as if it was a gun. But suppose that the defendant's perceptual experience was influenced by an ill-founded unconscious presumption—a form of racism, for example—that men who resemble the man the defendant sees are dangerous.

If the reasonableness of the person depends only on the interface between experience and subsequent belief, and not on the psychological background of the experience, then the belief that the man is dangerous (because he is holding a gun) might seem to be reasonable. But if the gun-experience itself detracts from the subject's rational standing because it is inferred from an ill-founded presumption, then when we assess what a reasonable person under similar circumstances would believe, we need not hold constant their experience. A reasonable person in similar circumstances would not have an experience that they inferred from the ill-founded presumption. Just as a reasonable person's beliefs would be by and large shaped by reasonable presumptions, their perceptual experiences would be shaped that way as well.

The minimal positions locate the epistemic problem at the interface between perceptual experience and belief. They fail to respect the idea that if there was something wrong with the presumptions that gave rise to the experiences, then to the extent that the experience elaborates those presumptions, there should be something wrong with having the experiences as well. The Rationality of Perception gives voice to this idea, and the concept of an epistemic charge that can be modulated by inference shows how it can be developed in detail.

2.5 What Kind of Normative Property Is Epistemic Charge?

The Rationality of Perception solves the problem of hijacked experiences by invoking the idea that those experiences are epistemically charged. I've said what epistemic charge is by describing in the broadest terms what it does. By virtue of being epistemically charged, a mental state redounds well or badly to the subject. In this way, epistemically charged mental states manifest an epistemic status.

An example of an epistemically charged mental state is a belief that is either justified or unjustified. As justification is usually construed, beliefs themselves are the bearers of this epistemic normative status. The Rationality of Perception says that perceptual experiences can, in themselves, manifest an epistemic status.

To bring the concept of manifesting an epistemic status into sharper focus, some distinctions may be useful.

First, we can distinguish between a perceptual experience manifesting a normative status, and merely enabling other mental states or actions to manifest a normative status. For instance, one might think that what a subject does is morally appraisable, only if she is capable of being in some phenomenally conscious mental states (such as pain), without holding that her conscious states in themselves manifest a moral status. Being capable of entering phenomenal states, on this view, enables one's actions to be morally appraisable, but that capability is not in itself moral or immoral to any degree. Similarly, one might agree with Cheryl Chen (2008) that having perceptual experiences is a precondition for having any beliefs at all, and therefore a precondition of having beliefs that manifest any epistemic status. But for perceptual experiences to play the role Chen highlights, they need not have any epistemic status of their own.

Second, we can distinguish between an individual belief manifesting a distinctive epistemic status, and an individual belief belonging to a larger unit that manifests that epistemic status. For instance, one might hold that the only thing that can be appraised as epistemically rational (relative to some precisification of that idea) is one's overall belief state—not one's individual beliefs. On this picture, individual beliefs are part of a minimal unit that manifests the epistemic status, but they are not such minimal units themselves. In contrast, epistemological accounts of the degree to which individual beliefs are justified presume that individual beliefs can manifest this epistemic status. The Rationality of Perception says that experiences can manifest the property of being epistemically irrational.

Finally, we can distinguish between a mental state's helping to determine the specific epistemic status that an individual belief has, and a mental state manifesting such a status in itself. When a belief in itself manifests an epistemic status, it occupies a position along a parameter of normative evaluation. The factors that determine what place it occupies on that parameter are typically taken to be extrinsic to the belief. For instance, having a perceptual experience presenting you with a red square might contribute to the positive epistemic status of a belief formed on the basis of the experience that there is a red square nearby, without the perceptual experience having the epistemic status itself.

For example, consider the coherentist theory of justification offered by Kvanvig and Riggs (1992). According to coherentism, what makes a belief justified is the relations of coherence it stands in to other mental states. On Kvanvig and Riggs's version of coherentism, coherence relations can hold between beliefs and experiences, as well as between beliefs and other beliefs. But Kvanvig and Riggs make a point of denying the Rationality of Perception, taking it to be obviously false:

It might be thought . . . that if coherentism were defined over both appearances and beliefs, then coherentism would be committed to the view that both beliefs and appearances can be epistemically justified. If that were so, there would be a problem, for it is obvious that appearance states are not suitable objects of epistemic appraisal. (p. 215)

Experiences that cohere with beliefs contribute to determining how well or poorly justified those beliefs are, but the experiences themselves cannot be either well or poorly justified, as they manifest no epistemic status at all.

In contrast, epistemically charged perceptual experiences manifest an epistemic status. They are not merely an enabling condition for other mental states to manifest such a status. Nor are they merely contributors to determining the epistemic status of beliefs as either well or poorly justified, though they play this role as well. In addition to this role, they manifest an epistemic standing in themselves.

This feature of epistemic charge leaves much else open. Is epistemic charge distinct from epistemic properties most analytic epistemologists have focused on, such as justification, ill-foundedness, well-foundedness, or evidential support?

A superficial difference is grammatical. "Epistemic charge" is grammatically different from the terms used to denote all of these other epistemic properties, in that "charge" marks out a parameter of epistemic appraisal. Epistemic charge is a valenced property, so that epistemically charged experiences can be negatively charged or positively charged. In contrast, "justified" (and "anti-justified"), "ill-founded" (and "well-founded"), and "evidentially supported" do not mark out parameters of epistemic appraisal. Instead, they presuppose such parameters, and denote positions on the parameter they presuppose. Grammatically, "epistemic charge" is closest to the somewhat strained senses of "justification" or "rational," in which those terms denote appraisability for justification or rationality.

Does the parameter of evaluation marked out by "epistemic charge" denote the same parameter that's marked by "justification," or by any other specific epistemic property that already figures in analytic epistemology, beyond the most general property of redounding well or badly on a subject?

The most conservative position is that positively charged experiences are justified, negatively charged experiences are anti-justified, and experiences in either category thereby have epistemic power to affect the justification of subsequent beliefs formed on the basis of those experiences. According to this position, the novelty attaches to the kinds of mental states that can be justified or anti-justified, rather than to the normative epistemic property itself.

At the other extreme, epistemic charge does not translate into any extant epistemic property, and the epistemic power of epistemically charged experiences does not affect the justification of subsequent beliefs at all. Their power to provide justification or anti-justification is untouched. Instead, one might say hijacked experiences have a power to *epistemically corrupt* beliefs formed on the basis of those experiences, and that such experiences have a hitherto ignored epistemic property of being epistemically corrupt themselves.[9] Here, the novelty attaches to the epistemic property. This option is pluralist, in that it posits a novel normative property distinct from the familiar property of providing justification, and allows that experiences can have both the novel property and the familiar one.

The pluralist and anti-pluralist approaches differ deeply in their dialectical consequences. On the extreme pluralist approach, perceptual hijacking would have no effects at all on the power of hijacked experiences to provide justification. It would instead adjust other powers of experience—powers that we would need new labels to describe. Hijacked experiences would then pose no challenge at all to any epistemological theory of perceptual justification. For instance, phenomenal conservatism (a view introduced in the Preface) predicts no effect at all on the power of hijacked experiences to provide justification. The extreme pluralist about epistemic charge can agree with this. Rather than constitute problem cases for phenomenal conservatism, on this picture, hijacked experiences show that phenomenal conservatism is not the whole story about the epistemic role of perceptual experience. The extreme pluralist can hold that phenomenal conservatism is not false, but merely incomplete, because it ignores an entirely separate dimension of epistemic evaluation.

My account of epistemic charge is not pluralist in such an extreme way. It says that perceptual hijacking can reduce the power of hijacked experiences to provide justification. When perceptual hijacking results in hijacked experiences, I argue in Chapter 4, it reduces the power of experiences to provide justification and with it, to make beliefs formed on the basis of those experiences well-founded. By using these terms to describe the epistemic situation that hijacked experiences put their subjects in, I mean to signal that the epistemological effect on experience is the same type that can occur by other means as well, such as defeat. In these ways, the account is at odds with phenomenal conservatism.

Matters are dialectically more complex when it comes to characterizing epistemic charge itself. My account of epistemic charge is neutral on whether it is or isn't identical with any normative property that philosophers have already identified. According to the epistemic profile I develop for epistemically charged experiences, epistemic charge affects

---

[9] Thanks to John Bengson and Farid Masrour for suggesting the term "epistemic corruption."

the powers of experiences to provide justification and to make subsequent beliefs well-founded or ill-founded, and these powers can be modulated by inference. I leave it to readers interested in such comparisons to see where specific theories of justification align with the account of epistemic charge offered here, and where they diverge.

The idea that experiences can be epistemically charged can be compared to a widespread response to what Laurence BonJour has called "Sellars's Dilemma."[10] According to one rendition of Sellars's dilemma, if experiences lack accuracy conditions, then they cannot provide justification for external-world beliefs (this is the dilemma's first horn), whereas if they have accuracy conditions, then they will be external-world beliefs themselves (this is the dilemma's second horn). Given these options, there is no way for experiences to provide justification, without needing to be justified themselves.

In the last decades of the twentieth century, many analytic philosophers rejected the second horn of Sellars's dilemma, on the grounds that experiences could both have accuracy conditions and provide justification for subsequent beliefs, without thereby needing to be justified by anything else.[11] I think this response succeeds. But all forms of the response I know of stopped short of claiming that experiences with these features could themselves manifest an epistemic status. The idea that experiences can be epistemically charged sits comfortably with the prominent response to Sellars's dilemma, and takes it one step further.

2.6 A Constructive Defense

On its own, the idea that perceptual experiences can be epistemically appraised leaves so many hanging threads that the entire epistemological fabric threatens to unravel.

---

[10] BonJour (1978). Sellars's (1956) discussion is structurally similar to the one described in the text but focuses on concepts rather than accuracy conditions.

[11] Some philosophers who reject the second horn of Sellars's Dilemma argue that experience can provide immediate justification (such as Pollock 1970, 1986, Peacocke 2004, Huemer 2007, Pryor 2000), whereas others who reject it argue that experiences provide non-immediate justification (Wright 2004 and 2007, McGrath forthcoming, Kvanvig and Riggs 1992). All of these thinkers take for granted that experiences have accuracy conditions. I argue for this claim in (2010), ch. 2.

To see what force the Rationality of Perception has, the most fundamental kind of defense that's needed is constructive. What's needed are responses to the principled objections to this idea, an explanation of how experiences could be epistemically appraisable, and a detailed account that highlights the epistemically relevant features of inferential routes to experience, shows what epistemic consequences they would have, and shows how those relations of epistemic dependence would impact the global structure of justification. In short, what's needed is an *epistemic profile* for experiences.

The first step in my constructive defense is to argue that nothing in the nature of experience precludes experiences from manifesting an epistemic status that can be modulated by the same kinds of inferences that modulate the epistemic standing of beliefs. In the next chapter, I provide such an argument, and define the property of epistemic charge.

3

Epistemic Charge

The Rationality of Perception recognizes epistemically significant relationships between experiences and their psychological precursors. The concept of epistemic charge helps us describe these relationships. It helps describe the epistemic impact of psychological precursors on perceptual experience, and the impact that those experiences can then have on subsequent beliefs. Once the notion of epistemic charge is on the table, we can consider the most plausible account of its scope and grounds, and its implications for the global structure of justification.

To start, let us consider the most powerful reasons to think that experiences are precluded from having a rational standing. Two aspects of experience might be thought to preclude them from being epistemically charged: our passivity in having perceptual experiences, and the fact that once we are having a perceptual experience, it seems impossible to change it just by exercising our rational capacities. I'll argue that when we look more closely at these aspects of perceptual experience, we find diagnostics of epistemic charge that would either rule out belief, or rule in perceptual experience. What we don't find, I argue, is a way to distinguish between experience and belief with respect to manifesting an epistemic status.

3.1 Does Anything Preclude Experiences from Being Epistemically Charged?

Ernest Sosa articulates the assumption (as was mentioned in Chapter 2, section 2.3) that perceptual experiences have no rational standing because in having such experiences, the subject is passive. What kind of passivity might underwrite the epistemic unevaluability of experience? We can distinguish between three kinds of passivity. I argue that none of them precludes experiences from being epistemically charged.

A first kind of passivity is phenomenological. It is not part of the phenomenology of perception that our experiences seem to result from mental activity of any sort. But the same is true of many of our beliefs. They do not seem to result from active reasoning either—we simply find ourselves believing that it is time for lunch, that the audience is pleased, that our neighbors are kind, or that the music is too loud. Phenomenological passivity is a poor diagnostic for epistemic charge.

A second kind of passivity is passivity with respect to reasoning of any kind. Could this kind of passivity underwrite the epistemic unevaluability of experience? We apply epistemic norms to all beliefs, even when they don't result from reasoning. For instance, self-ascriptions of experiences are sometimes not the result of reasoning, and cases where we simply believe our eyes are sometimes thought not to result from reasoning. And in some contexts, social allegiances can lead people to form beliefs in ways that may not involve any reasoning at all.[1] And yet none of these routes to belief precludes us from evaluating them as justified or anti-justified.

Perhaps the most powerful version of the idea that experiences are precluded from being epistemically charged draws on a third kind of passivity that contrasts with the upper-echelon rational capacities. These capacities include the capacity to deliberate about what to believe, to formulate one's reasons for what one believes or decides, and the capacity to revise or adjust one's conclusions in light of reflection on other things one believes, or on one's reasons for holding the belief. I'll abbreviate these capacities under the label "reflection." Any belief, it might seem, could in principle be formed by reflection. And that is why all beliefs are epistemically appraisable, according to this line of thought. The thesis that all beliefs could be formed epistemically *well* by reflection is stronger than the thesis at issue here, which is that all beliefs could be formed by reflection—whether they're formed epistemically well, or not.

The generalization that all beliefs could be formed by reflection seems false on either of two disambiguations. On one disambiguation, the generalization is that for any believer, all of that subject's beliefs could have been formed by reflection. But if believers need to have starting assumptions, the generalization won't be true. There will be initial prior beliefs that are needed to get a system of believing off the ground. Some

---

[1] Potential examples from the study of group identification and belief are given by Tamir and Mitchell (2013).

examples for human belief might be the built-in assumption that light comes from above, or assumptions about spatio-temporal continuity of ordinary objects, or unearned confidence in other people's testimony or the deliverances of perception.[2]

On a different disambiguation, the generalization is that for any belief, it could be formed by reflection—even if it isn't the case that all of a subject's beliefs could be. Beliefs with the content "I believe that p" could in principle be formed by reflection—even if they are typically formed by introspection and without reflection. The same point seems to hold for endorsements of perceptual experience, in which a belief with content P is formed on the basis of an experience whose content includes P. (I'll return shortly to the idea that a proposition could be the content of an experience.) Even if one could believe P by endorsing an experience with content P, that same belief could be reached by reflection.

In reply, making reflection the main diagnostic of epistemic charge treats beliefs formed in reflective ways as the ideal form of beliefs—leaving other beliefs as pale approximations. But belief in general may not have any ideal form. Even if it does, it may have multiple ideal forms.

A different paradigm of belief is the toddler's knowing, and hence believing, that her socks are on (after putting them on herself with much effort). The route to belief wasn't deliberation, which would require more self-conscious reasoning than she is capable of, but rather a mix of observation integrated with action.

A more mature subject could reach the same first-person belief ("I just put my socks on") by reflection. The toddler couldn't, yet her belief seems to contribute to her rationality just as much as the older subjects' beliefs contribute to theirs. And its role in the subject's mind seems just as "beliefy" as beliefs formed by deliberation: its felt strength comes in increments, and it belongs to the toddler's outlook on the world. The toddler's belief shapes her sense of possible futures: if her belief is firm, she might expect to put on her socks again tomorrow, whereas if her feeling that she can put on her socks is unstable, her putting them on might feel to her like an amazing surprise. The felt strength of her belief will shape her sense of herself and others: she can put her socks on—unlike a baby, who

---

[2] For a suggestion that our system of belief needs starting assumptions, see Railton (2013) and Hohwy (2013). For potential examples of starting assumptions about ordinary objects, see Carey (2009).

can't. It makes her disposed to respond to challenges as to whether she can or can't put on her socks.[3] These considerations suggest that the rational standing belief is not grounded in each belief's arising from a process that is either reflection or a pale approximation of it.

A different idea is that experiences cannot be epistemically charged, because they cannot be rationally adjusted in response to criticism. According to this idea, for a mental state to be epistemically charged, it must be possible for a subject to adjust it, in order to make it conform to any epistemic norms that can be used to evaluate it. It doesn't seem possible to adjust your experience, other than by looking away, covering your eyes, or otherwise closing off perceptual input (assuming the experience is not an internally generated hallucination). If the experience is over by the time you come to criticize it, there seems to be no way to adjust it at all, rationally or otherwise. So if being able to adjust perceptual experience without managing the intake of perceptual information is necessary for epistemic charge, then by this measure, it seems that experiences can't be epistemically charged.

In reply, we can distinguish between three kinds of adjustment of a mental state in response to rational criticism, any of which could result in getting rid of the mental state (since one way to adjust a mental state is to extinguish it). The three kinds of adjustment are adjustment by deliberation, adjustment by disowning the mental state, and adjustment by habituation.

If experiences were adjustable by deliberation in response to rational criticism, then in response to criticism, such as the information that the contents of one's experience is heavily influenced by vanity, or that the experience is irrational, one would have to be able to explicitly reason to a new experiential conclusion that rationally addresses the critical information.

Adjustability by deliberating about what to believe, including whether to keep a belief that one has already, is a poor diagnostic for epistemic charge. (Three paragraphs back, we considered whether all beliefs can be formed by reflection. Here what's at issue is whether all beliefs that one has already can be adjusted by deliberating about whether to maintain them as they are.) Beliefs in delusions cannot be adjusted by deliberation.

---

[3] I owe this insight about belief and self-conception to Peter Railton's discussion of epistemic authority in Railton (2013).

Rarely if ever has anyone been talked out of the monothematic delusional belief in Capgras syndrome, for example, or out of delusional beliefs in schizophrenia.[4] The background pathology prevents these beliefs from being revised. These beliefs seem to be paradigms of irrationality. Many beliefs are formed and adjusted without deliberation. The issue raised by Vivek's vain projection onto experience is whether his experience is like those beliefs in that respect.

An opponent might suggest that it is only this background pathology that makes the beliefs unadjustable—and in themselves, the beliefs are adjustable. So for all the delusion example shows, according to the skeptic, adjustability using reflective capacities is a good diagnostic of epistemic charge.

In reply, in schizophrenia, it makes little sense to distinguish the beliefs from the background pathology that precludes their adjustment. The pathology consists in having the beliefs to begin with. Absent the pathology, one would not be left with beliefs that one could adjust (such as the belief that one's friends have formed a secret league for persecution, or that the city in which one lives is an elaborate sham-city). One would not have these beliefs in the first place.

The second kind of adjustment is disowning a mental state. If this kind of adjustability is a good diagnostic of epistemic appraisability, then experiences satisfy it. Even if you couldn't make yourself stop having the experience, you can cease to rely on it in your reasoning and action. Ceasing to rely on an experience can even be done to a past experience. So there is such a thing as disowning an experience. When we respond to rational criticism of beliefs by giving up the belief, or by weakening it, this is what we do: we cease to rely on what we believed in reasoning and action (or we cease to rely on it so heavily). So what happens when you cease to rely on a belief happens as well when you cease to rely on an experience.

There is also a difference. In the case of belief, ceasing to rely on a belief can't come apart from ceasing to have the belief.[5] But experience

---

[4] On monothematic delusions (in which people admit to the implausibility of the belief but still maintain it), see Bortolotti (2013) and Coltheart (2005). On schizophrenia and treatment, see Frith and Johnstone (2003) and Campbell (2001).

[5] Are monothematic delusions such as Capgras syndrome (in which the deluded subject reports with distress that a spouse has been replaced by an impostor) an exception to the thesis that ceasing to rely on a belief constitutes ceasing to have it? These delusions are sometimes described as "circumscribed" because the subject does not act in all the ways one

can persist, even if you don't use it in reasoning or action. If the experience persists, does that show that experiences are never fully rationally adjustable?

No. Consider the Müller-Lyer illusion. If you know the lines are not the way they appear, and you cease to rely on the experience, then there is no further rational adjustment to be made in the situation.

Contrast Vivek's experience when it arises from his vanity. If Vivek learned that his experience arose from his vanity, and the experience persisted because of his vanity, that would be a case of residual irrationality. Vivek's situation would be analogous to someone obtuse who disowns an attitude (e.g., disrespect for someone they treat badly), but lacks the understanding needed to correct all the perspectives that go with it. Sometimes the fact that an experience persists, even when a subject disowns it, constitutes this kind of residual irrationality.

The third kind of adjustment of a mental state works by the subject's controlling the conditions that tend to give rise to that type of mental state. We might call this adjustment by habituation—a strategy described by Pascal in his discussion of how one can make oneself believe in God.[6] For instance, suppose one can't bring oneself to believe that climate change will lead to large-scale human disaster (because it is so unfathomable), but wants to believe this. One might put oneself in circumstances that one thinks would lead to forming this belief, by exposing oneself to all the evidence for the drastic effects of climate change, and by talking often with people who are firmly convinced of the grim consequences. Beliefs may be indirectly adjustable by orienting oneself to the factors that shape belief.

The phenomenon of perceptual learning suggests that habituation can apply to perceptual experience as well. Suppose that one habitually uses eye and hair color to distinguish faces from one another, and then moves to a place where everyone's hair and eye color is the same. To code individual differences, one might then try to focus on features of faces that vary, such as distances between the eyes, or between eyes and nose,

would expect they would, given their desires, if the subject believed that an impostor had replaced their spouse (Bortolotti 2013). But the subject is relying on the impostor hypothesis for some subsequent reasoning and actions, and if they didn't, the delusion would be a poor candidate for being a belief to begin with. (For discussion of whether delusions are beliefs, see Currie and Ravenscroft 2002.)

[6] See B. Pascal, (1966), Part II.

or nose and mouth. By engineering the course of perceptual learning, one could come to have different experiences of other people's faces. Here, cultivating habits of attention goes with cultivating experiences that facilitate recognition. So if adjusting by habituation is diagnostic of epistemic appraisability, then once again, experiences satisfy this diagnostic.

So far, I have rejected what strike me as the most powerful kinds of reasons to think that experiences can have a rational standing: experiences are passive, and experiences are not rationally adjustable. Many varieties of passivity and unadjustability pertain to beliefs as well, and some varieties of adjustability pertain to experience. But if none of these factors ground the rational standing of beliefs, what does? And could it also ground the rational standing of experience?

A natural idea is that what grounds the rational standing of both states is their role in the mind. Perhaps there is no other feature of belief, or of routes to belief, that explains why beliefs can be evaluated as epistemically better or worse. Instead, it is their role as states that contribute to our outlook on the world.

We can distinguish between our considered outlook on the world, and our complete outlook on the world at a moment. An outlook may be unstable or temporary, or it may be better characterized by incremental states (such as credences) than binary ones. Parts of the outlook will be at odds with others, and not all parts will have equal weight in the subject's considered view. For instance, in drawing a conclusion from an inference, one might come to discover that one wants to disown the conclusion. Here one has discovered a conflict within one's outlook (possibly a temporary one). Any part of the complete outlook will belong to a perspective on how things are in the world.

Belonging to an outlook plausibly anchors appraisals of other mental states, such as fears and desires. In debates about whether desires are rationally appraisable, one kind of case for saying that they are (or that some of them are) rests on the idea that desires are constitutively linked to judgments or other responses to what is desired as favorable or unfavorable.[7] Compare the case of moral responses to a person's desires,

---

[7] Arpaly (2003), Smith (2005), Railton (2012). A somewhat similar idea is found in Johnston (2001), who argues that affect, a dimension of desire, gets its rational authority from the way in which it is a form of uptake in response to values that one confronts. But this form of response, according to him, is distinct from any representation or judgment.

in which one holds that person accountable for what she wants. The eligibility of desires for moral reactions (such as resentment or gratitude) might be thought to derive from the fact those desires are closely linked (whether causally or constitutively) to judgments about which ends or outcomes are worth pursuing. These judgments in turn contribute to what the subject takes herself to have reasons do to. Such judgments are clearly eligible for being appraised, epistemically and morally. Similarly, fears are most plausibly seen as rationally unappraisable when they are construed as neither causally nor constitutively linked to representations of anything as frightening.

Experience forms part of how things are from our perspective. Experiences that we disown or disbelieve might not belong to our considered outlook, but they are part of the complete outlook. Given that the various forms of passivity and unadjustability do not preclude experiences from having a rational standing, it becomes easier to see how their belonging to our outlook could ground their rational appraisability.

Section 3.3 develops the idea that a mental state has a rational standing because it belongs to the subject's outlook. First I'll look more closely at the idea that experiences are already a kind of belief. Since beliefs have a rational standing, if experience is a form of belief, then that would suggest that experiences have a rational standing too. And if—as I argue next—experience is not a form of belief, then if experiences can have a rational standing, this won't be due to their status as beliefs.

3.2 Experience and Belief

How can we tell whether experiences are beliefs? Experiences aren't beliefs, if they differ from beliefs in their basic structure. For instance, if beliefs are relations to propositions but experiences are not, then experiences will differ from beliefs. What might experiences consist in, if they differ from beliefs in this way?

A first proposal is that experiences are not directed toward the world at all: they don't even seem to present the subject with aspects of the environment distinct from them. Think of "seeing stars" from being hit on the head, or of the pink glow that one experiences with eyes closed in sunlight. According to this position, which I'll call the raw-feel view, all experiences are undirected toward external things. Complex experiences such as Jill's experience of seeing Jack's face are complexes of raw feels, on this view.

The raw-feel view entails that experiences are distinct from belief. But it does not easily fit with the idea that experiences form part of one's outlook on the external world. To the extent that they plausibly do form part of that outlook, the raw-feel view could not be the whole story about the nature of experiences.

A second proposal is that experiences, when they aren't hallucinations or any kind of illusion, are perceptions of external things and their properties. This structure for experiences is distinct from belief, since beliefs can be false, whereas perception as construed here can only relate perceivers to objects that exist and properties that those objects actually have. Call this proposal Naïve Realism.[8]

Like the raw-feel view, Naïve Realism entails that experiences are distinct from belief (on the assumption that beliefs are relations to propositions). But unlike the raw-feel view, Naïve Realism is compatible with the idea that all experiences—not just the ones that aren't illusions or hallucinations—are the kind of state that can be accurate or inaccurate about the subject's environment. Just as beliefs can be true or false, according to this idea, all experiences have accuracy conditions: conditions under which they would be accurate about the environment. Call this proposal the Content View. When Naïve Realism is combined with the Content View, some experiences are fundamentally relations to objects and properties that those objects have, but these experiences, like all experiences, have accuracy conditions.[9] Because they are assessable for accuracy, having an experience constitutes having an outlook on the world.

So far, I've considered two proposals about how experiences could differ in their basic structure from beliefs. Could experiences differ from belief, even if they don't differ in their basic structure?[10]

Consider the temporal profile that standardly attaches to experiences and beliefs. Beliefs have inertia that experiences lack. If you acquire a belief, then it tends to stay in the mind, with no need to re-establish it. Of course it is possible to forget what one once believed. But the inertia of beliefs facilitates their role in planning and guiding behavior, and to that

---

[8] For a defense of Naïve Realism, see Martin (2004).

[9] This claim deserves more discussion. For a defense see Siegel (2010), ch. 2, and for criticism see Travis (2013b) and Brogaard (2014).

[10] For defenses of experiences as belief, see Glüer (2009) and Byrne (2009), and the earlier accounts by Pitcher (1971) and Armstrong (1968), which are criticized by Dretske (1969), Jackson (1977), and Smith (2001).

extent forgetting is not typical. Suppose you learn that your friends' plane will land at 10 p.m. If your belief didn't last as long as your plan to meet them at the airport shortly after 10 p.m., then you'd have to revisit the plan. And if the world changes in a way that makes the belief false—for instance, if the plane is delayed—that fact alone normally tells us next to nothing about whether the belief will change. Analogous observations apply to occurrent judgment. If you occurrently judge that your friend's plane will land at 10 p.m., even when the judgment ends, the content is typically retained.

In contrast, experiences lack the psychological inertia that characterizes beliefs. Whether your experience persists typically depends on whether you remain in contact with the relevant part of the environment. If you see a skyscraper ahead, and then turn so that it is no longer in view, your skyscraper-experience comes to an end, but your belief about where the skyscraper is located will typically persist. Fading into the past extinguishes the experience, but not the belief. This temporal difference results in different modes in which belief and experience contribute to a subject's outlook on the world. Because beliefs persist by default, it is possible to rely on them in planning for circumstances that differ from the ones one is in at the moment of planning. For experiences to help with advanced planning for such different circumstances, they must be converted into memories.

These considerations suggest that if experience were a form of belief, then experiential beliefs would be short-lived, and the reason for their short lives would differ from the reasons for other beliefs' short lives. Experiences don't die from being forgotten, or from the subject's responses to counter-evidence.

A proponent of assimilating experiences to beliefs could respond that beliefs simply vary in the range of temporal profiles they can have— experiential beliefs have one profile, and non-experiential beliefs have another. But the substantive point would remain that experiences have a distinctive temporal profile, and one that precludes it from playing a central role of belief. And the more differences one finds between experiences and non-experiential belief, the less dialectical power an assimilation of experience to belief would have. For instance, if beliefs admit of a range of temporal profiles, perhaps they admit of a range of epistemic profiles as well. Given the diversity of beliefs that the proponent of the experience-as-belief thesis has to accommodate, they seem poorly positioned to use the fact that experiences are beliefs to claim that experiences and beliefs share an epistemic profile.

So there are good reasons to think that experiences aren't beliefs, and they apply to a wide range of theories of the underlying structure of experiences.

3.3 Epistemic Charge

If we wanted to analyze the epistemic impact of Vivek's vanity on his perceptual experience, a simple and natural suggestion would be that the poor epistemic status of Vivek's overconfidence that his audience likes him is transmitted by his perceptual experience to subsequent beliefs. The experience inherits a poor epistemic status from the overconfidence, and Vivek's subsequent strengthening of his belief inherits it from the experience.

This analysis entails that the experience has a rational standing, because Vivek's initial overconfidence can transmit an epistemic property to the experience, only if the experience can inherit that property. And the experience, in turn, can transmit the property to subsequent beliefs, only if it has the property to begin with.

This property that is passed along from overconfidence to experience to belief resembles electric charge. Drawing on this analogy, my label for this property is "epistemic charge." What kind of epistemic charge an experience has can be modulated by psychological precursors of the experience. And like justification, epistemic charge can be transmitted to subsequent beliefs.

Epistemic charge: A property of experience that can be modulated by psychological precursors of the experience and transmitted to subsequent beliefs, and in virtue of which a subject's experience manifests an epistemic status.

The comparison with electricity helps describe potential epistemic features of experience. Like any metaphor, it has its limits. Some aspects of electricity have no analog in any epistemic features of experience. For instance, only negatively charged particles (electrons) are transmitted, whereas both positive and negative epistemic charge can be transmitted. The main point of the metaphor is that it provides a label for a valenced property of experience that manifests the experience's epistemic status, and contributes to the valence and epistemic status of other mental states.

Like having a justified or a poorly justified belief, having an epistemically charged experience makes a pro tanto contribution to the rational standing of the subject. Consider two equally rational subjects, call them S– and S+, where S– has an ill-founded belief that p and S+ has a well-founded belief that p. The two subjects could end up equally rational, because S–'s other mental states compensate for the ill-foundedness of her belief that p. So we can't read off from the fact that S– has an ill-founded belief that p that she is less rational than a subject with a well-founded belief that p.

An analogous point holds for the relationship between an ill-founded belief B and the epistemic status of a belief B* formed on the basis of B. Since other factors besides B may determine the ultimate rational standing of B*, one can't read off from the facts that: (i) B is ill-founded and (ii) B* is formed on the basis of B, that B* is ill-founded as well. B's ill-foundedness might "wash out" on the route to forming B*.[11] But even if it washes out, B still transmits an epistemic property, by making a pro tanto contribution to the rational standing of B*. And if there are other mental states (besides beliefs) that make a pro tanto contribution to the subject's rational standing and are formed on the basis of B, then B can make a pro tanto contribution to the subject's rational standing as well.

A final observation highlights the constraints on how epistemic charge can be moved from an experience to subsequent beliefs (or even to other experiences). Consider Vivek's experience, which characterizes an audience member's facial expressions, as well as the color of her hair. Vivek's vanity affects the expression that Vivek sees (or seems to see) on her face, but not the color he sees in her hair. It might seem natural to say that Vivek has a single experience with contents that characterize her face (face-contents) and contents that characterize her hair color (hair-contents). On the epistemic charge analysis, is the single experience negatively charged, because vanity's exaggerations influence the face-contents, or positively charged, because the hair-contents arise in a perfectly epistemically respectable way?

---

[11] Suppose that a belief B is ill-founded, but it is part of a complex belief in a scientific theory, and the complex belief is well-founded. B's ill-foundedness washes out, if the fact that B is ill-founded makes no difference to the epistemic status of a subsequent belief B* formed on the basis of the complex theory.

To account for these variations, we'll have to say things like "in having content C, the experience can provide less than the usual amount of epistemic support." Epistemic charge will then be relativized to a specific content of the charged experience. In having face-contents, Vivek's experience will be negatively epistemically charged. It won't be Vivek's experience that is positively or negatively charged, but rather Vivek's experience, in having a certain content, that is positively or negatively charged.[12]

I've presented the notion of epistemic charge as a tool that provides a possible analysis of cases like Vivek's. To defend this analysis, at a minimum, one would have to defend the idea that it is irrational for Vivek to strengthen his belief that his audience is pleased. The minimal defense is coming in Chapter 4. For now, I'll focus on explaining three things about the Epistemic Charge thesis.

Epistemic Charge thesis: Some experiences are epistemically charged.

To assess the Epistemic Charge thesis and its role in the Rationality of Perception, further explanation is needed on three fronts:

Scope: What is the scope of epistemic charge among experiences?

Ground: In virtue of what do experiences have any epistemic charge at all?

Modulation: What kinds of factors can modulate the epistemic charge of an epistemically charged experience?

---

[12] Even when we focus only on the face-contents of Vivek's experience, if his face-experience has any epistemic charge at all, it might seem to be negatively charged, relative to believing the face contents, but positively charged, relative to the contents of the intro-spective belief that he has a face-experience. Does this observation give us reason to relativize epistemic charge twice over—once to the contents of the experience, and again to the contents that the experience (in having the selected contents) can justify believing? On that picture, epistemic charge would be a relational property of the face-experience, rather than a monadic property of it.

Whether there is reason to think that epistemic charge is relational in this way depends on the role of the face-experience in providing justification for the introspective belief. On some views, the structure of justification of the introspective belief comes from self-referential contents of the experience ("I am having a face-experience"), rather than the face-contents themselves (Kriegel 2009). On other views, it does not come from any contents of the experience at all, but rather from the route by which the introspective belief is formed (Byrne 2012). If either of these approaches to introspective belief is correct, then it removes the apparent motivation for thinking that a face-experience could be negatively charged relative to face-contents, but positively charged relative to the contents of an introspective belief that self-ascribes the face-experience.

The scope question asks whether all perceptual experiences have epistemic charge. Is having epistemic charge exceptional or standard? The ground question asks what features of charged experiences explain why they are epistemically charged at all, as opposed to having no epistemic charge.

The ground question bears directly on the scope question. The scope of epistemic charge will depend on the factors that ground the epistemic charge of experiences. For instance, if the factors are exclusively contingent features of experience—such as resulting from projected overconfidence—then only the experiences with those features will be charged, and these experiences may occur only occasionally. At the other extreme, if the grounding factors are constitutive of experience, then all experiences will be epistemically charged.

The modulation question assumes that experiences can be epistemically charged, and asks what kinds of factors can increase or decrease its charge, or flip its valence from positive to negative. Taken together, the ground and the modulation questions ask for an account of which features give an experience the specific epistemic charge that it has. We have already met a possible answer to the modulation question: inference can modulate epistemic charge. If experiences can be epistemically charged, this opens the possibility that at least some of the routes to experience that psychologists call "inferences" have conclusions that epistemically depend on their inferential inputs.

In the rest of this chapter, I sketch what strike me as the most plausible and powerful potential answers to the scope, ground, and modulation questions. The sketch lets us see more clearly what the Epistemic Charge thesis entails, and what impact it would have on the global structure of justification.

3.4 The Scope and Ground of Epistemic Charge

Let us start with the scope question. If some but not all experiences have epistemic charge, then the uncharged experiences can in principle still be unjustified justifiers. But if all perceptual experiences have epistemic charge, then the impact on the global structure of justification is different.

When we consider possible grounds, there's good reason to think that if any experiences are epistemically charged, then being charged is standard rather than exceptional. And some potential grounds for epistemic charge suggest that it is universal.

What are the most plausible grounds for epistemic charge of experiences? Earlier I suggested that the fact that experiences form part of our outlook on the world helps motivate the Epistemic Charge thesis, once the misleading apparent reasons to reject it are cleared away. In the case of beliefs, it is difficult to isolate a further feature that ground their role in the mind. By contrast, perceptual experiences have such a feature: their presentational phenomenal character. The phenomenal character of perceptual experience purports to characterize how things in the external world are. The presentational aspects of phenomenal character are closely tied to the presentation of properties in experience.[13] In the rest of the discussion when I mention the phenomenal character of perceptual experience, I am taking for granted that it is presentational phenomenal character.

Phenomenal conservatism is the thesis that having an experience with content P (where P is an external-world proposition) suffices to provide prima-facie justification to believe P. Both phenomenal conservatives and others say that the phenomenal character of perceptual experience endows experiences with powers to provide justification to subsequent external-world beliefs formed on their basis. The first proposal about the grounds of epistemic charge starts from a closely related idea: the presentational phenomenal character of perceptual experiences endows them with a rational standing of their own. This idea can be put in the form of an argument for a universal epistemic charge thesis.

The Phenomenal Ground Argument

P1. All perceptual experiences have presentational phenomenal character.

P2. The presentational phenomenal character of perceptual experiences gives them epistemic charge.

Conclusion: All experiences have an epistemic charge.

The key premise of the Phenomenal Ground Argument, P2, raises several questions. In order to see what kind of impact phenomenal grounds for

---

[13] This type of phenomenal character is discussed under different labels, such as "assertortic force" (Heck 2000), and "perceptual consciousness" (Smith 2002), and "perceptual acceptance" (Price 1932), though Price's notion has further features. For further discussion, see Siegel (2010), Bengson (2013), Chudnoff (2012).

epistemic charge would have on the global structure of justification, I'll consider how these questions could most plausibly be answered.

First, if experiences are epistemically charged just by having a presentational phenomenal character, then what valence (if any) does the charge have, and how much? A plausible answer respects the observation that it is very often reasonable to believe one's eyes and other senses. If you want to know whether the sunset has started, you can find out by looking. Ordinary perceptual experiences like this one can provide a baseline amount of justification for believing the contents of those experiences, or closely related contents. These observations suggest that in the pervasive situations in which it is reasonable to believe your eyes, if perceptual experiences have any epistemic charge at all, they have a positive epistemic charge.

But what exactly is the role of phenomenal character in giving experience positive charge? Here we can distinguish between three roles for phenomenal character in grounding epistemic charge: weak, strong, and intermediate.

In the weak role, phenomenal character merely makes it the case that experience is epistemically charged, and other factors combine with the phenomenal character to determine which valence it has and in what increment. Since there is no such thing as having an epistemic charge but lacking any determinate charge, for this option to develop the Phenomenal Ground Argument as it stands (with its universal conclusion), the other factors would have to be present in all cases. In this respect, experiences would resemble beliefs as they are often construed. Beliefs are often thought to have an epistemic status no matter what, but which epistemic status they have depends on factors besides the mere fact that one has the belief. Whatever factors these are, there is no escaping them.

At the opposite extreme, the strong role for phenomenal character makes experiences more closely analogous to beliefs as epistemological conservatism construes them. According to epistemological conservatism, merely having a belief gives it a positive epistemic status.[14] In the strong role, merely having a perceptual experience gives it a pro tanto

---

positive epistemic charge, where that amount can be augmented or reduced by other sources of positive or negative epistemic charge. For instance, Vivek's vanity could modulate the epistemic charge of his experience of the faces in the audience, making his experience negatively charged. And to reach a baseline relative to which experiences provide pretty good reason to believe one's eyes, other factors besides experience may be needed, such as the negative conditions that there are no defeaters or epistemically bad-making relationships to psychological precursors. (See Chapter 4, section 4.1.2 for discussion). But in the strong role for phenomenal character, there is a minimum positive charge that an experience always has. Because it is analogous to epistemological conservatism, this option would be aptly labeled *phenomenal conservatism*, were that label not already used for a different position. I'll call it "strong perceptual conservatism."

Finally, in the intermediate role, phenomenal character suffices to give experience baseline positive charge, absent defeaters or epistemically bad-making etiologies. Either kind of bad-making factor would prevent the phenomenal character of experience from bestowing baseline positive charge. For instance, in the case of Vivek, the contest between phenomenal character and vanity would be explanatorily prior to bestowing such epistemic charge.

Compared with strong perceptual conservatism, the intermediate role makes experiences less closely analogous to beliefs as epistemological conservatism construes them. I'll call it "intermediate perceptual conservatism." All three versions of premise P2 support the conclusion that all perceptual experiences are epistemically charged, and all of them contribute to the constructive defense of the Rationality of Perception. I am officially neutral between them. But they have different implications for the global structure of justification.

3.4.1 Phenomenal grounds and the structure of justification

If a universal Epistemic Charge thesis is true, as per the Phenomenal Ground argument, then no experiences will be unjustified justifiers, according to the usual sense whereby unjustified justifiers are not admissible for being justified or anti-justified. If there are no unjustified justifiers in this sense, does that entail that the justification of belief must either continue in a regress, or consist in coherence relations between beliefs and other mental states?

No. If epistemic charge were phenomenally grounded, then the overall structure of justification could be in many respects the way that foundationalists take it to be.

Perceptual conservative varieties of phenomenal grounds could introduce self-justifying experiences. These experiences would be similar in one respect to the traditional unjustified justifiers: nothing else would justify them. But rather than being epistemically neutral, these experiences would be epistemically charged by their own features. If at least some self-charged experiences are self-charged positively, then they can play one of the roles of unjustified justifiers: they contribute to justification, without needing to be justified by anything else. They could be self-justifying justifiers.

Could a belief be immediately justified by a positively charged experience, on perceptual conservatism? (The difference between strong and intermediate perceptual conservatism won't matter. Perceptual conservatism is the disjunction of the strong and intermediate versions.). A subject S's belief that P is immediately justified by an experience, just in case there need be no further propositions that S must be justified in believing from a source other than the experience, in order for the experience to justify her in believing that P—or if there are, being justified in believing those propositions need not play a role in S's getting justification to believe P from her experience.

Consider first whether an experience with content p (a p-experience) could immediately justify a belief that p, if perceptual conservatism is true. Even if the p-experience came to have its positive charge in part by the influence of an antecedent psychological state with content p*, it is an open possibility that the p-experience could justify believing that p, without relying on justification for believing p*. For instance, the positive charge bestowed by presentational phenomenology might be enough to provide justification for believing p, and the psychological antecedents might be responsible for providing an increment of positive charge that goes beyond what is needed. On this scenario, the experience with content p could provide immediate justification for believing p.

The situation is no different when we consider the role of a positively epistemically charged experience with content p in justifying a subject in believing a different proposition q. Even if justification from the p-experience for believing p plays a role in providing the justification for believing q, this justification need not come from a source distinct from experience. So epistemically charged experiences can immediately justify beliefs, and those beliefs, together with the experiences that immediately justify them, could in principle form a foundation for knowledge.

Matters are less definite, if phenomenal character plays a weak role. Schematically, on this option, presentational phenomenal character plus factor X suffices to give experiences an epistemic charge (where factor X is not just a negative condition, such as the absence of defeaters or epistemically bad-making etiologies). Whether positively charged experiences can provide immediate justification, on this picture, depends on what factor X is. If X is a factor that only a few experiences have, then the weak role for phenomenal character will not do justice to the idea that experiences manifest an epistemic standing because they belong to the subject's outlook. This consideration favors the perceptual conservative options, among the phenomenal ground hypotheses.

In addition to asking whether self-charged experiences could provide immediate justification (they can), we can also ask whether they have to provide immediate justification. Here, the answer is No. If the minimal unit needed to provide justification includes more than just an epistemically charged experience, then even a positively charged experience will not be able to provide immediate justification.

The Phenomenal Ground Argument develops the idea that experiences are epistemically charged because they belong to one's outlook on the world. One might ask whether highly inattentive experiences contribute to one's outlook in a way that grounds epistemic charge.[15] The phenomenal ground approach could be refined by excluding highly inattentive experiences from the class of epistemically charged experiences. But since most experiences fall outside the category of highly inattentive ones, even this adjustment would make the scope of epistemic charge far-reaching. Epistemically charged experiences would still be standard rather than exceptional.

The phenomenal ground idea could be developed either in a way that takes the foundation to include beliefs that are self-ascriptions of experiences, or in a way that takes the foundation to include beliefs about the external world.[16] The important point is that from the fact that all

---

[15] For discussion of the epistemic role of highly inattentive experiences, see Siegel and Silins (2014).

[16] If experiences are positively self-charged in having the self-reflexive content "I am having this experience," then the foundation can include self-ascriptions of experiences. If

perceptual experiences are epistemically charged by their presentational phenomenal character, it does not follow that foundationalism is false, or that it is true, or that experiences cannot provide immediate justification, or that they can. These positions can only emerge from further commitments, beyond the commitment that all experiences are positively epistemically charged by virtue of their presentational phenomenal character.

3.4.2 Inference: ground vs. mere modulator

I've been discussing the hypothesis that the presentational phenomenal character gives experience an epistemic charge. This hypothesis is one way to develop the idea that experiences are epistemically charged because they belong to one's outlook on the world.

According to a different way to develop this idea, experiences have a rational standing exactly when they result from the kinds of inference that establish epistemic dependence relations. We draw inferences from information (including misinformation) we have already. When the information we infer from belongs to our outlook, the conclusion we draw in making those inferences will belong to it as well. For instance, if Vivek's perceptual experience of the faces arises from unconscious reasoning, then it is epistemically charged, whereas if his other perceptual experiences arise from merely causal routes, then they have no epistemic charge. In general, on this view, the scope of epistemic charge will extend exactly to the range of experiences that result from inference.

Compared to the phenomenal grounds, inferential grounds might be thought to integrate experiences more deeply into a subject's outlook. Even if the subject does or would on reflection disown the inference leading to the experience, the inference leading to the experience and the experience that grows from it reflect a bigger part of what the person is like psychologically, compared to what an experience on its own reflects.

A different role for inferences is to modulate epistemic charge, rather than grounding it. As a modulator of epistemic charge, an inference to experience adjusts an epistemic charge that is grounded in something other than inference.

experiences lack self-reflexive contents, and their only presentational phenomenology is reflected in external-world contents, then the foundation can include beliefs about the external world.

Which inferences could plausibly modulate epistemic charge? One might think that even if Vivek's projection operates by an inference that makes his experiences epistemically charged, the inferences that operate over processes internal to the visual system are the wrong kind to modulate any epistemic charge.[17] More radically, one might deny that any inferences to experiences could modulate epistemic charge. To analyze Vivek's epistemic situation, some other modulating factors would be needed.

If inferences to perceptual experiences can merely modulate their epistemic charge in ways that are analogous to the epistemic effects of inference on belief, then the inputs to the inference must have epistemic standing as well. We can ask about the ultimate sources of epistemic support for the inferential inputs to experience. Here the options are the same as the ones we find when we ask about the ultimate sources of justification of belief: there is an infinite chain of inferences, or a non-linear structure by belonging to which a belief can be justified, or a structure that contains some elements that provide their own epistemic charge—for example, via a phenomenal ground.

In the end, if one starts from the idea that experiences are epistemically charged because they contribute to the subject's outlook, then the most plausible development of that idea leaves us with one main choice point. Either perceptual conservatism is true, which allows experiences to provide immediate justification and entails that all experiences are epistemically charged, or else perceptual conservatism is false, and the consequences for the global structure of justification depend on the features external to experiences that determine epistemic charge. Both choices can do justice to the cases that motivate the Rationality of Perception. The perceptual conservative options have articulated coherence on their side, as they provide a fuller story of how epistemic charge impacts the global structure of justification.

---

[17] For discussion see Siegel (2015) and Jenkin and Siegel (2015).

PART II

Defending the Solution: The Epistemic Profile of Experience

The Rationality of Perception is motivated by the cases of hijacked experiences that populate the previous chapters. My constructive defense of the Rationality of Perception relies on four conceptual ingredients. We met the first ingredient already: epistemic charge. The chapters in Part II introduce the other three ingredients: epistemic downgrade (Chapter 4), inference (Chapter 5), and the workings of epistemic power (Chapters 6 and 7). These ingredients allow us to analyze the epistemic roles played by perceptual experience, if the Rationality of Perception is true. They are the building blocks in constructing the epistemic profile of experience.

We can see the epistemic profile at work in the analysis of a simple example of hijacked experience: the case involving Jack and Jill, which I'll call the anger case. The analysis consists in four claims. It is neutral on the scope and ground of epistemic charge.

The epistemic charge analysis of the anger case

Charge: Jill's experience, in having anger-content, is negatively charged.

Power: Jill's experience, in having anger content, has less epistemic power to support the belief that Jack is angry, than it could have if it weren't influenced by her fear that Jack is angry.

Inference: Jill's anger-experience is the conclusion of an inference that modulates its epistemic charge.

Ill-foundedness: Jill's subsequent belief that Jack is angry, formed on the basis of her anger-experience, is ill-founded because the experience is negatively charged.

The ill-foundeness component specifies that Jill's subsequent belief is ill-founded because it is formed in response to an experience that is negatively charged. The experiences's reduction in epistemic power is a consequence of its being negatively charged. And it is negatively charged, because of the way it results from inference.

Abstracting from the anger example, the epistemic charge analysis applies to the main hijacked experiences I've discussed. In those cases, the Epistemic Charge analysis in schematic form goes like this, where content C is the content that the perceptual experience has as the result of a psychological precursor:

The Epistemic Charge analysis

Charge: The perceptual experience, in having content C, is negatively charged.

Power: The perceptual experience, in having content C, has less epistemic power to support a belief with content C than it could have if it weren't influenced by the psychological precursor.

Inference: The perceptual experience with content C results from inference that modulates its epistemic charge.

The claims about ill-founded beliefs can be divided into beliefs formed on the basis of the hijacked experience, and beliefs that are related or are closely related to the psychological precursors.

- *Ill-founded belief in C*: The subsequent belief in C or closely related content, formed on the basis of the perceptual experience, is ill-founded, because the experience is negatively charged.
- *Ill-founded strengthening of precursor*: The subsequent strengthening of the psychological precursor is ill-founded because it is strengthened in response to the experience, and the experience is negatively charged.

In this schematic analysis of the epistemic situation into which hijacked experience put their subjects, epistemic charge is simply a label for the epistemic status manifested by the hijacked experiences. The rest of the analysis articulates what epistemic charge does.

To explain what epistemic charge does, the concepts of epistemic power and inference need to be carefully defined and properly motivated. In Chapter 4, I introduce the idea of epistemic powers of experience, use this idea to define the notions of epistemic downgrade, and argue that hijacked experiences are epistemically downgraded. Chapter 5 defends a theory of inference, and argues that perceptual experiences can result from epistemically evaluable inferences. Chapters 6 and 7 put the pieces together and explain how perceptual experiences can lose and gain epistemic power from inferences that produce them.

4

Epistemic Downgrade

When experiences become negatively charged, they lose epistemic power to support subsequent beliefs. Loss of epistemic power by experiences is illustrated by the idea of defeat. If you learned that you were hallucinating rather than seeing, you could thereby have less reason to believe your eyes than you normally would. If you learned that Jack looks angry to you because you're afraid that he is angry, then you could thereby have less reason from your experience to believe that he's angry, than you normally would.

My label for loss of epistemic power of experiences is *epistemic downgrade*. (A more exact definition comes later.) The Epistemic Charge analysis entails that experiences can be epistemically downgraded by virtue of being influenced by what a subject fears, suspects, wants, or believes, even if she isn't aware of that influence.

My first step is to introduce the notions that help articulate the epistemic roles of perceptual experience. I introduce the idea of baseline epistemic powers of experience and define several kinds of reduction in these powers (section 4.1). After the notion of epistemic downgrade gets its official definition (section 4.2), I argue that perceptual hijacking can epistemically downgrade experiences (sections 4.3–4.5), and explain the consequences for some plausible theories of perceptual justification (section 4.6). The rest of the chapter (section 4.6–4.7) summarizes the notions of epistemic powers and modulations of it that will allow us to analyze the effects of different kinds of inference on experience in Chapters 6 and 7, after the relevant notion of inference is introduced in Chapter 5.

I begin with the idea that experiences have baseline epistemic powers.

4.1 Baseline Epistemic Powers of Experience

Here are two ordinary perceptual situations.

- You're served a pink drink. It looks pink to you. Because of the way the drink looks to you, you form the belief that the drink is pink.
- You look outside and see a bird on the fence fly away. Because of how the scene looks to you, you form the belief that the bird is flying away.

A common sense presumption about situations like these is that the beliefs are well-founded. The normative notions of well-foundedness and ill-foundedness are defined in terms of the generic notion of rationality that figures in the Rationality of Perception hypothesis (Chapter 2, section 2.2). A belief is ill-founded if it detracts from the subject's rational standing, due to how the belief is formed or maintained. A belief is well-founded if it benefits the subject's rational standing, due to how it is formed and maintained.

Well-foundedness is sometimes called "doxastic justification." I've avoided this term, because it obscures the difference between different types of epistemic downgrade, as we'll soon see.

The notions of ill-foundedness and well-foundedness at work here license no inferences about whether beliefs with these normative properties do or don't count as knowledge. A belief could be well-founded but false, and so being well-founded does not suffice for being knowledge. And being ill-founded is conceptually distinct from whether a belief fails to be knowledge. For all the concept of ill-foundedness specifies, there could be a variety of ill-foundedness that attaches to belief, but is compatible with the belief being a case of knowledge. For instance, the following kind of insensitivity to the evidence on the basis of which a belief that p is held does not obviously preclude one from knowing that p on the basis of that evidence: S has evidence that supports believing that P, and S believes that P in response to that evidence. But were the evidence to weaken, S would keep on believing that P.

Skeptics about justification for external-world beliefs dispute the common sense presumption that beliefs in the bird case and the pink-drink case are well-founded. I am taking the common-sense, anti-skeptical presumption as a starting point in constructing an epistemic profile for experiences that entails the Rationality of Perception. According to this presumption, the experiences in these examples and other ordinary cases of perception typically provide baseline justification for believing one's eyes.

The baseline is high. It is not, for instance, an amount of justification that would support only a very low credence in the proposition that the drink is pink. The amount of justification, however, is different from the structure of justification. Baseline justification need not be immediate justification (on immediate justification, see Chapter 3, section 3.4.1).

To understand more exactly what it means for experiences to provide baseline justification, we need to look more closely at the roles that perceptual experiences play in making beliefs like these well-founded. A first question is whether they play any role at all.

For a long time analytic philosophers held that perceptual experience had at most a roundabout role in providing justification for external-world beliefs. Quine didn't talk about perceptual experience at all in discussing belief formation—only about "sensory stimulation." Davidson famously held that only a belief can justify another belief.[1] Early foundationalists shared Quine's (and perhaps Davidson's) impoverished construal of perceptual experience. They took the main challenge for the theory of empirical knowledge to be to explain how the transition from introspective beliefs ascribing such impoverished "sensory inputs" to beliefs about the external world could be rational.[2]

A shift occurred when analytic philosophers began to analyze perceptual experience as states that were themselves imbued with meaning, and could be accurate or inaccurate—just as beliefs and sentences can be true or false. In neighboring phenomenological traditions, this connection between perceptual consciousness and meaning had been drawn already.

My discussion of perceptual experiences assumes that they have contents pertaining to the external world, where contents are a form of accuracy condition. This assumption is less committal about the metaphysics of

---

[1] Davidson (1986). Quine (1960) worked with notions of *experience, observation,* and *evidence,* but never assimilated sensory stimulation or perception to any of these.

[2] Ayer (1940).

experience than it may seem (as I noted in section 3.2). I am not relying on the idea that if experiences lacked accuracy conditions, they couldn't play any epistemic role beyond the minimal one of causing beliefs—an idea thought to pose a dilemma for epistemological foundationalism (see the discussion of Sellars's dilemma at the end of section 2.5). I make accuracy conditions central to my discussion, because they provide a perspicuous way to describe the epistemically important relationship between experience and belief, and because for experiences to have accuracy conditions, they need not be fundamentally structured as a propositional attitude. All that's needed, for an experience to have accuracy conditions, is that such conditions can be defined out of properties that the experience presents as being instantiated by things in the external world.[3]

If perceptual experiences can be correct or incorrect about occurrences in the external world, a natural next idea is that they contribute to justifying beliefs about the external world, without needing a detour through introspective beliefs in which one ascribes the experiences to oneself. Here are two conceptual tools for describing the epistemic role of the perceptual experiences in the pink-drink and bird-watching situations.

Reason-power

- Your visual experience gives you excellent reason to believe that the drink is pink.
- Your visual experience (in which the bird looks to be moving) gives you excellent reason to believe that the bird is flying away.

Forward-looking power

- If you form the belief that the drink is pink on the basis of the visual experience, ceteris paribus, you'll have a well-founded belief.
- If you form the belief that the bird is flying away on the basis of your visual experience (in which the bird looks to be moving), ceteris paribus, you'll have a well-founded belief.

Both kinds of power fall under what is sometimes called "propositional justification," where this is a kind of epistemic support for believing a proposition that you can have, whether or not you actually believe the

---

[3] As noted earlier (Chapter 3, n. 9), this claim needs defense. I argue for it in Siegel (2010), ch. 2.

proposition.[4] I've avoided using this label, since propositional justification could be either of these kinds of power.

If the pink-drink experience has both kinds of epistemic powers, it is natural to suppose that the experience has the forward-looking power because it has the reason-power. But it is useful to distinguish between the two powers. They underlie different kinds of epistemic downgrade. In addition, a world of philosophical complexity surrounds the idea that experiences give reasons for beliefs, and it is useful to see that there's a notion of baseline epistemic power that avoids them.[5]

Both kinds of epistemic powers, on the face of it, seem apt for characterizing the common sense presumption illustrated by the pink-drink and bird cases. I'm taking it as a starting point that the common sense presumption is at least sometimes correct. If it's correct, then it identifies a level of epistemic support for the beliefs that are well-founded. (There is likely a range of levels. The baseline is best thought of as a range, rather than a single amount.) The pink-drink experience has baseline forward-looking power to support the belief that the drink is pink. And if it makes sense to talk about experiences providing reasons, then the pink-drink experience has baseline reason-power.

4.1.1 Minimal bearers of baseline epistemic powers

My descriptions of the forward-looking powers of the pink-drink and bird experiences can give the impression that each of these experiences has baseline epistemic power all by itself. The same impression could be easily conveyed whenever one asks (as I did in the Preface, and earlier in this chapter) whether perception and experience have or lack baseline

---

[4] For discussions of some distinctions in the vicinity that go under this label, see Turri (2010), Silva Jr. (2013), Kvanvig (2003), Smithies (2014) and (2015), Conee and Feldman (1998), Tucker (2010a).

[5] Some of the complexities: if reasons are facts, then experience does not seem guaranteed to provide a reason in all of the cases in which, intuitively, having an experience makes it reasonable to have an external-world belief. For instance, in the pink drink case, is the fact *that you have a pink-drink experience* your reason to believe that the drink is pink? Or is it rather that experience relates you to a fact that is the reason? What if the experience is an illusion, and it is reasonable to believe that there's a pink drink in front of you, even though that belief would be false? In that case, there is no external-world fact that is available to be the reason. Some of these considerations push against the idea that reasons are facts, while others push in favor of the view that the reason is the fact that you have the experience, rather than any putative fact about the external world that your experience presents to you. For discussion, see Dancy (2000), Byrne (2015), Ginsborg (2006), and Audi (2015), ch. 3.

epistemic powers. Asking this question seems to assume that experiences are bearers of baseline forward-looking power all by themselves.

It is implausible that experiences simply have baseline forward-looking power on their own, without help from any other factors. Having the pink-drink experience does not suffice to provide baseline justification, if the subject has a defeater, for instance. So far, my locutions "the pink-drink experience provides baseline justification" or "the pink-drink experience has baseline forward-looking epistemic powers" have not been intended to attribute to the experience the property of being sufficient to have forward-looking power or provide baseline justification. The property they attribute to the experience is instead the property of belonging to a minimal unit that provides baseline justification, or equivalently, has forward-looking power.

In the pink-drink and bird cases, one can end up with a well-founded belief by responding to one's experience. My description of the situations is not meant to pinpoint exactly which features the situations have, in virtue of which the beliefs end up well-founded.

The minimal unit that has the forward-looking power may include more than experience. For instance, according to the coherentist theories of justification defended by Kvanvig and Riggs (1992) and Gupta (2006), an experience provides support for belief, only together with other belief-like elements (Gupta calls these other commitments "views"). I am, however, holding fixed that experience have contents, and this assumption may be at odds with Gupta (2006) and (2011).

4.1.2 Epistemic powers are relativized to contents

The bird example helps us see that the baseline epistemic powers of an experience are tied to specific contents. You may have less justification from your experience to believe that the bird you saw is responding to a signal from another bird, than you have to believe that it is flying away. An experience's epistemic power is relativized to specific contents C1 of the experience—just as epistemic charge is (Chapter 3, section 3.3).

What exactly is the relationship between the contents for which an experience provides justification (C2), and the contents of the experience itself (C1)? It is often assumed that experiences with content p provide justification for believing p, so that the very same content could be the content of either an experience or a belief. This assumption will be an idealization, if it turns out that perception (including perceptual experience) belongs to a system of representation that differs so radically from belief that it is impossible for perceptions and beliefs to have the same content. But even if contents of experiences and beliefs cannot be shared, there will be some contents of beliefs that are closer to the contents of experience than others. In order to allow that the potential contents of beliefs might differ from the contents of experience, only because of differences in the nature of experience and belief contents generally, we could say that the content C of an experience is *close* to content C* of belief.[6] I have ignored this complication (for instance in the Power clause of the Epistemic Charge analysis), and talked as if experiences and beliefs could have the same contents.[7]

In ordinary perceptual situations like the pink-drink case, the common sense presumption is that there are experiences with baseline reason-power and baseline forward-looking power. The baseline epistemic powers described so far are powers that an experience can have, without manifesting any epistemic status themselves, and therefore without having epistemic charge. The Epistemic Charge thesis allows that these experiences could have baseline positive epistemic charge, which would entail that they have both kinds of epistemic power.

Putting these conceptual tools together, we can distinguish between two kinds of epistemic powers of experience, and both of them are relativized to contents in the same way. For appropriate contents C1 and C2, and keeping in mind that in some cases C1 and C2 can be the same, we can summarize the differences between these kinds of epistemic powers like this:

Reason-power: In having content C1, ceteris paribus, an experience provides the subject with reason to believe content C2.

---

[6] Some theorists would say that a belief's content C* is close to an experience content C, if C* is a "conceptualization" of C. (Compare Peacocke 2004, ch. 3 on "canonical correspondence" between non-conceptual and conceptual content.) Others, such as McDowell (1994), hold that experiences could not justify beliefs unless the contents of experience could be believed without any additional transformation. Self-ascriptions of experiences are also close to the contents of experiences, even if the experiences are not self-representing.

[7] Besides cases of "conceptualization" as Peacocke understands it and self-ascriptions, there is another way in which the content C of experience might be close to a proposition for which it provides justification, without being identical to it. Suppose that if you see Franco sitting down, the content of your experience would be the same whether you're seeing Franco or Franco's twin. Arguably your experience provides justificatory support for believing a proposition about Franco. Seeing Franco sitting can give you excellent reason to believe that Franco is sitting. This case is discussed in Silins (2011).

Forward-looking power: In having content C1, ceteris paribus, an experience has the power to make a belief formed on its basis, with content C2, well-founded.

4.1.3 Epistemic powers and baseline epistemic powers

The distinctions drawn so far allow us to identify an ambiguity in the locutions "experiences provide justification" and "experiences have epistemic powers" (and in the same locutions relativized to contents). The ambiguity did not matter much in the discussion in previous chapters (except in distinguishing between weak, strong, and intermediate roles for phenomenal character in bestowing epistemic charge, in Chapter 3 section 3.4). But it is important for defining epistemic downgrade and upgrade, and for explaining their role in the epistemic profile that will be constructed in the rest of the book.

On the first interpretation, the locutions "experiences have epistemic power" and "experiences provide justification" attribute to experiences the following property: the property of belonging to a minimal unit that provides baseline justification. On this interpretation, the locution leaves implicit that the bearer of epistemic power is a minimal unit, and that the justification it provides is a baseline amount.

The second interpretation leaves less implicit, and attributes a property of providing epistemic power to experiences all by itself. Although this property is in some sense simpler than the one just described, it is not part of the common sense anti-skeptical assumption I've been making that there is any such property. Whether there is depends on whether the minimal unit that provides baseline epistemic power fractionates into an experience that is all by itself the bearer of epistemic power. Common sense presumably takes no stand on this question, just as it doesn't take a stand on whether baseline justification is immediate or not, or on exactly what properties bestow epistemic powers on beliefs like the pink-drink belief. It is conceptually possible that experience, all by itself, is a bearer of epistemic power, but is never by itself a bearer of baseline epistemic power.[8]

---

[8] It would not be useful to characterize this pared-down epistemic power in terms of forward-looking power, since that kind of power was defined in terms of generating a well-founded belief that receives baseline justification from experience.

To picture how a minimal unit providing baseline justification could in principle fractionate, consider the possibility (noted briefly in Chapter 3, section 3.4) that the minimal bearer of baseline epistemic power consists in experience which always comes with a proprietary epistemic power all unto itself, plus other factors that make up the minimal unit, such as a negative condition (lacking defeaters), or justification for background beliefs, or another factor. The locutions "experiences have epistemic powers" and "experiences provide justification," on the second interpretation, attribute to experience an epistemic power that those experiences are a minimal bearer of. An example is the positive charge posited by the strong version of perceptual conservatism. This positive charge will not suffice for baseline justification, because it is compatible with defeat that precludes the experience from having forward-looking power. The minimal bearer of this kind of epistemic power or justification is experience itself, nothing larger.

The notions of epistemic downgrade and upgrade are defined in terms of baseline epistemic power.

4.2 Epistemic Downgrade

We saw in section 4.1 that an experience's epistemic power is relativized to a content. Since epistemic downgrade is loss of baseline epistemic power, it too is relativized in the same way.

We can see the relativization in action. Epistemic downgrade can be localized to some contents of an experience without attaching to all of them. Jill's visual experience when she sees Jack is multi-faceted. She sees his face, the way he walks, the bag he is carrying, and his immediate surroundings. Her experience thus has many contents, each of which characterize a different aspect of how these things look to her when she sees them. His face looks angry, his movements look bouncy, his bag looks heavy, and so on.

If Jill has a single experience with multiple contents, then it might be only the contents characterizing Jack's facial expression that result from her fear, not the contents characterizing the pace of his walk or the bounce of his bag or the path beneath his walking feet. If the fear is the only factor that downgrades the experience, then the downgrade will be localized to some contents of Jill's experience without attaching to all of them. If we want to distinguish between the propositions Jill's experience provides baseline support for believing, and the propositions it provides less (if any) support for believing, we'll have to say things like this: "in having content C1, the experience provides justification below the baseline for a content C2, while in having other contents distinct from C1, it provides baseline justification for contents C2*, which may or may not be distinct from C2."

Schematically, we can say that for any content C, in having content C, an experience is epistemically downgraded. This gives us a general definition of epistemic downgrade.

Epistemic downgrade: An experience E is epistemically downgraded in having content C, iff E's epistemic powers stemming from C fall below the baseline.

The epistemic powers of E differ depending on whether what's reduced below the baseline is reason-power, forward-looking power, or both.

One form of epistemic downgrade is undercutting defeat. An undercutting defeater, for a putative source of justification for a proposition p, is a factor that removes the putative source of justification for p. For instance, suppose you are having an experience as of liquid ahead, but you know you're in a desert and prone to illusions that make certain surfaces look shinier than they really are. Your experience may still give you justification to believe that the terrain ahead is hilly, or that the sun is bright on the sand. But given what you know about your experience of shininess, that experience doesn't give you the usual amount of justification to believe that there is water ahead. Absent good reason to think you are having an illusion, you would have good reason to think your surroundings are as liquidy as they appear, just as you have to think that your surroundings are as hilly and bright as they appear.

From now on, I'll use "defeaters" to denote defeaters that are inside the subject's ken. If perceptual hijacking operates without the subject's awareness of it, where the subject could not become aware of its operation by reflection alone, then its operation by itself cannot be a defeater. Perceptual hijacking could also operate alongside defeaters. For example, if Jill found out that her anger-experience is chiefly due to the influence of her ungrounded fear that Jack is angry, she could gain a defeater for her experience. But gaining a defeater would be adding something to the hijacked experience itself.

4.3 The Downgrade Thesis

The main thesis of this chapter is that the core cases of hijacked experiences lead to epistemic downgrade in forward-looking power without defeat.

> *Downgrade Thesis*: The core cases of hijacked experiences are epistemically downgraded in forward-looking power, without defeat.

Here are the core cases of hijacked experiences, which we have met before. They specify what the contents of experiences are, and how the experiences come to have those contents.

> *Anger*: Before seeing Jack, Jill fears that Jack is angry at her. When she sees him, her fear causes her to have a visual experience in which he looks angry to her. She goes on to believe that he is angry.

> *Preformationism*: When spermist preformationists (who favored the hypothesis that sperm cells contained embryos) look at sperm cells under a microscope, their experiences have embryo-content, due to their favoring preformationism. They go on to believe that the sperm cells contain embryos, and to strengthen their confidence that preformationism is true.

> *Gun*: After seeing a face of a man who is black as a conscious prime, a participant whose task (in an experiment) is to decide whether a subsequent object he is shown is a tool or a gun has a visual experience of a gun when seeing a pair of pliers. He goes on to believe that the object is a gun, and the outlook which associates between black men and guns is strengthened.

> *Vivek*: Vivek is a vain performer. He is irrationally overconfident that his audiences as well as casual observers look at him with approval. When he sees their faces, he has visual experiences in which those faces look approving, even when their expressions are in fact neutral.

The Downgrade Thesis is motivated by the idea that in the core cases of hijacked experiences, where the subjects are unaware of the influence of their fears, suspicions, or presumptions on their experiences, they don't seem to be in a position to rationally strengthen the fears, suspicions, or presumptions on the basis of those experiences. For instance, Vivek has no inkling that how things appear visually to him is influenced by his vanity, and yet he seems not to be in a position to rationally strengthen his expectation that audiences are pleased by his performances, on the basis of his experience of their faces as pleased.

In the rest of this chapter, I respond to what I take to be the three most powerful challenges to the Downgrade Thesis. These three challenges grant that the fear, hypothesis, racialized outlook, and overconfidence make an epistemic impact, but they deny that the impact takes the form of epistemic downgrade of hijacked experiences. The three challenges locate the adverse epistemic impact in three different places. The first two challenges deny that the subsequent beliefs (Jill's belief that Jack is angry, the experimental participant's belief that the object is a gun, or the preformationist's belief that the sperm cell contains an embryo, and Vivek's belief that his performances please the audience) are ill-founded. The third challenge grants that these beliefs are ill-founded, but denies that the hijacked experiences play any role in making them ill-founded.

4.4 Are the Subsequent Beliefs Ill-founded?

According to the first challenge to the Downgrade Thesis, the hijacked experiences give rise to well-founded beliefs, but not knowledge. This challenge minimizes the epistemic problem of hijacked experiences. Jill's subsequent belief that Jack is angry is not knowledge, but it is still well-founded, thanks in part to being based on her experience of his face as expressing anger. The epistemic effect of perceptual hijacking merely precludes *knowing* propositions that could be otherwise be known on the basis of the experience, if those experiences weren't influenced in the ways illustrated by the cases we started with. On this view, the only epistemic shortcoming imposed by Jill's fear that Jack is angry is that her belief that he's angry cannot count as knowledge, even if it is true and well-founded by her experience (and formed on the basis of the experience). If Jack really is angry, Jill would be something like in a Gettier case. Similarly, in the gun case, the belief that the object is a gun is not knowledge, but it is well-founded, by virtue of being formed in response to the experience.

A second challenge denies that any epistemic shortcoming attaches to Jill's subsequent belief. Instead, Jill's experience simply loses some of its reason-power to support the belief. It either neglects to provide her with any reason at all to believe that Jack is angry, or else it provides her with exclusively poor reasons to believe this. This loss of reason-power, however, does not reduce the forward-looking power of the experience. It therefore fails to diminish the rationality of forming or strengthening the belief that Jack is angry, and so fails to make Jill's subsequent belief ill-founded. Jill can form a well-founded anger-belief on the basis of her anger-experience, just as she could in a case where her perceptual experience was untouched by her fear or suspicion.

Both of these challenges grant that there is an epistemic problem in perceptual hijacking. Yet they both allow that it is rational to strengthen the outlook behind the influence on experience, such as Vivek's vanity or Jill's fear. It therefore does little to explain away the sense that strengthening fear in response to fear-generated experience is epistemically problematic. It leaves that aspect of the problem unaddressed.

The option that limits downgrade to the reason-power of experience also minimizes the epistemic relevance of an experience's reason-power for belief. Losing reason-power has no effect on the beliefs formed on the basis of experience. This disconnection between reason-power and forward-looking power calls into question what exactly reason-power consists in. Jill isn't prevented from using her experience as a basis on which to form or strengthen an anger-belief. When the loss of reason-power seems not to have any effect at all, reason-power itself seems to get watered down.[9]

If the subsequent beliefs in our cases of perceptual hijacking are ill-founded, we can ask whether they are ill-founded because they are defeated, or not.

4.5 Do Hijacked Experiences Generate a Defeater?

The Downgrade Thesis says that the experiences in our cases of perceptual hijacking are downgraded without defeat. But what if hijacked

---

[9] Turri (2010) assimilates reason-power to forward-looking power, in the guise of a theory that defines propositional justification in terms of doxastic justification. If reason-power is assimilated to forward-looking power in this way, then there is no such thing as downgrade limited to reason-power. What would get watered down is reason-power when it is not assimilated to forward-looking power.

experiences always generate a defeater? In that case, the experiences would be downgraded because they are defeated. Let us consider what the defeater might be.

One might think that Jill is in a position to notice that her experience conforms to what she already believes. Perhaps this should give her pause. Maybe the fact that her observation confirms her antecedent belief raises the bar for perceptual justification. We can formulate this proposal as the following principle:

Double-check-1: If you notice or are in a position to notice that you have an experience that p when you antecedently believe p or favor p as a hypothesis, then your experience that p by itself does not suffice to justify the belief.

We can compare Double-check-1 to the rationale for triple-blind studies, in which the interpreter of experimental data (e.g., a statistician) does not know which hypothesis the data were collected to test. A rationale for triple-blind studies is that knowledge of which hypothesis was being tested might influence the analyst's interpretation of the data.

Double-check-1, however, is not a promising principle. Consider your belief that you have hands. If Double-check-1 were true, then experience could not provide justification for believing that you have hands. Double-check-1 therefore makes perceptual justification less frequent than we can reasonably suppose it is. Before entering a classroom for the first time, you may expect that it will have chairs in it. But if Double-check-1 were true, then your experience upon seeing the chairs in the classroom could not provide justification for your belief that the classroom contains chairs. More generally, we nearly always have expectations about what we'll see, and if these expectations weakened the justificatory force of experiences, then experiences would only infrequently provide the kind of justification for belief that seems characteristic of them.[10]

---

[10] We could also formulate a principle much like Double-check-1 according to which it is enough if you suspect that your experience conforms to your belief, even if it does not actually so conform. This proposal would replace non-factive suspecting with factive noticing. It would face the same difficulties.

In response to these difficulties, one might revise the principle to make the need for double-checking less pervasive. Perhaps the need to double-check arises not merely when your experience manifestly conforms to antecedent expectations, but when your experience is manifestly influenced by those expectations. A principle that captures this idea is Double-check-2:

> *Double-check-2*: If you notice, suspect, or are in a position to notice that: you have an experience that p when *and because* you antecedently believe p or favor p as a hypothesis, then your experience that p by itself does not suffice to justify the belief.

Double-check-2 entails that if you suspect that your experience results from an influence by a belief or suspicions, then your experience will be undercut as a source of immediate justification. As such, it would prevent experiences by themselves from justifying beliefs (mediately or immediately), even in cases where the influence seems epistemically good or neutral. For instance, suppose you remember how different the trees in the endangered forest looked before you learned that they are Eucalyptus trees. Intuitively, this should not prevent your experience from justifying the belief that the trees are Eucalyptus trees. Or suppose you are a reformed villain, and when you see a thief pick someone's pocket on the subway, you find that whereas before you would have admired the pickpocket's grace, now your most salient reaction is disapproval, and you attribute this shift to your reformation. On the assumption that your visual experience represents that this act of theft is wrong and does so as a result of cognitive penetration by freshly acquired virtue, mere awareness of this sort of transformation from villainy should not prevent your experience from justifying you in believing that the act is wrong.

4.6 The Downgrade Thesis and Theories of Perceptual Justification

The Downgrade Thesis challenges a range of theories of perceptual justification, and constrains an even wider range. Let's start with the relationship between the Downgrade Thesis and the overall structure of justification of an individual subject's beliefs.

By itself, the Downgrade Thesis does not constrain the overall structure of justification. For instance, it can allow that perceptual experiences provide immediate justification at the baseline.[11]

So the Downgrade Thesis is not at odds with immediate justification per se. The Downgrade Thesis constrains when experiences could ever provide immediate justification, since it constrains when experiences can provide baseline justification of any kind, immediate or not. If, in general, an experience with content p can provide immediate justification for a belief that p, an epistemically downgraded experience with content p either provides less than baseline immediate justification, or provides no justification for p at all, and therefore provides no immediate justification.

According to the reliabilist theory on which experiences provide immediate justification by virtue of arising from a reliable process (Goldman 2008), the Downgrade Thesis constrains the exact sort of reliable process that is needed, according to a reliabilist theory of immediate justification, to produce justified belief.

The Downgrade Thesis also constrains theories of perceptual justification that disallow immediate justification, such as coherentism. It entails that any coherence relation among mental states that confer justification on beliefs is sensitive to which experience, if any, is downgraded. If an experience is epistemically downgraded, its contribution to the coherence relation is weakened. Similarly, Wright (2007) rejects the idea that experiences can provide immediate justification, in favor of the idea that for an experience that p to justify believing that p, ancillary background entitlements are needed.[12] According to Wright, these include entitlements to believe general propositions, such as the proposition that there is an external world. Here too, the Downgrade Thesis imposes an additional constraint on perceptual justification, beyond the experience and ancillary entitlements.

The Downgrade thesis is therefore not at odds with foundationalism, coherentism, reliabilism, or the thesis that experiences provide immediate justification per se. It is at odds with any version of these positions

---

[11] On immediate justification, see section 3.4.1. Compare Silins (2008), who suggests that an experience that p can immediately justify a belief that p, only if certain background conditions are met.

[12] See also Wright (1991).

that fails to respect the idea that some cases of perceptual hijacking weaken the epistemic powers of experience.

When it comes to phenomenal conservatism, the Downgrade Thesis is less tolerant.[13] Phenomenal conservatism belongs to the class of theories of perceptual justification that allow experience to provide immediate justification for beliefs.[14] It says that in the absence of defeaters, having an experience with content p suffices to give the subject immediate justification for believing p. The Downgrade Thesis opposes this claim, at least on the interpretation where experience (absent defeaters) suffices to provide immediate justification at the baseline. And phenomenal conservatism has to mean that, to have any bite against external-world skepticism about justification. Its bite against skepticism is its primary motivation.[15]

If phenomenal conservatism is to play its advertised role in answering the external-world skeptic, then it must be a theory of both reason-power and forward-looking power. Consider the following version of phenomenal conservatism that limits its theory to reason-power: in the absence of defeaters, having an experience with content p suffices to provide reason to believe p, but allows that a belief formed on the basis of the experience would not thereby be well-founded. This position is power-less against a skeptic who claims that skeptical scenarios weaken or even eliminate the forward-looking power of experience. Reason-power has no cash value in producing well-founded belief.

Limiting phenomenal conservatism to reason-power waters down the thesis that phenomenal conservatives usually defend. It is also at odds with a powerful idea often invoked to defend phenomenal conservatism: the idea that if a subject lacks a defeater for their experience, then there would be nothing epistemically wrong with the belief formed by endorsing the

---

[13] The challenge to phenomenal conservatism is discussed by Markie (2006), Tucker (2010b) and (2013), Jackson (2011), McGrath (2013a, 2013b), Huemer (2013), Lyons (2011a, 2016), Fumerton (2013), Sylvan (2015 and ms), Teng (2015, 2016, and ms), Brogaard (2013), Vance (2014), as well as Briscoe (2015), Lowe (2015), Pagondiotis (2015), Zeimbekis (2015).

[14] A few of the many defenders of the position that experiences suffice to provide prima-facie immediate justification for external-world beliefs include Pryor (2000), Huemer (2007), Pollock (1970, 1986), Pollock and Oved (2005), Tucker (2010b) and (2011). For discussion of related positions and oppositions, see Siegel and Silins (2015).

[15] See Pryor (2000).

experience.[16] The epistemic powers of experience are weakened, to the point where an experience could harbor justification, you could have no defeaters of any kind, but if you endorsed the experience, your belief would end up ill-founded by virtue of the influences from psychological precursors. This position gives up on the idea that forming beliefs is epistemically appropriate, when the subject does the best she can in responding to her experiences.

The distinction between reason-power and forward-looking power lets us formulate a much less ambitious version of phenomenal conservatism—one that does not try to answer the skeptic, and concedes that the reason-power of an experience may have zero impact on whether a belief formed on the basis of that experience is well-founded. The core cases on this view leave the reason-power of experience untouched, but that power becomes inaccessible for forming well-founded beliefs.

This position bears little resemblance to the standard versions of phenomenal conservatism, and has none of its motivations. For phenomenal conservatism to play its advertised role in resisting the skeptic, then, it has to apply to both reason-power and forward-looking power. As such, it is at odds with the Downgrade Thesis. The Downgrade Thesis allows that even absent defeaters, experiences lack baseline forward-looking powers. So the Downgrade Thesis opposes phenomenal conservatism.

4.7 Epistemic Upgrade and Enrichment

So far, I have argued that perceptual hijacking leads to epistemic downgrade. Specifically, it leads to epistemic downgrade in the forward-looking power of hijacked experiences. A second potential modification of baseline epistemic powers is more complex. It is that experiences are *epistemically upgraded*, rather than epistemically downgraded. What is epistemic upgrade?

Consider two phenomenally identical experiences in which a banana looks yellow to the perceiver. Suppose these two experiences differ in how much justification they provide for believing *x is yellow*, where x is

---

[16] Along with BonJour (1985), Jackson (2011) and Lycan (2013) go further, and suggest that refusing to believe your eyes, absent defeaters, would be irrational. See also Zagzebski (2009). Sylvan (ms) and Smithies (2016) argue more weakly that it would be less than fully rational not to believe one's eyes, absent defeaters for experience.

the banana in each case. (We can set aside whether the experience has a singular element that picks out a particular banana, and it won't matter whether the banana is the same each time.) Since it won't matter whether the justification the experiences provided is reason-power, forward-looking power, or both, I'll use the coverall term "justification."

The baseline experience provides justification at the baseline for this belief. If the magnitude of justification provided by the other experience is above the baseline, then that experience is upgraded. More exactly, this experience is upgraded, in having the content *x is yellow*.

Is it sensible to suppose that there is such a thing as upgrade? Here it is useful to distinguish between two ways of exceeding baseline justification.

Q1.   Is it possible to have justification above the baseline for believing: *x is yellow*, from an experience that is phenomenally identical to the baseline banana experience?

Q2.   Is it possible to have justification above the baseline for believing: *x is yellow*, from any source or combination of sources at all?

Q1 is the kind of question we are asking, when we ask whether upgrade is possible. We are not asking whether you could gain justification for believing "x is yellow," beyond what you already have from an experience, by adding other factors such as further experiences (you look at the banana in different light), or testimony (someone assures you that x is yellow). And we are not asking whether you could get more justification for p from one experience, than you could get for p from a phenomenally different experience. For instance, consider a tree expert and a non-expert who look at the same pine tree, and the expert gets more justification to believe it's a pine tree than the non-expert gets, because the expert's experience has the content *x is a pine tree*. Instead, when we ask Q1, we are asking whether it is possible to have justification above the baseline from an experience that is phenomenally identical to the baseline banana experience.

If there is such a thing as upgrade, then the answer to Q1 is yes. If the answer to Q2 is no, then there is no such thing as upgrade. I'll argue in Chapter 7 that the answer to both questions is Yes. In response to Q2, it is possible for a subject to possess justification above the baseline for believing *x is yellow*, and in response to Q1, it is possible for that magnitude of justification to come from experience.

A closely related modification of baseline epistemic powers is epistemic enrichment. An experience's baseline epistemic powers are epistemically enriched, if they lie at the upper range of the baseline. For instance, suppose the presentational phenomenal character of perceptual experiences can bestow them with a positive charge, as per the two versions of perceptual conservatism discussed earlier (Chapter 3, section 3.4). In principle, alongside the positive charge bestowed by that phenomenal character, an epistemically appropriate inference could give rise to the experience, and bestow it with another increment of positive epistemic charge, with the result that the experience has a positive epistemic charge at the upper range of the baseline. I argue in Chapter 7 that some inferences to experience can have this enriching effect.

Upgrade, downgrade, and enrichment are analytic tools for describing the epistemic powers of experiences. Since those powers are part of epistemic charge, these tools are needed to describe the epistemic profile of epistemically charged experiences. To fill in the profile, what's needed is a specification of the kinds of routes to experience that could modulate epistemic charge. The specification developed in the rest of Part II is that the epistemic charge of experiences can be modulated by inference. So the next natural step is to examine the nature and psychological anatomy of inference.

5

Inference without Reckoning

In the mind, we find many ways of responding to information. Observing at dusk that the sky is growing dark, you recall that you need to buy lightbulbs. A different response to the information that it is growing dark outside would be to burst into song, or into tears, or laughter. None of these responses would be cases of drawing a conclusion from the information that it is dark outside. None of them is a case of inferring.

Is there a kind of response that is distinctive of inferring? Here is a hypothesis, which I'll call the Response hypothesis: inferring is a distinctive kind of response to an informational state, or to a combination of such states, that produces a conclusion. An informational state can take the form of a belief, but it can also take the form of a perceptual experience, a supposition, or an attitude (in the psychologists' sense). The distinctively inferential kind of response to information is formed when one reaches a conclusion.

The kind of conclusion drawn in distinctively inferential responses can be a belief, but the characterization of inferential responses I'll offer abstracts from the type of mental state that embodies the responses. The result of abstracting lets us see how responses could result in perceptual experiences. But to start, I'll focus on cases where they produce belief.

The Response hypothesis might appear trivial. With a broad enough notion of response, it can seem obvious that inferring involves responding to an informational state. But it is far from trivial to identify the kind of response that is distinctive of inference. And in principle, the mental activity distinctive of inference could differ from any response that produces the conclusion (a possibility discussed by Mark Richard).[1] So the Response hypothesis is a substantive claim. In this chapter, I defend it.

---

[1] Richard (forthcoming).

A large handful of thinkers who have defended the Response hypothesis have claimed to analyze the distinctively inferential response further. One type of proposal, arguably found in Frege and discussed by many thinkers after him, is that one draws an inference by registering some information (where information can include misinformation), and reckoning that it supports the conclusion, with the result that one reaches the conclusion.[2] If this picture of inference had a slogan, it might be that in inference, one concludes because one reckons, where reckoning is taking some information to support a conclusion. I'll call this model of inference the reckoning-model (a more exact definition of it is coming later), which has been discussed in connection with the idea that inference involves a "taking condition": the condition that one draws a conclusion because one takes informational input to support it.[3]

I argue against the reckoning model on the grounds that reckoning is not necessary for inferring (though reckoning may occur in some inferences), while offering reasons to favor the hypothesis that inferring is a distinctive kind of response to information that produces the conclusion. The nature of inferring can be illuminated, even if we don't analyze it in terms of other mental states and processes that can be characterized independently of inferring. Perhaps there is an analysis of inferring, distinct from the reckoning model. But even if inferring has no further analysis, we can understand quite a bit about what inference is, by contrasting it with neighboring mental phenomena, and reflecting on what underlies these contrasts. We can understand enough about inference to see how inferential responses could result in perceptual experiences. This chapter is an exercise in illumination without analysis.

The labels "inference" and "inferring" are used widely in Psychology, Philosophy, and other modes of inquiry, with great variation in meaning. Before explicating the Response hypothesis and criticizing the reckoning model, I define the kind of inference that I'm purporting to illuminate. These phenomena satisfy three starting assumptions. I'll argue that they include the phenomena that proponents of the reckoning model (as well as many of its other opponents) claim to illuminate.

---

[2] Frege (1979).

[3] Discussion of the taking condition is found in Audi (1986, 2001), Boghossian (2014), Broome (2014), and Chudnoff (2014), all of whom defend it, and Wright (2014), who rejects it.

5.1 Three Starting Assumptions

The first starting assumption about inference is that it is a psychological phenomenon with an epistemic upshot. Inferences establish an epistemic dependence of the inference's conclusion on its inputs. The conclusion of an inference is thus both its psychological endpoint, and an epistemic upshot.

The epistemic upshot of an inference bears on the subject's rational standing. If a subject draws a poor inference, then her drawing it detracts from her overall rationality. If the inference is poor and the conclusion is a belief, then the belief is ill-founded: it is formed epistemically badly, and that status, too, detracts from the subject's overall rational standing.

When the conclusion of an inference is a belief, the well-foundedness of the conclusion depends on the well-foundedness of the inputs to the inference. Even if the inputs include perceptual experiences, and if such experiences are not the kinds of states that can be well-founded (contrary to the Epistemic Charge thesis defended in Chapter 3, section 3.3), the well-foundedness of the conclusion still epistemically depends on the experiences. If the experience lacks epistemic power, for instance because it is defeated, then the conclusion will not be as well-founded as it could be, if the experience had more epistemic power.[4]

The psychological ingredients of inferences are conclusions and inferential inputs to those conclusions. It can be natural to use both "conclusion" and "input" to label something closely related to these psychological entities: propositions that are their contents. Both uses of these terms can be useful. But it is psychological states, not propositions, that stand in relations of epistemic dependence of the sort characteristic of inference. If you infer a state with content Q (a Q-state) from a state with content P (a P-state), then your Q-state epistemically depends on your P-state. But if the inference is poor, then the proposition Q may not depend logically, semantically, or in any other way on the proposition P. Other relations of epistemic dependence could be defined for propositions, but those

---

[4] I'll set aside inferences from suppositions in this discussion. One might think that the conclusion of an inference from a supposition is a conditional belief *If P then Q*, where P is the content of the inferential inputs, and Q is the content of the conclusion. Even then, it will still involve a response to P or to the informational states. The Response hypothesis says it is a distinctively inferential kind of response.

dependence relations are not necessarily the kind that is established by inference.[5]

Often the conclusion of an inference is a belief. Other psychological states can be conclusions of inference as well. Some inferences begin from suppositions, and issue in conclusions in which one merely accepts a proposition, without believing it. Here one uses inference to explore the consequences of a supposition, when it is combined with other things you accept or believe. In other cases, one might accept a proposition for practical purposes. That kind of acceptance can be either an input of an inference, or a conclusion. Later on (section 5.6) we will see how inferential responses can result in perceptual experiences.

Consider a case where the conclusion of an inference is a belief. Reaching the conclusion by inference should not be identified with initially forming the belief. You might already have the belief, before you make the inference. For instance, suppose you believe that the person who works at the counter in your local post office is kind. Although you have never met the person who works in the post office, you've been left with the impression that she is kind by numerous stories you've heard from people about their transactions at the post office. When you finally go to the post office yourself, you meet the person who you've heard about. She sells you postage stamps. You then understand how other people got the impression that she is kind, and you share this impression yourself. By making an inference from your observations, you add a new basis to the belief you had before you went to the post office. Here, your inference is a way of adding to the basis of a belief you had already, before you drew the inference.[6]

---

[5] For instance, Laplace (1814) and Chalmers (2012) explore relationships of knowability, in order to probe what else you could know a priori, if you knew all the propositions in a carefully defined minimal subclass.

[6] Wright (2014), while discussing what he calls "acceptances," of which beliefs are meant to be a species, writes: "Inference is . . . basic mental action: the formation of acceptances for reasons consisting of other acceptances." The Response hypothesis also identifies inference with a kind of mental action, but there is reason to deny that it is the action Wright describes. One might already believe (or otherwise accept) a conclusion prior to inferring it. But Wright's definition seems to either rule out that you could already believe Q before inferring it from P, or else to require that if you already believe Q and then infer it from P, you believe Q twice over, with two instances of the same belief in the mind. The post office case, where inference adds to the basis of a pre-existing belief, suggests that both options are implausible.

A final note about the first starting assumption concerns the grammar of "response." In English, "response" can denote a mental state that one comes to be in by a certain dialectical process. For instance, a response to a question can be an answer. X's response to Y's claim can be to deny it. A response to a line of reasoning can be a belief. For instance, suppose you rehearse for me your reasoning that the apricots are ripe, because apricots ripen when they're pale orange, and the apricots on the tree are pale orange. In response to the part of your reasoning that follows "because," I too, like you, might form the belief that the apricots on the tree are ripe. It would be natural to say that one of my responses to this part of your reasoning is the same as your response: it's to believe that the apricots are ripe.

These observations about English suggest that when we examine inference as closely as one has to when trying to understand its nature, we will find several different things in the same vicinity, all of which are natural to call "responses." First, there is the route by which one came to the belief, which in the apricot example is: inferring. Attempts to analyze the inference need a label for this route. In contrast, there is the conclusion at the end of this route, which in the apricot example is a belief. Finally, there is the conjunction of these two things, and this conjunction is arguably what's denoted by the most natural uses of "response" in English. When we say "Y's response to X's claim that P was to deny it," we are denoting not only Y's claim that P is false, independently of what prompted it. We are also saying that Y claimed that P is false, in response to X. We are identifying a mental state in part by the type of route by which it was formed. In the apricot example, this kind of response is the belief that the apricots are ripe, together with the route by which that belief is formed.

In my constructive defense of the Rationality of Perception, it will be useful to talk about perceptual experience both in the simple sense as the mental states that result from inference, and also as inferential responses themselves. Drawing on the various natural uses of "responses," "Experiences can be inferential responses" means the same as "Experiences can be formed by inference." In the rest of this book, I will talk both about experiences as inferential responses (tracking the most natural way to use the English "response"), and about experiences as results of inferential response (in a more fine-grained sense of "response," which is useful when exploring the nature of inference).

The second starting assumption concerns the relationship between inference and consciousness. The process of inferring doesn't have to feel like anything. You don't necessarily have to think anything to yourself, in inner speech or otherwise. You don't have to rehearse the reasoning that brought you to the conclusion. For example, while walking along a rainy street, you might come to a puddle and think that it is too big to hop across, so you will have to go around it. You need not think to yourself that you have to walk around the puddle if you want to keep your feet dry. A child playing hide and seek might not look for her opponent on the swing set, because the swings provide no place to hide, and hiding in plain sight is an option she doesn't consider.[7]

These inferences do not involve any more cognitive sophistication than what's needed to play hide and seek, or to keep one's feet dry. Yet it is clear that the thinkers in these cases end up at a conclusion by responding to information they have, and that the conclusion epistemically depends on the information they respond to. If you underestimate your own puddle-hopping abilities because you are excessively fear-ridden, your conclusion that you have to go around is ill-founded, and it is ill-founded because it is based on an ill-founded assumption that you can't jump such long distances. This case differs psychologically from cases of inference in which one rehearses the premises or conclusion to oneself or someone else. But its upshot is the same relationship of epistemic dependence of a conclusion on another psychological state.

Although drawing a conclusion doesn't have to feel like anything, on some occasions, drawing an inference has a conscious profile. For instance, one might be aware of the exact moment at which one concludes that there is not a rock in one's mouth, after biting into a forkful of crunchy salad, wondering whether the crunch was entirely due to nuts and other bits of food, and trying discreetly to find out. This transition is an example of ending a search by reaching a conclusion. That kind of transition sometimes has a conscious profile, and is often an inference from information gained from the search.

The third and final starting assumption I'm making is that inferences are not always illuminatingly reconstructed as drawing conclusions from premises, when premises are propositions. ("Premise" has the same

---

[7] A similar example is given by Boghossian (2014).

ambiguity between psychological and logical uses as "conclusion." From here to the end of this section, I'll use "premise" and "conclusion" to denote a proposition rather than the psychological inputs and upshot of inference.)

Consider the simple case of responding to an experience whose contents include P, by forming the belief that P. For example, you look at a display containing colored shapes, and your visual experience includes the content that would be aptly characterized by saying "a reddish square is above a green triangle." Let P be the content that a reddish square is above a green triangle. If you believe your eyes, then you'll believe that a red square is above a green triangle in the display.

If you wrote down the inference from experience to belief as a premise and conclusion, it would be an inference from the experience with content P, together the beliefs just described, to the conclusion that P. Focusing only on the contents of states would lead to including P in both premise and conclusion. And yet the response to the experience generates a relation of epistemic dependence that closely parallel the kinds found in paradigms of inference.

The notion of inference that includes all three assumptions denotes a kind of epistemic dependence that does not stand or fall with the subject's consciousness of drawing a conclusion, or with reconstructibility into epistemically relevant semantic and logical relations between propositions. There are arguably sub-categories of epistemic dependence that are defined by either of these features. But whether these three assumptions I've outlined demarcate a natural kind of epistemic dependence or not, they frame the kind of inference that I am purporting to illuminate.

5.2 What Kind of Response Is Inferring?

Putting the three starting assumptions together, we have a notion of inference according to which: inference establishes epistemic dependence of a conclusion on inferential inputs, inference involves a link between an input and conclusion that need not leave any mark in consciousness, and inference is not always illuminated by the model of an argument with premises and conclusions.

By themselves, these starting assumptions do not speak to the nature of inference. The Response hypothesis is that inferring is a distinctive way of responding to an information state that produces a conclusion. If the Response hypothesis is true, then the distinctively inferential response is a locus of epistemic appraisal. An adequate theory of that type of response should identify the dimensions along which inferences can be epistemically better or worse. When the conclusion of inference is a belief, these will be dimensions of well-foundedness. A belief is well-founded if it is formed and maintained epistemically well, and ill-founded if it is formed or maintained epistemically badly.

In explicating the notion of response, I'll initially talk as if inputs are evidence. But the status of inputs as evidence is not essential to the notion of response. What's important is that the inputs are information that the subject has.

What is it to respond to evidence that one has? Consider ordinary updating of beliefs. If you see someone in the room walk through an exit, normally you'll believe they are not in the room anymore. This is an automatic adjustment of belief in response to changing perceptions. Responses to evidence are often less automatic when it takes some effort to recall the relevant facts (how far are you from your destination? how many miles per gallon does the car get?) and to think the matter through. In both cases, responses to evidence involve some ordinary sense in which you appreciate the force of the evidence you are responding to, even if the "appreciation" does not take the form of a higher-order belief that the evidence rationally supports the proposition you come to believe.[8] It seems doubtful that the mental activity involved in responding to evidence can be explained in terms of any other psychological notion.

The notion of a response can be brought further into focus by contrasting it with six different relations that a subject could stand in to psychological states, distinct from inferentially responding to them. These relations group into three kinds: failures to respond to informational states; responses to something other than informational states; and non-inferential responses to informational states.

---

[8] For discussions of other forms the appreciation might in principle take, see Fumerton (1976), Audi (1986) and (2001), Tucker (2012), and Boghossian (2014). Since "appreciation" is factive, these examples must be construed as ones in which the evidence does in fact support what you come to believe.

5.2.1 Failures to respond

The first relation highlights the difference between responding to an informational state inferentially, and being in an informational state that one fails to respond to in any way at all.

First, suppose that after looking in three rooms for your passport, you form the belief that it isn't anywhere else in the house. The mere sequence of searching and then forming the belief does not settle what kind of response the belief is to the information you got from searching, if it is any response at all. You could form the belief spontaneously, without its being any sort of response to the information you got from looking—not even an epistemically poor response in which you jump to the conclusion that your passport is lost.

Two subjects' minds could move from the same mental states to the same conclusions, where only one of them is inferring the conclusion from the initial mental states. The other one's mind is simply moving from one set of states to another. Adapting an irresistible term from John Broome, we could call a transition from informational state A to informational state B "mental jogging" when state B is not any kind of response to state A.[9] What's the difference between mental jogging and inferring? A natural suggestion is that whereas there is no response in mental jogging, there is in inference. If you drew an inference from the information you got while looking for your passport, perhaps together with some background assumptions, you were responding to the information and assumptions.

In the case where information is evidence that a subject has, she could *bypass* that evidence, instead of drawing inferences from it. You could have some evidence that the café is closed on Mondays (for instance, by knowing that it is closed on Mondays), and yet nonetheless plan to have

---

[9] Broome (2013) uses "mental jogging" to denote a more limited phenomenon, which is a foil for reasoning as he construes it. Broome writes: "Active reasoning is a particular sort of process by which conscious premise-attitudes cause you to acquire a conclusion-attitude. The process is that you operate on the contents of your premise-attitudes following a rule, to construct the conclusion, which is the content of a new attitude of yours that you acquire in the process. Briefly: reasoning is a rule-governed operation on the contents of your conscious attitudes." (p. 234).

By contrast, Broome's mental jogging is an inference-like transition in which you reach the conclusion from them "automatically," rather than operating on them following a rule. The second and third starting assumptions entail that inference of the sort discussed here need not involve conscious premise-attitudes.

lunch at that café on Monday, failing to take into account your know-ledge that the café will be closed then. You are not discounting that evidence, because you are not even responding to it at all in believing that you will have lunch at that café on Monday.

Another example of bypassing evidence comes from a kind of change-blindness in which you fixate on an object that changes size, yet you fail to adjust your beliefs in response to the information about the size change that we may presume you have taken in, given your fixation on the object. This phenomenon is illustrated by an experiment that uses a virtual reality paradigm.[10] In the experiment, your task is to select the tall yellow blocks from a series of blocks that come down a belt, and move them off to one side. Short yellow blocks and blocks of other colors should stay on the belt. In the experiment, after you have picked up a tall yellow block but before you have put it in its place, the block shrinks (hence the virtual reality set-up). But many subjects keep on with their routine of putting the shortened block where it doesn't belong—in the place designated for tall yellow blocks. They are fixating on the block, and for the sake of illustrating bypass, we can presume they are experien-cing the block as short. But they are not discounting this information when they maintain their belief that the block belongs with the other tall yellow ones. They are not even responding to this information. Their belief that the block is (still) tall and yellow bypasses evidence that it is short.

Bypass is a special case of mental jogging, as these relations have been defined. The concept of bypassing evidence is useful, since it highlights a form of mental jogging that is epistemically detrimental.

So far, I've contrasted inferring with mental jogging from one informational state to the next, and bypassing the information in an informational state. The difference between inferring and these relationships is well captured by the idea that the subject is responding to information in inference, but is not responding to it in any way in the other cases.

The next two relations highlight the differences between what one responds to in inference, and what one responds to in other cases: processes fueled by rhythm and rhyme, and association between concepts.

---

[10] Triesch et al. (2003).

5.2.2 Responses to non-informational states

The second kind of relation consists of responses to non-inferential states. Suppose you say to yourself silently that 16 people fit in the room. If you went on to hear yourself think that there are 16 days 'til the next full moon, you might end up making this transition because these sentences (half-) rhyme and follow a rhythm ("How many people fit in this room? How many days 'til the next full moon?") In the guise of inner speech, the second thought would be a response to the rhythm and sound of the first innerly spoken thought. By contrast, inferring is not a response to rhythm and rhyme. It is indifferent to rhythm and rhyme.

Responding to information differs from responding to concepts. In associative transitions, one responds to the concepts in the informational state, rather than to any truth-evaluable portion of the state's content. For instance, suppose that observing at dusk that the sky is growing dark, you recall that you need to buy lightbulbs. This transition from observation to memory is fueled, let's suppose, by the fact that you associate the concepts 'darkness' and 'light.'

Abstracting from the example, the transition from a thought involving a concept X (X-thoughts) to thoughts involving Y (Y-thoughts), puts no constraints on which thoughts these are. Whenever one thinks a thought involving the concept 'salt'—such as that the chips are salty, or that the soup needs more salt, or that salt on the roads prevents skidding—one is disposed to think a thought—any thought—involving the concept 'pepper.'

Associations leave entirely open what standing attitudes the subject has toward the things denoted by the concepts, such as salt and pepper. A subject may have zero further opinions about salt and pepper. The concepts may be no more related in their mind than the words "tic," "tac," and "toe." Which thoughts are triggered is constrained only by the linked concepts, not by any attributions a subject makes using the concept, such as attributing saltiness to the soup. In contrast, inference involves responding to predicatively structured information.

5.2.3 Non-inferential responses

The third kind of relation consists of non-inferential responses. For instance, thinking that it is dark outside might make you imagine that you could turn on the sky by switching on a giant lightbulb. The image of tugging a chain to turn on the sky, in turn, makes you remember turning on your lamp, and finding that the bulb was burned out. You then recall that you need to buy lightbulbs. The transition in your mind from the dark-outside thought to the need-lightbulbs thought exploits what one knows about lightbulbs, darkness, and light.[11] rather than being an inferential response, it is a response to narrative possibilities generated by the states that one is in.

The example makes evident that you need not be drawing a poor inference from "It's dark outside" to "I need to buy lightbulbs," in order to respond to the information that it's dark outside. The norms for generating narratives differ from the norms for responding inferentially, even though one could respond in either way to the same informational state, such as a thought that it is dark outside. A single transition could be a good development of a narrative by the standards of vivid, engaging fiction, but poor by the standards of inference.

A different relation to informational states is to direct one's attention. For instance, suppose your belief that there are pelicans nearby heightens your awareness of potential pelicans. It puts you on the lookout for pelicans. You tend to notice pelicans when they're there. When you notice them, your belief that pelicans are nearby does not affect how you interpret what you see. It simply directs your attention to places where pelicans are likely to be, without otherwise influencing which experiences you have when you attend to those places.

In this kind of case, your belief that pelicans are nearby helps explain why you form beliefs that you'd express by saying "I am now seeing a pelican" or "There is another pelican." This explanation, however, is mediated by your perception of pelicans. And those perceptions would normally give rise to the same beliefs, whether or not your attention had originally been directed to the pelicans by your prior belief that pelicans

---

[11] Boghossian's depressive (2014), who is supposed to illustrate a transition that isn't inference, has a wandering mind that creates a narrative depicting himself as isolated from those people in the world who are having fun, and resonant with suffering people. Upon thinking that he is having fun, the depressive goes on to think that there is much suffering in the world. The case is not described fully enough to identify what those responses are, but on many natural elaborations of it, they would involve inferences made in response to aspects of his outlook. When Boghossian describes the depressive's mental transition as an association, he is using a less fine-grained set of distinctions than those introduced here.

are nearby, and whether or not you had the prior belief that pelicans are nearby. In contrast, for you to infer that you're seeing a pelican (or that X, which you can see, is a pelican) from the belief that pelicans are nearby, you'd have to respond to the information (perhaps it's misinformation) that pelicans are nearby in a special way. This special way is neither necessary nor sufficient for the belief to direct your attention toward pelicans.

Schematically, the contrasts drawn so far are between inferring P from Q, and these other transitions from a Q-state to a P-state:

- *mentally jogging* from the Q-state to the P-state, for instance by *bypassing* the information in the Q-state in forming the P-state;
- *rhythm and rhyme*: moving from Q-state to P-state because words used to express Q and P rhyme or follow a rhythmic groove;
- *association*: moving from the Q-state to the P-state by associating a concept occurring in the Q-state with a concept occurring in the P-state;
- *constructing a narrative* from a Q-state using a P-state;
- *attention*: moving to the P-state because the Q-state directs your attention to a property that the P-state is about.

On the face of it, what's lacking from these cases is a distinctive way of responding to the Q-state that produces the P-state. These transitions fail to be inferences, because they lack this kind of response.

5.2.4 Epistemic differences between poor inference and non-inference

A useful test for whether the contrasts I've drawn help illuminate the distinctively inferential response is to consider if they shed any light on the difference between poor inferences, and the various other non-inferential relations.

Recall the example of bypass involving change-blindness. Suppose you do not respond to the change in the color of the block. You persist in believing that the block is yellow when in fact the block has turned blue and you have taken in this information but have not adjusted your belief or actions. Assuming that you have evidence that it is blue, in having the information that the block is blue, your belief that the block is yellow is maintained in a way that fails to take account of some highly relevant evidence.

This epistemic situation involves bypassing the information that the block is blue. Contrast bypassing that information with drawing a poor inference from it. You start out believing the block is yellow and then, after the block changes color, you freshly infer that the block is yellow, irrationally discounting the blue appearance. Here, too, a belief is formed in a way that fails to give some highly relevant evidence its proper weight.

There's a level of abstraction at which the epistemic flaw in both cases is the same: one fails to take proper account of highly relevant evidence. The belief that P, in both cases, lacks propositional justification for P. Going with that similarity, in both cases, the information that the block is blue defeats the belief that the block is yellow. And at the same high level of abstraction, in both cases, the subject's ultimate belief that the block is yellow (after the block changes color) is ill-founded: it is formed (in the inference case) or maintained (in the bypass case) epistemically badly.

Alongside these similarities, there is also a major epistemic difference between the bypass and inference cases. According to the Response hypothesis, the locus of epistemic appraisability in inference is the response to P. It's the response to P that's epistemically bad-making. The epistemic badness is found along a further dimension that is missing in the bypass case. Its badness is not just the negative feature of failing to be based on adequate propositional justification, or failing to take relevant evidence into account. Nor is it the generic feature of being badly based, simpiciter. Instead, the badness of the inference is located in the response. If one inferred from a blue-block experience that the block is yellow, without any assumptions that explain the disconnect between color and apparent color, that would be a poor inference.

More generally, according to the Response hypothesis, the epistemically relevant features of inference reside in the distinctively inferential responses. I next consider a way to oppose the idea that distinctively inferential responses also produce the inference's conclusion. These are attempts to analyze inference in terms of regulatability. I argue that they overextend the domain of epistemic appraisability in the next section.

5.3 Responding by Regulating

It may seem trivial that inferring a P-state from a Q-state is a kind of response to the Q-state. But it is not trivial that in inferring P from Q, inference is a kind of response that produces the P-state. An alternative proposal is that a subject's inferring consists in her playing the role of an overseer who allows an epistemic dependence to be established.[12] On this view, which I'll call the regulatability approach, inference proceeds on its own momentum, without the subject's having to do anything special, such as deliberate, or consciously feel the force of any inferential inputs. But a subject can disown the inference once it is made.

On the regulatability approach, the distinctive feature of inferring is the ability to disown a conclusion, not its formation. We can distinguish between two versions of this approach.

In the first version, the fact that you can overturn the conclusion of a transition that lands in an informational state makes the transition an inference.

If disownability of a conclusion was a sufficient condition for inference, then the proposal would seem to overgenerate. You could in principle disown a belief that you land in via mental jogging, by ceasing to rely on it in reasoning and action (a possibility discussed in section 3.1), but this would not make that belief result from inference. The same objection could be made using experiences, fears, or desires. You could disown an experience by not relying on it in thought or action, or disown a fear you find yourself with as unfounded, or decide not to pursue a desire. But none of these acts of disowning would establish that the mental state came about through an inference. Disownability of a conclusion seems like a better candidate for characterizing transitions into or out of certain mental states as exercises of mental agency, regardless of whether the capacity for such exercises bestows those states with the status of being inferred from their inputs.

In a second version of the regulatability approach, what makes a transition to a conclusion an inference is the fact that you can disown the process that leads to the conclusion. Here, the possibility that matters is the possibility of disowning the process leading to a mental state, rather than the possibility of disowning the mental state itself. But this version of the disownability approach will overgenerate as well.

Suppose someone thinks that P ("I have to buy lightbulbs") and then, to their dismay, thinks that Q ("I could easily be harmed"). To this person, Q-thoughts often come unbidden, and he wishes his unbidden thoughts were less agitating. As he tries with some success to cultivate

---

[12] I thank Mark Richard for discussion of this view.

new mental habits that avoid the frequent occurrence of Q-thoughts, he is disappointed when such thoughts come to him anyway, and in that sense, he disowns the process that leads to the Q-thoughts. The disownability of such a process would not suffice to make the transition from the P-thought to the Q-thought an inference. To appropriately restrict this condition, then, we would need further constraints on which kinds of processes or which kinds of regulatability are diagnostic of inference. At that point, however, regulatability is only part of the account of inference, and the regulatability approach is not necessarily an alternative to the reckoning model.

Consider another example. A subject's brain regularly takes as input some information about a pattern of light contrasts, and using stored information, regularly produces a representation of a pattern of edges. Then the subject learns that her brain computes in accordance with a rule that links edge patterns to light contrasts. She understands the rule, and ceases to rely on it in her reasoning and decisions. At the same time, and by an independent process, her brain changes, and it no longer computes those patterns of edges from those light contrasts. She disowns the rule in her explicit reasoning, and her brain ceases to use that rule as well. In these ways, it is possible for her to disown the process that led to the representation of edges, given representations of light contrasts.

The fact that it is possible in these ways for her to disown the process does not seem to show that the process of generating edges from light contrasts was an inference in the sense outlined by the first starting assumption. Disownability in this form does not suffice for the regulated state to bear on the rational standing of the subject at all. It therefore does not suffice for the regulatable state to depend epistemically on the inputs that lead up to it, in the way distinctive of inference.

5.4 The Reckoning Model

If the Response hypothesis is true, then we can ask: does the distinctive inferential kind of responding have any further structure? The regulatability approach just examined avoids attributing further structure to the response that produces the conclusion. But it seems to overgenerate, allowing too many relations to informational states to count as inferring.

The most developed positive account of structured responses comes from the reckoning model.

According to the reckoning model, inferential responses have two parts. First, there is a state of responding to inputs that constitutes those inputs' striking the subject as supporting the conclusion. We could call this kind of taking "taking as reckoning," where reckoning is the non-factive analog of appreciating. The term "appreciating" is factive: if you appreciate that P supports Q, then P really does support Q. But taking-as-reckoning can include cases in which P doesn't support Q.

A reckoning state is a specific state the subject is in whereby she reckons that P supports Q. A reckoning state can be a belief that P supports Q, a state of its seeming to her as if P supports Q, an intuition that P supports Q, or some other kind of representation with that content.

The second part of inferential responses as the reckoning model construes them is that the subject's being in the reckoning state explains why she actually reaches a conclusion. Concluding is distinct from reckoning. One could reach the conclusion that the clerk is kind after observing her interaction with a customer, including all the features of the clerk's manner (her tone of voice, etc.), without responding to those features in forming the belief. Conversely, you could reckon (or even appreciate) that some inputs support a conclusion, without yet drawing the conclusion. For instance, you might take your observations of the clerk to provide pro tanto support for the conclusion that the clerk is kind, but walk away from the post office thinking "I have no idea what she is like in other contexts" and so stop short of believing or otherwise accepting that she is kind. Or you might doubt that you could know what she's like, just from observing the one interaction. Here, you second-guess the conclusion that would be natural to draw from your reckoning.

According to the reckoning model, the reckoning state explains why the inferrer drew the conclusion. The relation between the reckoning state and the conclusion is the "becausal" relation: one concludes because one reckons. According to the reckoning model, it is this response—concluding because one reckons—that is distinctive of inference. By virtue of concluding because one is in a reckoning state, one is not mentally jogging from inputs to conclusions, or bypassing those inputs, or standing in any of the other relations described in section 5.2.

The reckoning model is motivated by a powerful consideration. If there were no reckoning state, then, it might seem, in drawing an inference, that one would proceed as if in ignorance of any relationship between the inputs and the conclusion.[13] And if inferring could proceed in this way, then its status as a rational activity might seem to be lost.

As many philosophers have noted, the reckoning model faces a problem similar to the one illustrated by Lewis Carroll (1895).

The problem is that the "becausal" role for the reckoning state threatens to force it into the role of another premise. Consider an inferrer who concludes Q from P and If P then Q, and responds to those premises in drawing the conclusion. If she must also respond to a reckoning state with the content: P and If P then Q supports the conclusion Q, then the fact that she is responding to it seems to add that reckoning state to the stock of premises. If every stock of premises needs a reckoning state, then we will have started a regress.[14]

I am not going to criticize the reckoning model on the grounds that it cannot solve the regress problem. Various ingenious solutions to this problem have been proposed by proponents of the reckoning model.[15] But none of them is necessary for giving a theory of inference, because there are reasons to think that inference does not in general involve reckoning.

If inference in general does not involve a reckoning state, then the regress problem does not arise. Since the Response hypothesis does not posit a reckoning state, it does not face this problem on its own. The problem arises only if the response distinctive of inference involves: concluding because one reckons.

Wright (2014) argues that one could not infer because one reckons, on pain of making inference into a super-task that could never be completed. This objection is directed at the role of the reckoning state in inference. In contrast, my objection targets the putative existence of a reckoning state, independently of any role in producing a conclusion. Many kinds of inference have no reckoning state, I will argue, because the subject cannot identify the information to which she responds, and therefore does not represent the putative support relation between that information and the content of the conclusion.

---

[13]   Chudnoff (2013), Boghossian (forthcoming), Audi (1986, 2001).

[14]   Some discussions of the problem of the role of the reckoning state in inference include Fumerton (1995) on the principle of inferential justification, Greco (1999), Boghossian (2014), Hlobil (2014), Chudnoff (2014), Wright (2014), and Broome (2014).

[15]   For instance, by Boghossian (forthcoming) and Chudnoff (2013).

5.5 Reckoning Is Not Needed for Inference

In at least four kinds of inferences, subjects draw conclusions from some information they cannot identify. The four kinds of inference involve categorization, responses to aggregated factors, spatio-temporal calculations, and searches for information. Here is a quartet of examples of transitions (some of which we have met before) that are epistemically evaluable in the ways that are distinctive of inference, despite involving no reckoning state.

Kindness (categorization): The person ahead of you in line at the Post Office is finding out from the clerk about the costs of sending a package. Their exchange of information is interspersed with comments about recent changes in the postal service and the most popular stamps. As you listen you are struck with the thought that the clerk is kind. You could not identify what it is about the clerk that leads you to this thought. Nor could you identify any generalizations that link these cues to kindness. Though you don't know it, you are responding to a combination of what she says to the customer, her forthright and friendly manner, her facial expressions, her tone of voice, and the way she handles the packages.[16]

Pepperoni (aggregated factors): Usually you eat three slices of pizza when it comes with pepperoni. But tonight, after eating one slice, you suddenly don't want any more. Struck by your own uncharacteristic aversion, you form a belief about your desire: you believe that you want to eat no more pepperoni. The desire is a response to a range of factors, and the belief is a response to those factors, too. Though you don't know it, the factors include the facts that (i) the pepperoni tastes too salty to you, (ii) it looks unappetizingly greasy, (iii) it reminds you of someone you don't like, who you recently learned loves pepperoni, and (iv) you have suddenly felt the force of moral arguments against eating meat. If the next bites of pepperoni were less salty, the greasy

---

[16] It is worth emphasizing that one need not be justified in ascribing kindness on this basis, in order to infer from these cues that the clerk is kind. You might be jumping to conclusions about how kind the clerk is from these cues. I am also assuming for the sake of argument that kindness is not represented in perceptual experience of the clerk. If it were, it would be a case of endorsing an experience, and would be less compelling as an example of being unaware of the inferential input to the conclusion. Similar judgments of kindness are discussed by Setiya (2012).

appearance turned out to be glare from the lights, you learned that your nemesis now avoids pepperoni, and the moral arguments didn't move you, the conclusion of your inference would weaken, and so would your aversion. You haven't classified your aversion to the pizza as an aversion to grease, salt, your nemesis, or the sad product of immoral practices. Nor are you consciously thinking right now about any of these things.

Too far north (spatio-temporal calculation): Walking in a group of people with a common destination, it occurs to you that you have walked too far north. Though you don't know it, you are responding to an assumption that it would take less time to get to the turn-off point than the time that has elapsed since the group departed. You could not formulate the assumption concerning how long it would take, or why it would take that long, or how long you have been walking.

Rockmouth (search for information): On the third forkful of a nutty meal, you bite down with a suspicious crunch. It might be a small rock that could chip a tooth, or it might just be a hard nut. You try to locate the source of the suspicious crunch, chewing carefully in case there is a rock in your mouth. After searching for a bit, you don't locate any hard morsel and conclude that there is no rock in your mouth.

The kindness example is a case of categorization. Categorizing someone as kind is a rational activity, so we should expect inference to operate in such categorization. In general, it should not come as a surprise that classifying a particular event, object, or situation as falling under a category can involve inference.

The pepperoni example is a case of aggregating factors (some might call them "reasons") that underlie a preference. Speaking schematically, where "phi" is a variable for an action, sometimes when you have a desire to phi, you want or prefer to phi, because of a combination of factors. In this example, a number of factors make it the case that you prefer to eat no more pepperoni. This domain is another place where we should expect to find inference.

The too-far-north example is a case of spatio-temporal calculations of time and distance. You draw the conclusion in the example because you were keeping track of time and distance, and bringing that information to bear on your goal. Bringing information to bear on a goal is the kind of mental activity that calls for inference.

The rockmouth example involves searching for something and concluding that it isn't there. The conclusion is drawn in response to the flow of information produced by the search for a rock.

In these cases, the subjects respond to some information that they have by forming a belief (and in the pepperoni case, a desire and an aversion as well). Subjects draw conclusions from information they have, and those conclusions depend on the information epistemically. But none of these cases can involve a reckoning state, because the subjects cannot identify the information to which they are responding, in the following sense: there is no X such that subjects know they are responding to X in forming the belief (or the desire).

For instance, in the kindness case, the subject cannot identify the cues she is responding to when she forms the conclusion that the clerk is kind. She therefore does not believe that those cues normally indicate kindness, nor do they seem to her to indicate kindness—either by a conscious intuition or some other kind of seeming-state. The case is also consistent with the subject having no disposition to judge that the very cues she responded to are cues for kindness. She cannot identify those cues and does not group them together in any other beliefs. She might be disposed to say "people who act like *that* are kind," but she isn't in a position to understand what the demonstrative expression picks out. Generalizing from the kindness example to other cases of categorization, inference in categorization does not need a reckoning state.

Analogous points hold for the pepperoni case, which illustrates aggregated factors leading to preferences. The pepperoni-refuser responds to an aggregate of several different cues. It is consistent with the case that she has no disposition to judge that if a piece of pizza is salty, greasy, and has a topping that an enemy likes, and was produced by harming animals, she will not want it. After all, she usually enjoys salty, greasy pepperoni pizza, and her enemies' tastes, she thinks, are irrelevant to her own. Perhaps feeling the force of moral arguments against eating meat would bring with it a disposition to judge (after a lot of reflection) that the conditions under which pepperoni is produced should generate some aversion to eating it. But by hypothesis, the pepperoni-refuser is responding to an aggregate of factors. And she need have no disposition to form a judgment that if just these factors are grouped together, then she will refuse pepperoni.

The rockmouth case makes the lack of a reckoning state even more vivid. Here, the case would become unrealistic if the thinker had a belief, a seeming state such as an intuition, or a disposition to judge that gathering just the information that was gathered by chewing salad supported the conclusion that her mouth contained no rocks.

Examples like these suggest that distinctively inferential responses do not require a reckoning state. They are therefore not in general structured as a "becausal" relationship, in which one concludes because one reckons.

5.6   The Scope of Inference in the Mind

I've argued that the reckoning-model is false for the category of inference defined by our starting assumptions: the assumptions that inference establishes epistemic dependence of a conclusion on inferential inputs, inference involves a link between an input and conclusion that need not leave any mark in consciousness, and inference is not always illuminated by the model of an argument with premises and conclusions.

The Response hypothesis does not purport to give a theory of responding that is entirely independent of inference. The notion of inferential responding does not amount to an explication of inference using notions independent of it, let alone an explication of inference in non-normative terms. It does not allow us to rule on difficult cases, such as whether the usual process by which one discovers that one is feeling a mild pain is an inference. But these features do not make the account uninformative. The point of describing a distinctively inferential form of response to information is that it lets us see, among certain phenomena, the unity that we might otherwise miss. It gives us clues as to where we can reasonably expect to find inference operating in the mind.

One place it might operate is in chaotic processes of thinking. Imagine trying to figure out why a device doesn't work. You try to identify the scope of the problem, form hypotheses about what might cause it, or see which other adjustments have any impact. This kind of inquiry can involve fits and starts, false leads, confusions, conflations, interruptions, and entanglements that make one hesitant and uncertain about how various bits and pieces all fit together, if they do—especially when the topic is demanding. If such a course of thinking were music, it might return often to the same notes and show hints of tension, but it would rarely have a melody, a harmony, or any other seemingly orderly development.

Suppose that after a period of mental chaos brought on by an effort to answer a question, you settle on a conclusion. There is some fact of the matter, let's suppose, about how you came to the conclusion. And being a reasonable sort of person, in drawing your conclusion, you responded to considerations that actually support it. If you knew what those reasons were, and if you could state them clearly, then you could rehearse for someone else (as a jury does) how you came to your conclusion. In rehearsing that reified reasoning, your mind would move from the inputs of the reasoning to the conclusion. That kind of movement of the mind is orderly, in contrast to the disorderly mental music that preceded it and made it possible.

The reckoning model takes the paradigms of inference to be as orderly as your rehearsal. Among its paradigmatic features are the fact that you formulate to yourself what premises support your conclusion, and that you are focused on the fact (as you see it) that those premises support your conclusion.

If our only paradigm of inference is this kind of case, then a great range of cases of reasoning would be excluded, including many of the types illustrated earlier. Yet those forms of reasoning easily satisfy our starting assumptions about inference. If inference had to involve a reckoning state, then the boundaries defining the class of inferences would be drawn too tightly.

Unreflectively produced inferential responses are exactly the kind that would occur in inferential routes to perceptual experience. Nothing in the nature of inference precludes experiences from being formed by inference. Together with earlier arguments from Chapter 3 that nothing in the nature of experience precludes this either, we have a significant part of the constructive defense of the Rationality of Perception.

The attempt to illuminate inferential responses does not leave us with guidelines that determine whether such responses can be found in the routes to perceptual experience. Assuming that not all routes to perception are inferential responses, even when they could be reconstructed as conforming to rules of deduction, or rules sensitive to informational features of states, there will be a limit that marks off which responses to informational states are inferences and which aren't. I'll call this the limit from below. In presuming that perceptual experiences cannot result from inferences in ways that would redound on the subject's rational standing, one is presuming that the limits from below preclude routes to perceptual experience from being inferences.

If there's a coherent and plausible epistemic profile of perceptual experiences that result from inferences of the sort that I've tried to illuminate in this chapter, then the profile must include some reason to locate the limits from below at a place that allows some responses to informational states to produce perceptual experiences. So far, I've concentrated on the nature of experience and the nature of inferential responses, in order to make the case that neither rules out that experiences could result from inferences.

Another way to discover where the limits from below lie is to focus on a more specific question. What kinds of informational states can inferential responses be responses to?

In general, if a state can be inferentially responded to, then it must be eligible for having epistemic power. The examples that motivate the Rationality of Perception involve states that can clearly be epistemically appraised, such as Jill's fear that Jack is angry, Vivek's belief that people like him, and the preformationists' confidence in preformationism. (The case of fear is discussed in Chapter 8, and the case of racial bias is discussed in Chapter 10.) But what about routes to perceptual experiences that involve stored expectations, such as the phenomenon known as memory color?[17] Could this kind of route to experience involve the kinds of mental states to which a subject can respond inferentially? In the rest of this chapter, I argue that it can. If it can, that gives us some reason to think that the limits from below allow that inferential responses are involved in memory color.

In memory color, the perceptual system stores information about colors things tends to have, and this information is used in generating perceptual experiences. For instance, once a perceptual system learns that banana-shaped-and-textured things tend to be yellow, this information is used in ways that run parallel to reasoning that combines generalizations with incoming information.

---

[17] The central experimental papers include Hansen (2006), Olkkonen (2008), Witzel et al. (2011). It is in dispute whether the influencing state is a belief, and if so, what its content is ("Bananas are yellow" or "Banana-shaped and textured things are yellow.") For discussion of this issue, see Deroy (2013). Jenkin (ms1, ms2) discusses the epistemic impact of memory color and object cognition on experience. I'm indebted to her for many illuminating discussions of these topics.

Many experiments support the phenomenon of memory color, but there are in principle different interpretations of these experimental results. Many researchers claim that the results show that stored information influences perceptual experience, though some argue that it only influences judgment.[18] I'm going to assume that it influences perceptual experience, so that we can explore the idea that those experiences result from an inference from stored information. I will also assume that the generalizations link color to shape and texture properties, and that these generalizations are stored in the perceptual system.

If memory color generates inferences to experiences, then there are two kinds of states that subjects could inferentially respond to. First, there are stored generalizations about the color of things that the subject sees regularly. (The experimenters use bananas, mailboxes, and other ordinary objects, in the experiments that highlight this phenomenon.) Second, there is a pre-conscious perceptual state that conveys information about the particular object one is seeing. This is the object that will end up being experienced as yellow and banana-shaped, for instance. I'll call a state "pre-conscious" if it is an unconscious part of a perceptual process that gives rise to a perceptual experience, and it is a constancy-implicating perception.[19]

Are either pre-conscious processes or perceptually stored generalizations eligible for harboring epistemic power?

Starting with pre-conscious perceptual states, there are reasons to think that such states can have epistemic powers, and so are eligible for

---

[18] Zeimbekis (2013).

[19] For discussion of unconscious perception, see Burge (2010) and Phillips (2015), and for a debate about the existence of unconscious perception which contains many potential examples and focuses on the significance of key experiments, see Philips and Block (2016). Block's case that some unconscious representations are perceptions focuses on unconscious representations that reflect the subject's values and understanding, and alleges that some of the properties that can be unconsciously perceived include gendered bodies (Jiang et al. 2006), fearful facial expressions (Yang et al. 2007), words whose meaning the subject unconsciously registers (Klauer et al. 2007), and anomalous scenes (Mudrik et al. 2011). He focuses on experiments involving "high-level" properties because he thinks they more directly support the conclusion that the representations are person-level. On the assumption that scenes, faces, and bodies are perceived in part by perceiving color, shape, and texture, these properties are unconsciously perceivable as well, if the higher-level properties are. By this reasoning, the grayness and banana-shape and texture of a banana would be unconsciously perceivable, and so these properties could figure in the contents of pre-conscious perceptions as defined here.

being states that can be inferentially responded to. One way to assess whether a state has epistemic powers is whether failing to respond to the state can influence the epistemic status of other processes or states in the mind.

For instance, compartmentalized beliefs can be unused epistemic resources that bear on the epistemic status of other beliefs. We saw an example in the earlier discussion of bypassing evidence. Suppose you believe that you'll meet with X alone at noon, and you also believe that you'll meet with Y alone at noon. You don't notice the conflict, and so you have scheduled conflicting appointments. Beliefs like these are compartmentalized. Each compartmentalized belief is accessible to sub-sequent reasoning and processing. For instance, you might plan to give X her umbrella back when you meet with her, and you might be keeping a list of things to talk over with Y. In addition, each belief has epistemic power to support subsequent beliefs. But at least one of these epistemic powers remains unused, for as long as each belief remains in its com-partment: each has the power to defeat the other. Your belief that you will meet with X alone at noon is a reason to think you won't meet with Y alone at noon, and your belief that you'll meet with Y is a reason to think you won't also at the same time meet with X.

Compartmentalized beliefs are not the only possible unused epistemic resources. Perceptual experiences can be unused resources as well. Con-sider perceptual experiences with a low degree of attentiveness. Just as each compartmentalized belief about your appointment can be made available for reasoning through recall, inattentive experiences can be made available through shifts of attention. Just as the compartmentalized belief retains its epistemic force when unaccessed, arguably the inatten-tive experiences do too.[20]

Some pre-conscious perceptual states seem to fit the same pattern. They could become conscious with minimal changes in informational content. Just as the inattentive experience could easily become attentive, so too the unconscious perception could easily become phenomenally conscious. In both cases, the result of the transition clearly belongs to the subject's epistemic resources. When only a minimal transition is needed to cross the threshold into the realm of unambiguously epistemic

---

[20] For discussion of inattentive experiences and their epistemic status, see Silins and Siegel (2015).

resources, such states are plausibly epistemic resources all along, and compartmentalization, inattentiveness, or unconsciousness are merely ways of limiting our access to them.

We've been considering whether pre-conscious perceptual states can have epistemic powers—a feature they would need, to be inferentially responded to. One way to have those powers is to be epistemically appraisable. Earlier, in discussing whether experiences could be epistemically charged, I suggested that what makes them eligible for epistemic appraisal is that they form part of the subject's complete outlook. Developing this idea further, we can ask: do any of the following distinctions mark a boundary between states that belong to an outlook and states that do not?

- phenomenally conscious states vs. states that are not phenomenally conscious;
- states that one can know and report that one is in vs. states that one cannot know and report that one is in, without extensive inquiry;
- generalizations that a person believes and are not stored in the perceptual system vs. generalizations stored in the perceptual system;
- person-level states vs. subpersonal states.

To start, there are clear examples of beliefs, unreflectively held presumptions, and fears that are epistemically appraisable, but are not phenomenally conscious, and that the subject fails to know she has. Angela Smith (ms) gives a vivid example: person A asks person B why B is sullen, B honestly denies being sullen, but after A points out B's sullen behavior, B sees that in fact he was sullen, and comes to see from noticing the pattern of his own behavior what he was responding to, and why. (In Smith's example, B discovers that he resented A's recent choices, and felt that they didn't properly take him into account.) The epistemically appraisable states are clearly not limited to phenomenally conscious states, or to states that one can easily report being in.

Focusing specifically on the learned generalizations stored in the perceptual system that link color to shape and texture, we can consider whether the process of perceptual learning can bestow epistemic power on the generalization that results from that kind of learning.[21] The more

---

[21] For extended discussion of perceptual learning, see Connolly (2014 and ms).

continuity we find between perceptual learning and cognitive learning, the less plausible it is that perceptual learning marks a cut-off point between states that are eligible for epistemic appraisal and states that are not, or between states that can harbor epistemic power and states that can't. And there is substantial continuity between the processes, as the psychologist Robert Goldstone (Goldstone and Byrge 2015) points out. For instance, perceptual unitization (clumping bits of perceptual information into units that can be recognized later) seems to differ from memory chunking only in how early it occurs. The same point holds for perceptual differentiation and building associations (as Goldstone and Byrge (2015) emphasizes). What's perceptual about the process is that adjustments are made to initial representations of external things, but the adjustments themselves are not always different in kind.

A different attempt to hive off the states of the mind that are epistemically appraisable or merely epistemically powerful, and the states of the mind that are neither, invokes the distinction between subpersonal and person-level states. Several distinctions do business under the label "personal vs. subpersonal." One approach simply defines subpersonal states as those states that are epistemically unappraisable. (Something like this distinction is proposed by Hornsby 2001.)[22] But this version of the distinction would give no traction in identifying which states are epistemically unappraisable.

Cutting across the different distinctions, however, we find two paradigmatic examples of a subpersonal state or process: early vision, and states of grammatical processing. What do these two systems have in common? They are widely thought to be insulated from information in the rest of the mind, and in that sense, to form a subsystem.[23] But by itself, being an informational state that is insulated from other information is a poor diagnostic for being epistemically unappraisable. As we saw earlier, compartmentalized beliefs are to some extent insulated from other information, but they are epistemically appraisable. There is also evidence that some of our most basic assumptions about the physical

[22] Drayson (2012), who discusses several versions of the distinction, including those by Dennett (1969), Rowlands (2006), Machery (2009), Burge (2003), Kriegel (2012), argues that none of the standard glosses underwrite the distinction that hives off a mechanistic, normatively unappraisable domain of the mind.

[23] For instance, early vision and grammatical processing are Fodor's two main examples of modules in Fodor (1983).

world and social world are informationally insulated—such as our assumptions about how objects move through space (they move as bounded wholes), which spatio-temporal processes are processes of mechanical causation (the ones without big spatial or temporal gaps), and which events are exercises of agency.[24] It is far from obvious that these working assumptions of our cognitive and perceptual systems lack epistemic power, or that they are exempt from epistemic appraisal.

Putting together all of the considerations so far suggests that perceptual experiences, preconscious perceptual states, and learned perceptual generalizations can all harbor epistemic powers. This makes them eligible for being the kinds of states to which subjects inferentially respond. And given what we know about the role of some such states in the mind, it is plausible that subjects do inferentially respond to them. Compare the responses Vivek makes to his generalizations (which we can assume are stored in his mind as beliefs, rather than being stored in the perceptual system). Vivek believes that people tend to like him, and he inferentially responds to this generalization when he faces his audiences. He may be at most only dimly aware, if he is aware at all, that he is responding to this generalization when he forms the impression that his audience is pleased. The fact that Vivek's responding to this information (or as the case may be, misinformation) lies outside his awareness does not stop it from being an inferential response.

Given the assumption that perceptually stored generalizations harbor epistemic power, we should put responses to those generalizations on a par with Vivek's responses. If one kind of response can be the kind of response that establishes relationships of epistemic dependence characteristic of inference, then so can the other. Memory color has no features that put it squarely on the side of the epistemically unappraisable processes.

Psychologists have long argued that perceptual experiences, like many other perceptual states, result from inference—or at least, from a process they have happily called "inference."[25] By and large, those interested in the epistemic role of perceptual experience have not concluded that experiences epistemically depend on the inferences psychologists describe. But if the process of combining stored generalizations with

---

[24] For further discussion and examples, see Carey (2009).

[25] Psychologists who posit perceptual inference include Alhazen (1989/ca. 1030), Helmholtz (1867/1910), Rock (1975). For discussion see Hatfield (2002).

incoming information from a particular situation operates over epistemically powerful (or even epistemically appraisable) states, then it has all the hallmarks of the inferential responses described in this chapter.

If memory color is an example of inference leading to a perceptual experience, we can ask what kind of epistemic status its influence bestows on experience. A more general version of this question is the focus of Chapter 6, where we will see what kind of epistemic profile experiences can have, when they result from inference.

6

How Experiences Can Lose Power from Inference

The Rationality of Perception is stated at a high level of abstraction: experiences can be rational or irrational, and so can the processes by which they are formed. One such process is inference.

I have argued so far that inferential routes to experience are not precluded either by the nature of inference (Chapter 5) or by the nature of experience (Chapter 3). In the rest of Part II, I offer a proof of concept for the Rationality of Perception, by outlining a coherent profile of epistemic effects that inference can have on experiences. This proof of concept is also a proof of concept for the Inferential Modulation thesis.

Inferential Modulation thesis: Experiences can be formed by inferences that can modulate their epistemic charge.

By distinguishing between different kinds of epistemically evaluable inferences, we can see in detail how the psychological precursors of experience could affect the epistemic roles of experience.

One epistemic role of experience is in supporting a belief that is an *endorsement* of that experience. An experience is endorsed, when one forms a belief that P on the basis of an experience whose contents include P. An epistemic profile should illuminate the epistemic role of endorsed experiences, when those experiences result from inference.

In addition, the epistemic profile for inferred experience should be constrained by a plausible account of the relationship between the epistemic powers of inferred and uninferred experiences.

By outlining an epistemic profile of experience that illuminates these relationships, I illustrate the plausibility of the Rationality of Perception. The proof of concept I offer can explain the epistemic downgrade that

I've argued we find in hijacked experiences (Chapter 4), using the notion of inference developed in Chapter 5.

If experiences can result from inferences, then the epistemic effects of inference will be effects on the epistemic powers of experience. I begin by discussing the ways in which experiences can lose epistemic power from inference. After distinguishing three ways that inferences in general can be epistemically inappropriate, without yet assuming that experiences can result from inferences (section 6.1), I consider how inferences that are epistemically inappropriate in each of the first three ways could affect experiences (section 6.2). The resulting epistemic profile for inferred experiences can explain the epistemic downgrade we find in hijacked experiences (section 6.3). Whether experiences can gain epistemic power from inference is the topic of Chapter 7.

The epistemic profile constructed in this chapter and the next shows how the epistemic charge of experience can be modulated by inference. When an experience is epistemically downgraded as a result of a poor inference, its epistemic powers fall below the baseline, and the experience is negatively epistemically charged. When an experience is epistemically upgraded due to an inference, its epistemic powers rise above the baseline, and it has even more positive charge than experiences have when their epistemic powers lie at the baseline.

As we have seen, the purpose of the concept of epistemic charge is to express the idea that experiences can manifest a rational standing. Since modifications of epistemic charge of experiences entail modifications of their epistemic power, the epistemic profile for experiences constructed in this chapter and the next is described in terms of epistemic powers. Nothing would be added by describing it in terms of epistemic charge, beyond highlighting the idea that experiences manifest an epistemic status. If experiences didn't manifest any such status, then they could not stand in the relations of epistemic dependence characteristic of inference. The idea that experiences are epistemically charged is therefore implicit in the epistemic profile constructed here.

The epistemic dependence of conclusions on inferential inputs can be divided into epistemically bad inferential routes to conclusions and epistemically good ones. Here are three ways for inference to produce epistemically bad conclusions.

6.1 Three Kinds of Inappropriate Inference

In a first kind of poor inference, the conclusion of the inference inherits epistemic inappropriateness from one or more of the inferential inputs.

Inherited inappropriateness: If belief Y is epistemically inappropriate, a subsequent belief Z inferred from Y may inherit Y's inappropriateness.

What if you infer Z from both an inappropriately formed Y– and an appropriately formed Y+? Is Z's inappropriateness diluted by Y+? With a complex enough Y+, Y–'s badness can wash out.[1] For instance, suppose the content of Y+ is a conjunction with 18 conjuncts. Conjoining those with the content of Y– would yield a conjunction with 19 conjuncts, where the only culprit is the belief in the 19th conjunct. Belief in the 18 conjuncts of Y+ would be well-founded, and would provide support for belief Z. Under these circumstances, Z might not inherit any significant epistemic inappropriateness from Y–. But although not every ill-founded input to inference transmits significant ill-foundedness to its conclusion, some ill-founded inferential inputs do transmit significant ill-foundedness to their conclusions. These are cases of inherited inappropriateness.

A second kind of poor inference is jumping to conclusions.

Jumping to conclusions: You infer Q from P, in an inference to a Q-state from a P-state. But P doesn't support Q.

For example, suppose you see a creature and you have the following thought about it: There's a dog and Jim always wanted a dog (=P). If you infer that the creature belongs to Jim (=Q), you are jumping to conclusions. I won't try to give a general account of what support relations between propositions are. There are clearly inferences in which the inferential inputs fail to support the conclusions adequately, or fail to support them at all. In these cases, the conclusion is not necessarily inheriting any epistemic inappropriateness from the inputs, as the inputs might be perfectly appropriate. Jumping to conclusions is therefore a different kind of flaw than inherited inappropriateness.

---

[1] We met this possibility in Chapter 3, section 3.3.

Table 6.1. Composite inference 1

Inference 1a	
Belief 1:	Bananas are yellow
Belief 2:	o is a banana
Belief 3:	o is a yellow banana
Inference 1b	
Belief 3:	o is a yellow banana
Bad Strengthen Bel 1:	Bananas are yellow

Perhaps the most complex kind of poor inference involves circularity.

Circularity: For some roles of X in inferentially supporting a conclusion Y, Y cannot provide rational support for X. If Y is strengthened in response to X, then Y is epistemically inappropriate.

Circularity is illustrated by the composite inference in Table 6.1. The conclusion of the first inference (Inference 1a) is a premise of the second inference (Inference 1b). Beliefs 1, 2, and 3 are components of this composite inference. Because Belief 3 is the conclusion of an inference from Belief 1 and Belief 2, you cannot rationally strengthen Belief 1 on the basis of Beliefs 2 and 3 (see Table 6.1).

To illustrate, suppose that o is behind a curtain. You know that o is a banana, and you know that bananas are yellow. It is then a good bet that o is yellow. So you have some rational support for believing that o is yellow, prior to seeing o.

Let us assume that while o is behind the curtain, your only source of rational support for the belief that o is yellow is this inference. Does your conclusion that o is yellow give you any additional incremental support for the belief that bananas are yellow? (You might not *need* any more support for the conclusion to be knowledge, but we can still ask whether drawing the conclusion provides any.)

No. By hypothesis, you concluded that o is yellow by drawing only on Beliefs 1 and 2. You were in a position to draw on the propositions

Table 6.2. The Oracle inference

The Oracle inference	
Belief 3:	o is a yellow banana
Oracle tells you:	If o is a yellow banana, then bananas are yellow.
Strengthen Belief 1:	Bananas are yellow

bananas are yellow and *o is a banana* because you believe them, and you were in a position to draw on them rationally because (let's suppose) you know them.

Even though it would be epistemically inappropriate to use Belief 3 to strengthen Belief 1, Belief 3 could still be used to support other beliefs, such as the belief that x is not purple, or the belief x is the color of my house.

It is not in general true that if you infer Y from X, then Y can't rationally strengthen X. It depends what else you rely on, once you have inferred Y, to strengthen X. Consider the inference from Belief 3 given in Table 6.2. Putting its etiology aside, Belief 3 is a natural unit of inductive support for Belief 1. Factoring in its etiology, Belief 1 is used to support Belief 3 in both the Oracle inference, and Inference 1b. So why does the Oracle inference seem better than Inference 1b?[2]

The Oracle inference seems better, because the Oracle provides independent support for the induction, whereas in Composite Inference One (Table 6.1), the only support for this unit of inductive support comes from Belief 1 and Belief 2. But although it is not true in general that inferring Y from X precludes strengthening X on the basis of Y, there are some cases in which such strengthening is precluded. These are cases of the mode of epistemic inappropriateness that I've labeled Circularity.

6.2 Inferentially Inappropriate Routes to Experience

What would each kind of bad inference do to experiences? The concepts of epistemic powers and epistemic downgrade help specify the impact that each of these kinds of poor inferences would have on experiences.

---

[2] Thanks to Jeff Speaks for discussion of this case.

Table 6.3. Composite inference 2

Inference 2a	
Belief 1:	Bananas are yellow
Experience:	<u>o is a banana</u>
Experience 1A:	o is a yellow banana

Inference 2b	
Experience 1A:	<u>o is a yellow banana</u>
★Bad★ Strengthen Bel 1:	Bananas are yellow

6.2.1 Circularity and inherited inappropriateness

Regarding inherited inappropriateness: If an experience inherited inappropriateness from it inferential inputs, or resulted from jumping to conclusions from inferential inputs, then it would be formed in a way that is epistemically inappropriate.

Regarding circularity: An experience could play the role of Belief 3 in Composite Inference One. Consider Composite Inference Two (Table 6.3), which is just like Composite Inference One, except that the first part of the inference results in an experience instead of a belief, and has an experience as one of its inputs.

We can think of Experience 1A as having reduced epistemic power to strengthen Belief 1, relative to the power it could have if Belief 1 didn't play that role in its etiology. (A parallel observation about the Oracle applies here too).

In Composite Inference Two (Table 6.3), the epistemic flaw of circularity has a different structure than the epistemic flaws of jumping to conclusions, or inherited inappropriateness from inferential inputs. For all that the circular structure in Composite Inference Two shows, the experience may be formed via an epistemically good inference. But the experience nonetheless loses epistemic power that it could (and normally would) otherwise have to strengthen belief in one of the inferential inputs (Belief 1). Here it is the role of experience as an input to inference (Inference 2b) that is epistemically inappropriate, not its role as a conclusion of inference (Inference 2a). But its role as an input to

Table 6.4. Composite inference 3

Inference 3a	
Bad → Belief 1:	sperm cells contain embryos
Belief 2:	x is a sperm cell
Experience 3:	x contains an embryo

Inference 3b	
Experience 3:	x contains an embryo
★**Bad**★ Strengthen Bel 1:	sperm cells contain embryos

Inference 3c	
Experience 3:	x contains an embryo
★**Bad**★ Bel 3:	x contains an embryo

inference is made inappropriate by virtue of the fact that the experience was the conclusion of another inference.

Despite the difference between circularity and the other kinds of poor inference we have considered, in all three cases the impact on experience can be understood in terms of losing epistemic power. Consider the preformationism example, which can illustrate both Circularity and Inherited Inappropriateness. In the preformationism example, an experience loses power to provide support for believing that the sperm cell contains an embryo, due to the role of that belief in producing the experience, and the fact that the belief was epistemically inappropriate. (See Table 6.4).

As we have seen, because of circularity, it is bad to strengthen Belief 1 in response to Experience 3 (barring any extra contributions from the Oracle, or another source of inductive support for Belief 1). But the preformationism case exemplifies another source of badness: the embryo-experience (Experience 3) inherits the epistemic inappropriateness of Belief 1 (assuming that all the inferential inputs are pictured so there are no other ones to wash out Belief 1's badness). Since the embryo-experience inherits epistemic badness from its inferential input (Belief 1), it has not only reduced epistemic power to support that very input, but also reduced epistemic power to support believing its own contents. That is why Inference 3c is bad. In having the content "x contains an embryo," the experience would be epistemically downgraded relative both to believing "x contains an embryo" and to believing "sperm cells contain embryos."

Both Circularity and Inherited Inappropriateness can occur in Bayesian routes to perceptual experience. Section 6.2.2 and the rest of this section describe how these epistemic flaws operate, when experiences are formed in the way characterized by Bayesian theories of content-determination. Of all the kinds of inferences, it is worth focusing specifically on Bayesian inferences, since this kind figures in many theories of purely perceptual processes, as well as in discussions of memory color and similar effects that are potential examples of perceptual hijacking.

In their simplest form, Bayesian theories of content-determination for experience describe how an experience comes to have a content, such as "this is yellow." They posit that, in the process leading up to the experience, prior assumptions are combined in a Bayesian way with information that the subject takes in from her current situation. I'll continue to call that information "pre-conscious perception," or "pre-conscious perceptual input," with the caveat that nothing in the Bayesian process per se entails that the information is perceptual (in the sense debated by Phillips and Block 2016). I am working with the assumption that in memory color, the unconscious representation on which prior assumptions are brought to bear is an unconscious perception.

The Bayesian calculation results in a new probability distribution over a space of hypotheses, and then a selection rule selects one of the hypotheses to be the content of experience.

To see how this process works using an oversimplified example, consider a case in which a gray banana looks yellow. Here are some useful abbreviations:

o = the gray banana
E = pre-conscious perceptual input from the banana
H_Y = (also: *yellow*) = o is yellow.

H_Y belongs to a set of hypotheses. Each hypothesis H_i in the set differs according to the color that it assigns to o. Another such hypothesis is:

H_G = *gray* = o is gray.

By Bayes's theorem, $P(H|E)$ is proportional to the product of two other probabilities: $P(E|H)$ and $P(H)$, and a normalizing constant. (For simplicity, I'll leave out the constant, since it is a constant function of the other values in Bayes's theorem.) "P(H)" is called a *prior*, and "P(E|H)" is called a *likelihood*. Applied to our current example,

P(*yellow* | E)
is proportional to:
P(E | *yellow*) x P(*yellow*).

If P(*yellow*|E) is higher than P(*gray*|E) and P(H_i |E), for all the other H_i's besides *yellow*, then the content of the experience will be: o is yellow. In pure English: if the probability that the banana is yellow, given the pre-conscious information, is higher than the probability that the banana is gray (or any other color), given that same pre-conscious information, then the banana will be experienced as yellow.

Within the structure of a Bayesian inference, there are at least two places to locate potential inappropriateness that the experience could inherit: in the prior probability, and in the selection rule. The prior probability that the banana is gray (or that it is not yellow) could be too low (and the prior probabilities that it is yellow could be too high), or the conditional probability that P(E|*yellow*) could be too high. Alternatively, the probabilities could be as they should be, but the selection rule could be a rule to select the hypothesis that is congruent with one's desires.[3] This last alternative arises, because of the limits of Bayes's theorem. Bayes's theorem provides a way to calculate the set of conditional probabilities (the values of P(H|E), for each H_i), from other information. But it does not speak to which of the resulting probabilities are the contents of experience. That role is for the selection rule.

With this background, we can describe the flaw of circularity in Bayesian inference. Because of the complexity of Bayesian inference, the circularity flaw is more complex than it is in the badly circular inferences considered previously.

---

[3] Later on (section 7.2) I discuss whether the conditional probability P(E|H_Y) adequately reflects the idea that the perceptual input in the banana inference is given its proper weight. More generally, when a selection rule selects H to be the content of experience because it figures in P(H|E) and E is a perceptual input, we can ask whether the reverse conditional probability P(E|H) adequately reflects the weight given to E.

Another potential place to locate inheritable inappropriateness is in hyper-priors. Informally, the hyper-priors of a system are its representations of how confident to be in its priors. Hohwy (2013), Chapter 6 leans heavily on hyper-priors in his explanations of how experiences get their contents.

6.2.2 Circularity in Bayesian theories of inference

The hypothesis that Bayesian inferences determine the content of experience opens the possibility that those inferences might give rise to a kind of circular reasoning that has been discussed, using different examples from the ones I'll discuss, by Jona Vance (2015). I will illustrate it using memory color.

As before, someone is seeing object o, which is a gray banana. Prior to seeing o, according to the Bayesian theory of content-determination, the perceiver had opinions (and these opinions may be encoded in her visual system) about how likely something is to be yellow, if it has the properties represented in the pre-conscious perceptual input labeled by "E." I'll call these properties "E-properties." An example of E-properties might be the characteristic shape and texture of bananas. To describe the circularity flaw, however, it does not matter what the E-properties are.[4]

These opinions take the form of a distribution of probabilities over a space of hypotheses concerning the percentage of things with E-properties (for short: 'E-things') that are yellow (in a domain that we can leave unspecified). For instance, let's suppose the subject assigns a low probability to "100% of the E-things are yellow," an even lower probability to "no E-things are yellow," and much higher probabilities to analogous percentages above 50%. We can call these hypotheses H_{100}, H_{95}, and so on.[5]

When the subject sees banana o, she takes in the information that o has E-properties. Using Bayes's theorem, she combines this information with her prior opinions, represented by the hypotheses in H_i about the percentage of E-things that are yellow, and calculates a probability distribution over a space of hypotheses concerning the color of o. We met some of these hypotheses before. H_Y is the proposition that o is yellow. $H_{\sim Y}$ is the proposition that o is not yellow. The more likely it is, according to the subject, that something with E-properties is yellow, the higher the probability of H_Y.

The selection rule for determining the content of experience selects from among these hypotheses. Suppose the selection rule selects H_Y (the proposition that o is yellow) as the content of the experience. It

---

[4] In Bayesian theories of content-determination for color perception, E-properties will be processed (that is, they will come to be represented by the perceptual system) before color. If that is not true of shape and texture properties, the example is unrealistic in that respect.

[5] I'm ignoring complications arising from having infinitely many hypotheses in this hypothesis space, since they are irrelevant to the basic structure of circularity.

might select H_Y because the rule is to select the color hypothesis with the highest probability, and H_Y is highest.

In this scenario, the hypotheses H_{100}, H_{95}, and the others in the same space of hypotheses have played a role determining the color content of the perceptual experience our perceiver has when she sees banana o. The circularity problem consists in the person's using that color experience to strengthen her credences in those hypotheses. For instance, suppose she takes herself to have learned from her experience that o is indeed yellow. Assuming that the experience has no way to reflect the nuance of H_Y, any strengthening of the hypotheses in the space that contains H_{100}, H_{95}, and so on will be illicit.[6]

The danger of this kind of circularity is easily hidden by the fact that Bayesian inferences to experience occur outside the subject's awareness. A subject might consciously strengthen prior probabilities about the color of bananas in forming beliefs in response to experience, without knowing that those same probabilities have been used already in generating the experience.

6.2.3 Jumping to conclusions

So far I've considered what it would be like if experiences were susceptible to epistemic inappropriateness from circularity and from inherited inappropriateness. What about jumping to conclusions? How could an experience result from jumping to conclusions? I'll describe this kind of flaw in the simplest case first, and then consider a form it can take in Bayesian theories of content-determination.

In the Jack and Jill case, Jill could come to experience Jack as angry by jumping to conclusions from another experience, after seeing his face. Since the experiences in the example could and would normally occur simultaneously, I'll call them "sub-experiences."[7] In Table 6.5, I render Jill's experiences of Jack using "x" instead of "Jack."[8]

---

[6] The fact that this nuance cannot be reflected in experience gives rise to the rounding-off problem, discussed in section 6.2.4 and by Teng (2016) and (ms). For related discussions, see Vance (2015), Morrison (2016), Moss (forthcoming), and Munton (forthcoming and ms).

[7] The term "sub-experience" might seem to suggest a metaphysical structure to experiences where they are built out of other experiences. But the idea that experiences are metaphysically structured in this way isn't necessary for the examples. Jill's sub-experience that Jack has a blank stare can equally well be thought of as the fact that the Jill has an experience whose content includes "Jack has a blank stare."

[8] For more on the complications concerning what contents experience have when they attribute properties to a particular item that you see, see Siegel (2010), ch. 7, Schellenberg (2010), Logue (2014).

Table 6.5. Jumping to conclusions: Composite inference 4

Inference 4a	
Sub-experience 1:	x has a blank stare
Bad Sub-experience 2:	x is angry

Inference 4b	
Bad Sub-experience 2:	x is angry
Bad Belief:	x is angry

Jill's fear that Jack is angry might cause her experience of Jack as angry (sub-experience 2) to depend on her experience of him as having a blank stare (sub-experience 1). Both sub-experiences might belong to the same experience, and she might have both sub-experiences at the same time. Even so, within the single experience, one of the sub-experiences might depend on the other one, because of the background fear. The dependence could have all the marks of inference.

Jill might have the anger-experience, in part because she fears that Jack is angry, and she sees his blank stare (and experiences it as such). Her fear makes her respond to the blank stare by experiencing Jack as angry, just as in a case of fearful thinking, it might make her respond to the blank stare by believing that Jack is angry.[9] Here, experiences are responses to other experiences, just as conclusions are responses to inferential inputs. And like inferential responses generally, responses to experiences can be explained by the subject's rational sensitivity to the relations, as the subject sees them, between Jack's blank stare and the rest of her outlook concerning Jack and anger.

Just as in the case of fearful thinking, the conclusion would be ill-founded to the extent that the subject, due to her unfounded fear, jumped to the conclusion that Jack is angry from seeing his blank stare (as such), an experience could likewise be ill-founded if it arose

---

[9] McGrath (2013a, 2013b) introduces this kind of dependence relation and calls it "quasi-inference." It is discussed further in Chapter 7, and in Siegel (2013b).

in an exactly analogous way. That experience would be downgraded, in having the content *x is angry*.[10]

Besides developing the epistemic profile of experiences that result from epistemically inappropriate inferences, it is also natural to consider what happens to the epistemic profile of an experience if a subject loses a belief from which that experience was inferred. Consider the inferred experience 1A (Table 6.1), with content *x is a yellow banana*. What happens if the subject loses the belief that bananas are yellow (a belief which helped generate this experience), while still having an experience with that content? If the experience persists without the inferential input, then it doesn't depend on the inferential inputs any more. For all that, the experience could retain the same epistemic status, if it depended on something else. The Inferential Modulation thesis makes no further predictions about the epistemic status of the experience, absent further specification of the case.

We can also ask what happens if one of the inferential inputs to an inferred experience becomes ill-founded while the experience still depends on it. For instance, suppose you gain reason to think that x isn't a banana. If the experience comes to depend on an ill-founded inferential input, then the experience will inherit this inappropriateness and lose epistemic power, unless the ill-foundedness washes out given the rest of the inferential input.

6.2.4 Bayesian inference to binary experience: the rounding-off problem

The epistemic flaws in inference that I've discussed under the heading of "Jumping to conclusions" have an analog in Bayesian inferences to experience.

Traditionally, philosophers who find the idea that experiences have content useful for analyzing perception have presumed that experiences are binary states with non-probabilistic content. A less orthodox and less common approach would hold that they could be binary states with probabilistic content, or incremental states analogous to credences.[11]

---

[10] In section 6.3 I consider whether jumping to conclusions is the only epistemic flaw in the anger case. I am using one version of the examples to illustrate this mode of epistemic flaw, not giving a full analysis of the example.

[11] The less orthodox view is explored by Morrison (2016), Munton (forthcoming), and Teng (ms), but not Hohwy (2013), despite the global ambition of Hohwy's theory. Credences are standardly operationalized in terms of betting behavior, and the scale of

One of these non-traditional options is needed for experiences to be the conclusion of Bayesian inference in a way that reflects the incremental nuances of those conclusions. Suppose the upshot of the Bayesian inference is that the probability that banana o is yellow is less than 1. On the traditional view of experiences, there is no way for experience to reflect this incremental nuance. It can't be reflected in the type of state that experience is, since by hypothesis it isn't a state that comes in increments. And it can't be reflected in the content of experience, since by hypothesis, experiences have non-probabilistic content. On the traditional view, there is no way for an experience to be the conclusion of a Bayesian inference.

If the Bayesian theory of content-determination for experience is combined with a traditional theory of experience, the combination creates a potential epistemic problem, first formulated (to my knowledge) by Lu Teng.[12] On this picture, the transition from the conclusion of the Bayesian inference to an experience is analogous to the transition from the information that the probability of a hypothesis that o is yellow is less than 1, to a full belief that o is yellow. If there are rules for which transitions from incremental states to binary states (with non-probabilistic contents) are rational, then some transitions from conclusions of Bayesian inferences to full beliefs with non-probabilistic content will be reasonable transitions to make. But presumably, not every such transition will be reasonable. The possibility of unreasonable transitions to experience gives us another potential epistemic flaw in an inferential route to experience: an inappropriate transition from the conclusion of a Bayesian inference (either in the form of a belief with probabilistic content, or an incremental state), to an experience construed as a binary state with non-probabilistic content. This flaw is a variety of jumping to conclusions.

As Teng (ms) observes, if all experiences had their contents determined in a Bayesian way, and none of them reflected incremental nuance in their contents or in the type of state they are, then experiences

credences is defined in relation to the credence that equals 1. If a subject has credence that equals 1 in a proposition p, she would be prepared to bet anything against p. Since the operationalization of incremental states in terms of betting behavior presumably does not apply to unconscious states of perceptual processing, it remains for Bayesian theories that posit such states to specify how else they should be understood.

[12] Teng (ms and 2016).

would be systematically downgraded. This conclusion accords with external-world skepticism about justification. Both positions hold that we normally take experiences to have more epistemic power than is warranted.

For this skepticism to be avoided, either experiences must not uniformly have their contents determined in a Bayesian way, or else something in their nature or contents must reflect probabilistic information.

6.3 How Inference Can Explain Epistemic Downgrade

According to the Downgrade Thesis (Chapter 4), some cases of hijacked experiences lead to epistemic downgrade. The epistemic profile for experiences described so far can explain why these experiences are epistemically downgraded.

In arguing that the epistemic profile can explain the Downgrade Thesis, I'll focus on two cases. The first case is the preformationism case, as before:

Preformationism: When spermist preformationists (who favored the hypothesis that sperm cells contained embryos) looked at sperm cells under a microscope, their experiences had embryo-content due to their favoring preformationism. They go on to believe that the sperm cells contain embryos, and to strengthen their confidence that preformationism is true.

The second case, as before, is an oversimplified and fictionalized form of memory color. A gray banana looks yellow, due to your belief that bananas are yellow. That belief prevents you from seeing the grayness of the banana for what it is.[13]

Banana: Due to one's true and well-founded belief that bananas are yellow, a gray banana looks yellow.

Both of these cases are good candidates for being epistemically downgraded.

---

[13] The example in the text is fictional because it stipulates both that the influencing state is a belief, and that the subject experiences the banana as yellow, whereas in the real case it is experienced as yellowish (though see Zeimbekis 2013 for an argument that it is simply experienced as gray, with no effect on color experience at all).

Earlier, I argued that in the preformationism case, the experience of an embryo in the sperm cell does not provide much if any support for either preformationism, or for the belief that the sperm cell contains an embryo.[14] In the banana case, analogous epistemological questions arise. Let's focus just on the potential for Circularity. We can ask whether your yellow-banana experience provides as much support as it might otherwise provide for strengthening your belief in the generalization that bananas are yellow. The main argument for the Downgrade Thesis suggests that it wouldn't.

The epistemic downgrade in these cases can be straightforwardly explained by the hypothesis that the experience is the conclusion of an inference whose inferential inputs include the beliefs that help generate the experience. In the banana case, if the yellow-banana experience results from Belief 1 and Belief 2 (in Table 6.1), then it will lose epistemic power to support the generalization that bananas are yellow. The hypothesis that the experience results from inference explains this reduction in its epistemic power. Similarly, the hypothesis that the embryo-experience results from inference 3a explains the loss of epistemic power depicted in the diagrams of Inferences 3b and 3c (Table 6.4).

6.3.1 Is inference irrelevant to epistemic downgrade?

I've argued that inferential routes to the experiences in the preformationism and Banana cases can explain the epistemic downgrade in those cases. An objection to this hypothesis grants that epistemic downgrade occurs in these cases, but denies that inference is relevant to explaining the downgrade. According to this objection, in order to explain the epistemic downgrade of the experience in the preformationism case, it is neither necessary nor illuminating to posit an inferential relationship between the experiences and the beliefs that help generate the experiences. There are several versions of this objection.[15]

A first version is that inference is not necessary, because other ways for psychological precursors to influence experience also seem to epistemically downgrade those experiences. Suppose Jill's *fear* that Jack was angry helps explain why she has an anger-experience—and not a belief

---

[14] Chapter 4.
[15] Some of these are developed by Lyons (2011a), (2016), Ghijsen (2016), and Brogaard (2013).

that Jack is angry. Here we have something superficially similar to the epistemic flaw of Circularity. If Jill's experience had its usual baseline epistemic powers, then Jill's fear could be confirmed by her experience. If Jill's fear can't reasonably be confirmed by her experience, that suggests that her experience lacks baseline epistemic powers.

But this version of the anger case would be a case of Circularity, only if the fear is an inferential input. Believing that Jack is angry might be an input to an inference, but can fearing that Jack is angry play the same role? For that matter, could desire? If they couldn't, then in some cases we would need a non-inferential explanation of downgrade. Inference could explain epistemic downgrade only by giving up on having a unified explanation of epistemic downgrade in the banana, preformationism, anger cases, and wishful seeing.

One might question the assumption that fear can't be an inferential input in the same way that belief can. (I argue against this assumption in Chapter 8.) But let us grant for the sake of argument that if Jill fears that Jack is angry without believing that he is, she is not in a position to infer that Jack is angry directly from her fear, in exactly the same ways that she can infer that Jack is angry directly from her belief. Still, fears or desires could control which inferences are made. For instance, Jill's fear could produce an anger-experience that is inferentially flawed as a result of jumping to conclusions from other mental states, such as other experiences or from pre-conscious perceptual states.[16] Fear-based explanations are thus compatible with inference explanations.

A different version of the objection focuses on modes of influence on experience that are superficially similar to the anger case, but that don't, according to the objectors, lead to epistemic downgrade. Lyons (2011a) imagines a perceiver whose fear of snakes improves his visual acuity, leading him to see snakes more often when they are around.[17] Lyons's perceiver becomes more sensitive to snakes. Since the relationship

---

[16] McGrath (2013a, 2013b) discusses inferences from experiences to other experiences.

[17] In Siegel (2013a), I considered a similar example (a belief that you are a hawk increases your visual acuity) in order to distinguish improvements in acuity from experiences that are downgraded by their psychological precursors. I suggested that experiences would be epistemically downgraded if their relationship to their psychological precursors was sufficiently similar to a relationship between those same precursors and belief, where that latter relationship would make the belief ill-founded. Lyons (2011a), Ghijsen (2016), and Vahid (2014) criticize this proposal on the grounds that it left underspecified what kinds of similarity matters. The inferential approach provides a way to develop this idea that avoids

between fear and acuity is causal, the fact that the influencer is a fear is not relevant. A belief that snakes are around could play the same role, and that belief's own epistemic status would be irrelevant. In this case, Lyons reasons, the snake-experiences would not be downgraded.[18]

On its own, the snake case is not a counterexample to the inferential modulation thesis. As we saw in an earlier discussion of pelicans, if the gain in acuity comes from the way the psychological precursor directs the perceiver's attention, then the relationship between the experience and the precursor (desire, fear, belief) is not inferential. The perceiver may be responding to her fear, desire, or belief when she looks for snakes and finds them, but her response is not an inferential response.[19] In his rendition of the objection, Lyons takes himself to be showing that inference is irrelevant to downgrade, by finding a case in which a state that's eligible to be an input to inference, namely an unjustified belief, causes an experience that is not epistemically downgraded. But since the belief merely causes the experience, and is not also a state to which the experience is an inferential response, this case is not a counterexample to the inferential explanation of downgrade. It could be turned into a counterexample only by assimilating inference to causation.[20]

The fact that a fear, desire, or belief could lead to an accurate experience, or to a pattern of them, entails nothing about whether the experiences are inferred. Nor do they entail anything about whether those experiences

---

the need to appeal to similarity at all, by directly identifying inference as the relationship between experience and a precursor that modulates the experience's epistemic status.

[18] Ghijsen (2016) and Vahid (2014) follow Lyons's line of reasoning.

[19] See Chapter 5, section 5.2.

[20] The cases of improved sensitivity are also under-described. Sensitivity is a measure of how often experiences are accurate. But it is not fine-grained enough to determine how the accuracy on any given occasion arises. Two experiences could arise from equally sensitive processes, even if one process belonged to a modally robust pattern in which each experience was accurate because the perceiver saw them without any interference at all (innocuous or otherwise) from desire, fear, or prior belief, while the other belonged to a modally robust pattern in which the perceiver inferred the experiences from an ill-founded belief. Lyons's presumption that neither experience would be downgraded suggests that sensitivity, for Lyons, is sufficient for having baseline epistemic powers. That assumption would count as justifying the true beliefs about the outdoor temperature of Keith Lehrer's character TrueTemp (Lehrer 1990), who regularly and accurately forms beliefs about the temperature, solely because those beliefs are sensitive to the truth about the temperature. Lyons (2011b) grants that this verdict on TrueTemp is counter-intuitive.

Table 6.6. Bad circularity and beliefs

	Bad circularity	Beliefs
Premise	Well-founded belief:	X
Premise	Well-founded belief:	Y
Bad conclusion	Strengthen	X

are downgraded. They therefore do not make a strong case that inference is irrelevant to epistemic downgrade.

A powerful alternative to inference as an explanation of epistemic downgrade is reliabilism, which takes the varieties of poor inferences as different manifestations of a single more basic epistemic flaw: unreliability. I'll focus on process reliabilism.[21] According to process reliabilism, a belief is ill-founded to the extent that it results from a process that is not conducive to producing true beliefs, and well-founded to the extent that it results from a process that is conducive to producing true beliefs. For any ill-founded belief, reliabilism predicts that the epistemic flaw will ultimately consist in the fact that the belief-forming process that operates is not truth-conducive.

Reliabilism seems to lack the resources to identify the epistemic problem with badly circular inferences that lead to epistemic downgrade.[22] Consider first an uncontroversial case of inference from beliefs to other beliefs. Suppose S infers belief Y from belief X. Then she strengthens her belief X, in response to her belief Y. Let's assume we're in a case where this circularity ill-founds belief X (see Table 6.6).

But now suppose that before belief X was strengthened in response to Y, it was formed by a highly reliable process. The process of strengthening X in response to Y does not seem any less truth-conducive than the process that generated X in the first place. It seems equally truth-conducive: whatever process made belief X true across the relevant range of circumstances before it was strengthened would seem to make it true across the same range after it is strengthened. Yet it is wrong that

---

[21] I focus on process reliability as opposed to indicator reliability, but the basic issues are the same. For more on the distinction, see Goldman and McGrath (2014).

[22] Perhaps the same general difficulty underlies the enduring challenges to reliabilism from bootstrapping (Vogel 2000, Cohen 2002), though I won't make the case here.

the original belief X and the strengthened belief have the same epistemic status. By hypothesis, the strengthening is illicit.

In response, a natural reliabilist strategy is to deny that the process that generated the original belief X is equally truth-conducive to the process that generates the strengthening of X in response to Y. This reply seems most promising if it identifies a process that is not individuated by the belief X, and that process is the process whose reliability matters for assessing the epistemic status of the strengthened X. In addition to identifying such a process, the reliabilist reply needs to give grounds for thinking that it will always be sufficiently unreliable, since by reliabilist lights, unreliability has to underlie the poor epistemic status of the strengthened belief.

One candidate for such a process would be circular inferences (with whatever modifications are needed to rule out cases like the one involving the Oracle discussed earlier). This proposal seems to back off from unreliability per se as the basic epistemic flaw, because it gives the notion of inference a non-derivative status. It is also not at odds with the hypothesis that circular inferences explain downgrade in hijacked experiences.

The challenge for reliabilism in identifying the epistemic flaw with badly circular inferences from highly reliable beliefs has an analog in the case of experiences. Suppose that Jill starts out with a highly reliable belief that Jack is angry, and that this belief generates an experience—not by guiding Jill to focus on the features of Jack's face that are cues for anger (or are manifestations of Jack's anger), but by influencing the content that Jill's experience has when she sees Jack's face. In response to her experience, Jill strengthens her belief that Jack is angry. Here's Jill's experience plays a mediating role between an initial belief and its strengthening. In the earlier example, belief Y played this role.

Reliabilism seems to predict that Jill's strengthened belief that Jack is angry is at least as well-founded as that belief was, before it influenced her experience. This prediction does not depend on whether Jill's experience is inferred from her initial belief or not. Either way, the prediction seems wrong. To identify the flaw with the belief, the reliabilist has to find an unreliable process in the picture, and make the case that it is the process whose reliability matters for determining the epistemic status of Jill's strengthened belief. The challenge seems no easier to meet here than it does in the case where by hypothesis, the relationship between the initial, well-founded belief and the middle state is inference. If a purely reliabilist treatment of circular inference is unpromising, then a unified reliabilist account of epistemic flaws in poor inference is unpromising as well. By comparison, the framework of inference can explain both the epistemic flaw of circularity in general, and the special case of it in the perceptual hijacking of the kinds we have discussed. And the framework seems more promising without reliabilism's commitment to assimilating every epistemic flaw to unreliability.

I've argued that inferential routes to experience can explain what makes hijacked experiences lose epistemic power. In Chapter 7, I turn from loss to gain, and consider whether inferences can bestow epistemic power on experience.

7

How Experiences Can Gain Power from Inference

The epistemic profile constructed in the previous chapter aimed to characterize the kinds of inference that could interfere with an experience providing baseline epistemic power. Baseline epistemic power to provide justification is the kind that sustains the commonsense assumption that often, perceptual experiences provide pretty good reasons to believe one's eyes. Epistemically downgraded experiences lack the power to provide baseline justification, and may lack epistemic power to provide justification at any level at all. I argued that this profile can explain what makes hijacked experiences epistemically downgraded.

Once it is granted that experiences can provide baseline epistemic power, the phenomenon of losing that power has natural exemplars. In contrast, gain of epistemic power by experiences beyond the baseline can seem elusive from one perspective and implausible from another. From these two perspectives, two challenges arise to the idea that experiences can be inferred, and both challenges center on the idea of epistemic upgrade.

Starting with the challenge that upgrade is implausible, one might be tempted to think it has no exemplars at all, on the grounds that baseline justification is a ceiling (a thick ceiling, if the baseline is a range). For instance, if the best possible basis for learning that there's a pig in the pigsty involves seeing the pig, then it might seem that the baseline epistemic power provided by the experience you have in seeing the pig is as much epistemic power as any experience could provide. No purely inferential route to learning that there's a pig in the pigsty could be as good, and an inferential route to a pig-experience could be at most as good as a non-inferential route to the same experience—not any better.

This line of thought might seem to rule out epistemic upgrade, as it suggests that to allow that an experience could provide epistemic power beyond the baseline would be to posit experiences with implausibly high amounts of epistemic power.

If epistemic upgrade is implausible, then the idea that experiences can result from inference might seem implausible as well. Inference to experience, it might be thought, inevitably bestows epistemic power to the experience, in some cases where the inferential inputs are well-founded. At the same time, the commonsense idea that we often have excellent reason from experience to believe our eyes does not seem sensitive to whether experiences are inferred or not. Putting these ideas together, the Inferential Modulation thesis seems to predict cases in which the epistemic power bestowed by an inference aggregates with the epistemic power that the experience can have independently of resulting from inference. In this way, the inferential modulation thesis might seem forced into predicting epistemic upgrade. And that is the first challenge to the Inferential Modulation thesis: in predicting epistemic upgrade, it predicts that some experiences accumulate an implausibly large amount of epistemic power.

From another direction, the very idea that inferred experiences could have so much as baseline epistemic power faces a different challenge. It might be thought that inferential routes to experience somehow dilute the epistemic power that uninferred experiences can have, by interfering with a potentially direct link to the particular object, event, or situation being perceived. If inferences to experience always dilute the epistemic power that the experience can provide to a point below the baseline, then all inferred experiences will be downgraded. And if all inferred experiences are downgraded, then any epistemic profile that details the differences in impact between epistemically good inferences to experience and epistemically poor ones will just amount to greater or lesser degrees of ill-foundedness. On the spectrum of epistemic powers of experience, the entire profile for inferred experiences would be confined to the part below the baseline.

This line of reasoning generates a second challenge, when combined with the hypothesis that ordinary everyday judgments, such as "that banana is yellow," are in fact made on the basis of experiences that result from inferences. If the inferences downgrade those experiences, then experiences are not providing us with as much epistemic support as common sense supposes. This result would be at odds with the starting assumption that the perceptual judgments that truly deserve their status as common sense are well-founded, thanks to their support from perceptual experience.

So there are two challenges to the idea that inference could produce experiences, both centered on the idea of epistemic upgrade by inference. According to the over-aggregation challenge, epistemic upgrade by inference is implausible, while according to the putative inevitability of downgrade by inference, epistemic upgrade by inference is impossible. Together, these two challenges put pressure on the coherence and plausibility of the inferential proof of concept for the Rationality of Perception. If there is no plausible epistemic role that epistemically appropriate inferences to experience could play, that might make one reconsider whether experiences can result from inference at all. The challenges jointly suggest that any answer to the question whether experiences can be epistemically upgraded by inference is problematic. In this way, they illustrate the need for a constructive defense of the Rationality of Perception.

In this chapter, after clarifying the potentially problematic ways in which inference could impact the epistemic powers of experience that figure in these challenges, I argue that both challenges can be met, and summarize the epistemic profile of inferred experiences constructed in this chapter and the previous one.

7.1 What Would It Be to Gain Power from Inference?

There are at least three things that could constitute an experience's gaining epistemic power from inference. Most straightforwardly, inference can bestow any epistemic power on experience, where the epistemic power does not yet result in the experience providing justification at the baseline. The Inferential Modulation thesis entails that experience can gain power from inference in this sense. If an experience is the conclusion of inference, then the inference establishes an epistemic dependence on the inputs of the inference. In at least some cases where those inputs themselves have epistemic power to provide justification, the experience will have that power as well.

At issue in the challenges to epistemic upgrade is whether an experience can end up with baseline power from inference (epistemic baselining), and whether an experience can gain power above the baseline from inference (epistemic upgrade). For instance, consider two experiences with the content *o is yellow* (see Table 7.1a). The inferred experience results from inference. The uninferred experience, let's stipulate, has baseline epistemic powers to support believing that o is yellow.

Let's focus on the epistemic power to support the belief that o is yellow. The two challenges raise these two questions:

Baselining Question: Can the inferred experience have baseline epistemic powers to support believing *o is yellow*?

Upgrade Question: Can the inference bestow the experience with epistemic powers *above* the baseline to support believing *o is yellow*?

We can address these questions by comparing two endorsements of experiences: an endorsement of the inferred Experience 5a, and an endorsement of the uninferred Experience 5b. The comparison of experiences in Table 7.1b (a continuation of Table 7.1a) holds constant the experience's phenomenal character and content, and varies the route to the experience, so that the impact of the inferential route can be assessed.

Table 7.1a. Two routes to experience

Inference		No inference	
Belief:	Bananas are yellow		
Experience:	o is a banana		
Inferred Experience 5a	o is yellow	**Uninferred Experience 5b**	o is yellow

Table 7.1b. Two endorsements

Inference 5a		Inference 5b	
Inferred Experience	o is yellow	Uninferred Experience	o is yellow
Conclusion-Belief	o is yellow	Conclusion-Belief	o is yellow

The comparison in Table 7.1b is distinct from other situations that might come to mind when considering whether experience can gain power from inference. These situations may help bring the Baselining and Upgrade questions into focus. (Readers for whom these questions are in focus already can skip to section 7.2 without losing the thread.)

First, suppose that an expert and a non-expert see a pine tree, and end up with phenomenally different experiences. If the influence of expertise on experience was usefully analyzed as an inference, then we could ask whether the expert's experiences had more epistemic power than the non-expert's experience to support believing that the tree is a pine tree. Here we would be holding constant the external thing seen (they are both seeing the same tree), and varying both the phenomenal character of each experience, and the route to each experience. In contrast, in Tables 7.1a and 7.1b, we are holding constant the phenomenal character of experiences, and varying the route to them.

Here is a different comparison. Consider two people who hear the note A-flat, and their auditory experiences are phenomenally the same. One perceiver has perfect pitch and can recognize the note as A-flat, whereas the other perceiver is not sure what note it is. By hypothesis, the perceiver with perfect pitch has more reason to believe that the note is A-flat than the other perceiver does. We could use this comparison to ask whether the contents of the experiences differ, where the difference in epistemic power comes from, and to what extent the difference in epistemic power is localized in the experience (as opposed to an extra-experiential factor, such as perfect pitch). In the A-flat case, we are holding constant the phenomenal character of two experiences, and starting out with a difference in epistemic situations of the subjects. In contrast, in Tables 7.1a and 7.1b we are trying to assess whether there is any difference in epistemic power between the experiences.

I'll argue that the answer to both the Baselining Question and the Upgrade Question is Yes. Inferences can leave experiences with baseline epistemic powers, and they can lead to upgraded epistemic powers.

7.2 Does Inference Always Lead to Epistemic Downgrade?

Let us begin with the idea that any inferential basis downgrades experience.

Consider a scenario we've met before. You know that an object o is behind a curtain, you can't see o, but you know that o is a banana. You've got some reason to think that o is yellow, but it doesn't come from perceiving o—it comes from your knowledge that bananas tend to be yellow. Compare your situation to someone who sees that the banana is yellow, and knows on that basis that it is yellow.[1] If you think that the power you get from your experience of seeing the banana to believe *o is yellow* is greater than any power you get from an inference, then you might conclude that the answer to the Baselining Question is No: the inferred experience could at best have only as much epistemic power as a good guess, well-informed by its inferential inputs, whereas an uninferred experience's baseline epistemic powers could have more.

The idea that perception can be more powerful than inductive reasoning may lie behind some responses to external-world skepticism. Consider J. L. Austin's suggestion that if you want to know whether any pigs are in the pen, seeing a pig "just settles the matter." According to Austin, seeing a pig does not provide evidence for the presence of a pig, from which you have to infer that a pig is present.[2] If seeing merely provided evidence for the presence of a pig, Austin seems to suggest, then presumably it wouldn't settle the matter of whether a pig is present or not. Since seeing the pig leaves you with no need to infer from evidence, seeing is epistemically more powerful than inferring from evidence.

McGrath (2013a) develops the idea that perception is more powerful than reasoning in a different way. Rather than focusing on the difference between reasoning from generalizations on the one hand, and perceptual contact on the other, he focuses on the distinction between two kinds of perceptual experiences: receptive and constructive. A constructive

---

[1] There is a range of psychological and epistemic states that it is natural to use the schematic locution "S sees that P" to denote. Here "S sees that the banana is yellow" denotes the state that S is in when S sees the banana, and sees it at least in part by having a visual experience that correctly and non-accidentally attributes yellow to it. It is a further question what more (if anything) has to be added to make a case of seeing that P a case of knowing that P. On the idea that there is an explanatorily primitive form of knowing that P that is also a case of seeing that P, see Williamson (2000). Williamson presumably means something different by "seeing that P" than what's meant by the locution here, since he takes it to entail believing that P. On the use of "S sees that P" here, the fact that S sees that P does not entail that S believes that P.

[2] Austin (1962), p. 115.

experience is the result of an inference from one sub-experience to another (he calls the inference "quasi-inference"), and a receptive experience does not result from inference.[3]

According to McGrath, experiences that result from quasi-inference (constructive experiences) cannot provide immediate justification for believing their contents, whereas receptive experiences can.[4] Even if the considerations he offers favoring this view support a difference between the structure of justification by receptive as opposed to constructed experiences as he construes them, they do not support a difference in the degree of justification that each kind of experience provides. They therefore do not support the conclusion that inferred experiences are always downgraded.

A relatively more promising route to the idea that inferred experiences are always downgraded starts with a comparison. Suppose you have a well-founded belief that 16-year-olds tend to be poor drivers. Then you meet your friend's 16-year-old daughter. It seems possible to learn that this individual is a good driver, unlike most 16-year-olds, by getting information directly about her. The information is about a particular 16-year-old, whereas your prior belief was a generalization. Why rely on generalizations to decide what to think about the 16-year-old, when you can find out about her directly? This kind of case might make it seem that information coming from a particular person or situation should not be diminished in favor of information in the form of generalizations when there is a conflict. Combined with the idea that perception is a channel for taking in information from particular things (such as persons, situations, and events), it might seem that perception is always more

---

[3] Quasi-inference as McGrath understands it is not limited to jumping to conclusions. Suppose someone's ability to recognize papayas on the basis of how they look results in an experience that attributes (to an object) the property of being a papaya. According to this account, the sub-experience with papaya-content results from quasi-inference from a sub-experience representing oblong shape and textured green and yellow surfaces. Or one's experience of a gray banana as yellow could result from a different quasi-inference: one that goes from a sub-experience attributing banana-like shape and texture properties to a thing, to a sub-experience attributing yellowness to that thing.

[4] McGrath seems to equate uninferred experiences to receptive ones and constructive experiences to inferred experiences. These equations overlook the possibility (discussed at the end of this section) of experiences that are at once receptive and inferred, as well as the possibility that some experiences are epistemically impacted by their precursors, but not by virtue of being inferred from them. In Chapters 8 and 9, I consider experiences that bring this option into focus.

epistemically powerful than inference from generalizations, when both bear on the same particular situation.

According to this line of thought, because perception is a means for getting information about particular situations, inferred experiences are always downgraded when they are inferred from generalizations—even if those generalizations are epistemically appropriate. Generalizations can produce good inferences when the banana is behind the curtain. But once one has the banana itself as a source of information, one can do no better than use the information about the banana that comes from it directly.

Something like this idea may be implicit in Charles Travis's discussion of perception. According to Travis, perception presents a subject exclusively with the particularity of a situation. When the subject witnesses a particular situation, she witnesses things as they are, in all their particularity (Travis 2013a, 2013b). Extrapolating, if an inference from a generalization such as "bananas are yellow" and "x is a banana" could never recover the full particularity of what one can witness in perception, then such witnessing might seem always to provide better grounds for beliefs about how things are than the relatively impoverished generalities which, according to Travis, are never present in perception.

In reply, the contrast between generalities and information coming directly from a particular situation is a poor guide to relative epistemic power. Sometimes evidence coming directly from a particular weighs more than generalizations, and other times it's the reverse. For example, suppose you meet a tall, composed, seemingly responsible nine-year-old, Cara. You observe that she is a student of traffic laws and a keen observer of how cars are driven, and you watch her help build a motor car from a build-your-own-car kit. When it's done she drives it once slowly down the driveway. The information you get about this car-focused nine-year-old is evidence that unlike most nine-year-olds, Cara could drive on the streets without putting herself or others in any more danger than most adult drivers.

Let's suppose your limited contact with Cara leaves it open whether she has ever driven in traffic, and whether she has somehow developed the kind of good judgment that often makes the difference between safe and reckless driving. If you were assessing whether Cara could drive safely in traffic, it could be reasonable to rely on the generalization that nine-year-olds generally make unsafe drivers, if they try to drive.

Generally nine-year-olds don't know what's important to pay attention to in traffic and what things to ignore, and they couldn't figure out on the spot the safest way to proceed when other drivers aren't driving the way they should. While you have some evidence that Cara could drive safely in traffic, you also have some other evidence that she couldn't, in the form of your well-founded belief in the generalization that nine-year-olds in general make unsafe drivers. Even putting aside any legal qualms and disappointment from your young car-loving friend, it would be reasonable not to lend Cara your car to drive through the neighborhood, on the grounds that she would likely drive it unsafely. Here's a case in which the evidence you get directly from Cara for believing that she can drive safely in traffic is ultimately weaker than the evidence you get against this proposition from the generalization that nine-year olds make poor drivers.

In addition, when we look more closely at what getting information directly from a particular object, event, or situation involves, we find that it can already involve inference. To see how an inferred experience might have baseline epistemic powers, consider an inferential response to partial color information. To fix ideas, think of this process in the form of a dialogue between the visual system and banana o:

    vs: What color are you?
    o: I don't know, but I'm a banana.
    vs: Well then you're yellow.

In principle, the information that the visual system draws on could take the form of an equal probability distribution over possible colors, where for each color, it is equally probable that o is that color and that o isn't that color. Alternatively, it could take the form of information that leaves color unspecified without a probability distribution.

We can distinguish two kinds of inferential responses to incomplete color information. (These two roles are depicted in Table 7.2.) In the first kind of situation, further processing distinct from the inference would generate more determinate information, but the inference doesn't allow the other processing to unfold. In the second kind of situation, there is no more determinate information to be had, without a contribution from inference. This second kind of situation is a good candidate for one in which the perceptual experience is as receptive of particularity as it can be, despite a role for an inference in generating that experience. Many processes that are paradigmatically receptive are structured in a similar way. For instance, experiences of convexity result from the processes that draw on the visual system's stored information that light comes from above. Psychologists have called this process "inference." But since the kinds of inferences they're discussing do not detract from or add to the subject's rational standing, the fact that they're inferences of a sort does not detract from making them purely receptive.

We can probe farther whether inference always weakens the epistemic power of experience if we contrast the role of an inference in responding to indeterminate information that is left over once a channel of information has been exhausted, with a different role that inference could play. Rather than responding to the information from the banana that is ultimately indeterminate with respect to the banana's color, an inference (resulting in an experience with the content *o is yellow*) could override a pre-conscious percept of grayness. In dialogue form:

vs: What color are you?
o: I'm gray.
vs: But you're a banana. You must be yellow.

The epistemic situation here can seem analogous to someone who ignores relevant counterevidence in the course of drawing an inference.

The idea that inference always leads to downgrade seems relatively more plausible for the case of overriding information, than it does for resolving leftover indeterminacy. This idea gives us a second reply to the charge that inference always leads to downgrade. When the inference merely resolves indeterminate information, then the grounds for holding that it has to produce a downgraded experience seem weak.

But what about when inference overrides pre-conscious information: does every case of overriding information lead to downgrade? Earlier (Chapter 5, section 5.6) I gave some reasons to think that pre-conscious percepts can in principle have epistemic power. If the information overrides epistemically powerful information, then overriding it can lead to downgrade. At the same time, if the priors are strong enough to outweigh the pre-conscious percept, then experiential conclusion, even if it's false, may nonetheless provide a baseline amount of justification for believing that o is yellow.

Table 7.2. Two roles for inference

Inference overrides a pre-conscious percept:

Inference	Pre-conscious perception
Bananas are yellow	
o is a banana	
	o is gray
o is yellow	

Inference resolves leftover indeterminacy:

Inference	Pre-conscious perception
Bananas are yellow	Bananas are yellow
o is a banana	
	<indeterminate color representation>
o is yellow	

These considerations suggest that the kinds of inferences displayed in my reconstruction of the memory color phenomenon, where the conclusion is a yellow-banana experience, are not uniformly cases of perceptual hijacking. Instances of the inference that fail to give pre-conscious input proper weight will be cases of perceptual hijacking. Instances that give this input proper weight will not be cases of perceptual hijacking. In principle, proper weight can even be given to pre-conscious percepts with color content that is different from the color content of the experience that's the conclusion of the inference.

Bayesian theories of perception provide a potential analysis of perceptual hijacking. Whether an experience is hijacked or not depends on whether its perceptual inputs are given proper weight. Does the Bayesian framework have the resources to analyze the weight of perceptual inputs? In our earlier example, E = a pre-conscious perceptual state with content concerning the banana, and H_Y is a color hypothesis. Can the weight of

E be analyzed in terms of $P(E|H_Y)$?[5] If it can be, then whether the experience is hijacked depends on whether that value is epistemically appropriate, and whether the state attached to the value is formed epistemically well.

If the idea of having proper weight is completely reflected by the value of P by $P(E|H_Y)$, then the Bayesian framework can distinguish banana inferences that lead to downgraded yellow-banana experiences, and banana inferences that lead to yellow-banana experiences with baseline epistemic powers, where both inferences are drawn from the same epistemically good priors. The yellow-banana experience is hijacked when formed by an inference in which $P(E|H_Y)$ is too high, and non-hijacked when formed by an inference in which $P(E|H_Y)$ is appropriately low.

This result allows for the possibility that some cases of overriding gray input generate non-hijacked experiences with baseline epistemic powers. These cases provide a reply to the charge that all inferred experiences are downgraded.

In contrast, if there is a notion of giving perceptual inputs proper weight that cannot be analyzed in terms of a prior probability like $P(E|H_Y)$, then even when this value is epistemically appropriate, the perceptual input can still fail to have its proper weight. A Bayesian inference that generates a yellow-banana experience could be downgraded, even if the values assigned to all of the components of the Bayesian inferences were epistemically appropriate. The best chance of defending the position that inference always leads to epistemic downgrade lies with identifying this other notion of the weight of perceptual inputs. That there is such a notion of weight has some plausibility, though I will leave it to others to identify it, and to make the case that it is not already expressed by some component of the Bayesian calculation.

Even without identifying a notion of weight that is not captured by a conditional probability, we have identified several other ways to distinguish between hijacked and non-hijacked outcomes of inferences leading to experiences in which a gray banana looks yellow, due to high priors that the banana will be yellow. Hijacked experiences could arise in at least two ways: first, from overly high priors that the banana is yellow

---

[5] The status of an experience produced by a Bayesian banana inference as hijacked or not is not sensitive to whether the state attached to $P(E|H_Y)$ is a binary state with probabilistic content, or an incremental state.

and overly low priors that it is gray; or second, from overly high likelihoods that a gray input would be generated by a yellow banana and overly low likelihood that a gray input would be generated by a gray banana. Non-hijacked experiences could also arise in at least one way and possibly two: first, by resolving indeterminate color information, rather than overriding a signal that the banana is gray; and second, by properly overriding a pre-conscious signal that the banana is gray with the prior probability that bananas are yellow, on the assumption that the weight of the pre-conscious signal can be analyzed in terms of the kind of prior probability that figures in Bayesian inference.

7.3 Can Inferences Ever Lead to Epistemic Upgrade?

Earlier, we distinguished between two questions about whether experiences can gain epistemic power from inferences.

Baselining Question: Can an inferred experience have baseline epistemic powers to support believing *o is yellow*?

Upgrade Question: Can the inference bestow the experience with epistemic powers *above* the baseline to support believing *o is yellow*?

So far I've argued that the answer to the Baselining Question is yes. Now we can turn to the Upgrade Question.

As we have seen, inference results in patterns of epistemic dependence between conclusions and inferential inputs. For instance, suppose you believe that o is yellow, by inferring it from the beliefs that *o is a banana* and *bananas are yellow*. Then your belief that o is yellow receives epistemic power from its inferential inputs to support subsequent beliefs, such as the belief that o is the color of your house. A natural hypothesis about inferred experiences is that when their inferential inputs provide support for believing *o is yellow*, the experience conducts that support to subsequent beliefs. If the experience conducts the support for *o is yellow* that the inferential inputs had already, then the inference bestows the experience with epistemic power to support believing *o is yellow*.

But now consider an uninferred experience with the content *o is yellow*. It too (we are supposing) has baseline epistemic power to support believing that o is yellow. What features bestow this epistemic power on the uninferred experience? This question asks only about the epistemic powers of the experience—abstracting from the other components of epistemic charge.

Some candidates for the factors that bestow these epistemic powers include: the phenomenal character of the experience, its contents, and the fact that there are no downgrading factors.[6] I'll call this last condition the absence condition. Let's work with the hypothesis that these factors bestow epistemic power, and call these bestowing factors Parity features, because what will matter most is that they can be shared by inferred and uninferred experiences.

> *Parity features*: Three features together bestow the uninferred baseline Experience 5b with baseline epistemic power to support believing *o is yellow*: (i) the phenomenal character of the experience, (ii) its contents, and (iii) the absence of any downgrade-inducing factors (absence condition).

The over-aggregation worry is that the experiences that result from epistemically appropriate inferences will end up with too much epistemic power.

I've chosen features (i)–(iii) as an example of potential bestowing factors. But ultimately, for the sake of assessing the plausibility of epistemic upgrade, what matters is that there are bestowing features that uninferred and inferred experiences can share. Exactly what those features are matters little in this dialectical context.

The Parity features are shared between the experiences we have been comparing: the inferred experience and uninferred experience with baseline powers (Experiences 5a and 5b, reproduced in Tables 7.1a–7.1b).[7]

---

[6] If presentational phenomenal character plays the role in providing epistemic character that I labeled the intermediate role in Chapter 3, section 3.4, then this role will identify the Parity features.

[7] As stated, the definition of Parity features does not specify whether the features are sufficient to bestow experiences with epistemic powers. Even if they had to be supplemented with other features to be sufficient, for instance by a condition specifying a way that the subject is embedded in her environment, we can focus on enlarged sets of features that are still shared by the inferred and uninferred experiences. Since the shared features of these experiences is what matters for the over-aggregation worry, we can set aside the complicated question of which features are sufficient to bestow experiences with epistemic powers. For discussion of possible Parity features, see Siegel and Silins (2015).

Table 7.1a. Two routes to experience

Inference		No inference	
Belief:	Bananas are yellow		
Experience:	o is a banana		
Inferred Experience 5a	o is yellow	**Uninferred Experience 5b**	o is yellow

Table 7.1b. Two endorsements

Inference 5a		Inference 5b	
Inferred Experience	o is yellow	Uninferred Experience	o is yellow
Conclusion-Belief	o is yellow	Conclusion-Belief	o is yellow

If the Parity features are shared, then given the hypothesis that the inference bestows the experience with epistemic power to support believing *o is yellow*, the epistemic powers seem to be bestowed on the inferred experience from both the inference and the Parity features. The inferential input provides support for believing that o is yellow, and the experience conducts this support. But the experience also supports believing this same proposition, by virtue of its Parity features. So there seems to be more support in the picture for believing that o is yellow in Inference 5a, compared to Inference 5b. The inferred Experience 5a ends up with more epistemic power than it would have with the Parity features alone. This is the aggregation prediction.

> *Aggregation prediction*: Inferred experiences with Parity features have more epistemic power to support believing *x is yellow* than uninferred experiences with the same Parity features.

According to the aggregation prediction, the inferred Experience 5a has more epistemic power than the a-rational Experience 5b to support believing *o is yellow*.

The over-aggregation worry is that the aggregation prediction is false. It might seem false, because Experiences 5a and 5b are phenomenally identical. Exactly the same information about x is conveyed to the subject by the two experiences. Perhaps further sensory exploration could give you more support for the belief that x is yellow, for instance if you looked more closely at x, or examined it in different lighting conditions. But when we compare Experiences 5a and 5b, we hold sensory exploration constant.

The prediction would be avoided if there were no Parity features. And there would be no Parity features if the features that bestowed Experience 5b with its epistemic powers included the absence of any inferential route to experience. In section 7.2, this idea was discussed and rejected, on the grounds that inferential routes to experience per se need not have this effect.

If there are Parity features, then the aggregation prediction seems unavoidable.

The inferred experience is on the receiving end of two independent sources of support for believing *o is yellow*: the Parity features, and the inferential inputs. The experience is analogous to a person who is on the receiving end of two sources of epistemic power that she can aggregate, where both support believing *o is yellow*. Consider someone who starts out with good grounds to think that o is a banana and bananas are yellow. We can suppose that the person is new to bananas, and sees a banana for the first time without knowing that it's a banana, and has the experience with the content *o is yellow*. She ends up with pretty good reason to think that o is yellow—a typical case of baseline support for believing her eyes. Then she learns that o is a banana and bananas are yellow. Such a person could aggregate these two bits of support, and end up with more reason to believe that o is yellow, than she would have with either the experience alone, or with the background beliefs alone.

The inferred experience is analogous to this situation, with the added twist that the inference is partly causally responsible for the fact that the experience has the Parity features. In this analogy, the parity features of the experience and its inferential inputs aggregate, just as (respectively) the experience and the background beliefs aggregate. The person's experience and background beliefs aggregate to produce more support for *o is yellow* than either factor could provide alone, and according to the analogy, so do the Parity features and the inferential inputs. The fact that the experience has one source of support (its Parity features) partly because of the other (the inference) does not stop it from having two sources of positive epistemic charge, giving it more than the usual amount of epistemic power.

Is the prediction that epistemic powers of inferred experiences aggregate with epistemic powers bestowed by parity features implausible? One might find aggregation implausible because one finds upgrade itself implausible. But any apparent implausibility of epistemic upgrade that stems from considerations about witnessing the particularity of the ways things are in perception is undermined by our earlier considerations. The idea that perceiving a particular situation (or an object, or event) puts one in a better epistemic position with respect to perceptible features of that situation than one could come to be in by inference is not well motivated by the considerations about particularity. And nothing in the commonsense starting point that perceptual experiences provide justification at the baseline speaks to whether some perceptual experiences could provide even more justification than that.

If inferences can result in experiences that provide the baseline amount of justification, then we should also expect that epistemically strengthening the inferential inputs to an experience will generate experiences with more epistemic power. How much power an inferred experience has depends on the power of its inferential inputs, and there is no obstacle to rising above the baseline.

A potential example of upgrade involves expertise. Consider a perceiver who believes on strong, multiple, independent grounds that bananas are yellow. She has seen many yellow bananas that are treated as normal bananas by everyone around her, knows that bananas (in her environment) ripen yellow, and even knows what makes bananas turn yellow when they are ripe. Any of these grounds would be enough to give her a reasonable belief from which she could infer that o, a banana she is about to see, is yellow.

Suppose this perceiver formed an experience with the content *o is yellow* by inference from a belief that bananas are yellow that had any one of these grounds. Given the inference itself doesn't lead to downgrade, it's plausible that the experience would provide at least as much justification as a baseline amount for believing that o is yellow. But if the fact that she has several such grounds gives her even stronger reason indeed to believe that o is yellow, then it's plausible to suppose that the inference from the combined very strong grounds to an experience yields an experience with epistemic powers that exceed the baseline. More generally, if inferences can result in experiences that provide the baseline amount of justification, then we should also expect that epistemically strengthening the inferential inputs to an experience will generate experiences with more epistemic power. How much power an inferred experience has depends on the power of its inferential inputs, and there is no obstacle to rising above the baseline.

Finally, aggregation of Parity features with inferential bases does not entail upgrade, since the baseline plausibly includes a range of increments of epistemic power, as discussed in Chapter 4 (section 4.1.2). A visual experience with less visual acuity, for example, could provide more epistemic support for believing there are cabbages on the table, than a visual experience with higher resolution, even if both experiences provide a baseline amount of support. Improving an eyeglass prescription can move the epistemic support provide by experiences to the higher end of the baseline. If the baseline encompasses a range of magnitudes of epistemic power, then aggregation of inference with parity features could simply make an experience provide epistemic support at the high end of the baseline. This result would be a case of epistemic baselining rather than epistemic upgrade.

Summing up, the full epistemic profile of inferred experiences is this:

Epistemic profile of inferred experiences: Epistemically inappropriate inferences can reduce the epistemic power of experiences by having flaws of circularity, inherited inappropriateness, or jumping to conclusions, and they can reduce these powers below the baseline. Epistemically appropriate inferences can bestow experiences with baseline epistemic powers, and can bestow them with epistemic powers above the baseline.

In constructing this epistemic profile for inferred experiences, I've focused on examples that lend themselves relatively easily to inferential routes to experience. Other routes to hijacked experiences might seem to sit less easily in the framework of inference. In Part III, I focus on hijacked experiences that motivate the Rationality of Perception, but that initially may not seem to be illuminated by this framework of inference. I argue that in a significant class of cases, even when hijacked experiences arise in these ways, the epistemic impact of perceptual hijacking can be analyzed in terms of inference.

PART III

Applications

Many of the hijacked experiences that motivate the Rationality of Perception figure in epistemic situations that are usefully analyzed in terms of inference. But other hijacked experiences that motivate the Rationality of Perception might seem to fit less easily in the framework of inference.

How powerfully does the inference model succeed as a proof of concept for the Rationality of Perception?

At one extreme, inference could be the only way to account for how psychological precursors to experience could modulate the epistemic charge of those experiences. In particular, it could be the only way to explain how perceptual hijacking could produce irrational experiences.

On the face of it, the odds seem to be against the extreme view. The sheer volume of potential psychological mechanisms by which perceptual hijacking could occur makes it unlikely that they could all be analyzed as inferences. Aside from the sheer volume, there are specific phenomena that seem resistant to analysis in terms of inference.

Regarding evaluative states such as fear and desire, the extreme view would have to explain how any mental state—whether it is an experience or not—could be inferred from evaluative states. If there are no inferences involved when experiences are hijacked by fear or desire, then the entire range of potential hijacked experiences arising from these evaluative states would fall outside the constructive defense of the Rationality of Perception offered so far.

Regarding mechanisms by which the hijacked experiences come about, these include selecting objects and properties to be experienced. Selection effects by psychological precursors on the face of it seem more like effects on attention than inference—one of the key contrasts that brought inferential responses into view in Chapter 5. If there is an epistemic flaw at all in experiences that arise from selection effects, the flaw might seem to lie in the collecting of evidence, rather than in one's inferential response to the evidence collected. The extreme view would have to argue that all selection effects leading to experience can be analyzed as inferences in which the experience is the conclusion.

Regarding the political examples of hijacked experiences where the precursor is a form of racialized bias, the extreme view would at a minimum have to make the case that these attitudes are the kind of state that can figure in inferences, or that they constitutively involve such a state. As we saw in Chapter 1, the potential mechanisms of hijacked perception are numerous. Any defense of the extreme view would have to make the case that *all possible* psychological mechanisms by which racialized attitudes could hijack experience can be analyzed as inferential responses.

To add to the challenge, some hold that racial attitudes take the form of associations between concepts. As we saw in discussing distinctively inferential responses in Chapter 5, associative movements of the mind from the activation of one concept to the activation of another are not inferences, and by themselves activations of concepts make poor candidates for being states to which one can inferentially respond. If the purely associative analysis of racial attitudes is correct, then no responses to them (either in the form of experience or belief) could be inferential responses.

One reaction to these challenges is that evaluative perception, selection effects, and effects arising from racial bias simply don't fit the inferential model. In Part III, I argue for a different reaction. Regarding evaluative perception, a significant category of experiences that are influenced by desire and fear can be analyzed in terms of inference. Regarding selection effects, perhaps surprisingly, some experiences hijacked by selection effects can be analyzed in this way as well. Regarding racial bias, contrary to how it is often characterized, it is the kind of state to which a subject can inferentially respond.

If these conclusions are correct, then the inferential model fits a wide range of hijacked experiences, including all of the core cases I've used to motivate the Rationality of Perception. The fact that it includes these kinds of cases strengthens the proof of concept of the Rationality of Perception. The constructive defense using the inferential model shows how inferences to experiences could figure in a coherent and plausible epistemology of perception.

8

Evaluative Perception

It is one thing to draw an inference from things you believe. But is it possible to draw inferences from fears or desires? If not, how can the influences of fear or desire make experiences irrational—as I've argued they do, in some cases of hijacked experiences?

Fear and desire are windows into what a subject values, including what she cares about and what she feels pressure to avoid. Perceptual experiences trigger fear and initiate desire, but fear and desire can also influence perception. Because of the close relationship between fear or desire and values, their complex interactions with perception result in a kind of evaluative perception.

In this chapter, I argue that we can find a structure of inferential responses in perceptual experiences generated by fear or desire.

8.1 Fearful Seeing

In a nutshell, my argument that fear can make perceptual experiences epistemically evaluable via inference is this. First, there is a type of outlook that's internal to fear. Like any part of a subject's outlook, it may be at odds with her considered outlook. Second, the outlook internal to fear is epistemically appraisable. Finally, given the earlier discussion of epistemic charge and inference, nothing in the nature of experience (Chapter 3) or inference (Chapter 5) precludes perceptual experiences from being inferential responses to this outlook.

8.1.1 The outlook internal to fear

Suppose you enter an apartment on the top floor of a building. Your host wants to show off the view from the balcony. Unfortunately for you, she does not know about your fear of heights. Once you step on to the balcony, your fear intensifies. The possibility of dangling precariously from the balcony is so vivid that you can picture it.

People who have acrophobia have a standing disposition to feel endangered when they believe that falling from a great height is *afforded* by their surroundings, and the affordances seem especially live or salient (I'll use "live" and "salient" interchangeably).[1] An affordance is a possibility of action for a creature in an environment. For instance, the balcony can be fallen from, and it is possible to slip down a steep mountain trail.

Underlying the disposition to feel endangered is an outlook on the world. According to the outlook, some ways of being high up off the ground—standing on a rocky trail high up on a mountain, or on an unenclosed balcony from which one could in principle fall—move the possibilities of falling closer than they'd be if one were on the ground, or if they were high up but protected by an enclosure. This outlook is internal to fear of heights.

Someone could believe that the possibility of falling is afforded by a balcony, without being anxious or agitated by that possibility, and without feeling that the possibility is live and pressing. In contrast, to the fearful subject, the possibility of falling feels live and pressing. It is especially salient to the subject, and the salience has an affective profile—agitation and anxiety. When someone believes that falling from a great height is afforded by their surroundings, or when they experience this affordance, it seems to them (either in belief, or in imagination, or in another kind of "seeming" state) that the possibility of falling is a nearby possibility, and they feel endangered.

A fuller philosophical analysis than I can offer here would explain exactly what it is for a possibility to be live and pressing, and specify a sense of "nearby" in which possibilities can seem closer or father off. With such an analysis in hand of what it is for a possibility to *seem* pressing, or equivalently, what it is for a possibility to be salient to a subject, we could then better understand what it is for a possibility to *be* pressing. Conversely, better understanding what it is to be pressing could help illuminate what it is to seem pressing. Further analysis is needed,

---

[1] Outright believing that one is high up seems to be neither necessary nor sufficient for acrophobia. But having a visual perspective or being shown visual imagery that makes salient the possibility of falling seems to trigger acrophobia. For discussion of possible psychological mechanisms of fear, see Coelho et al. (2009). Thanks to David Silbersweig for discussion.

because taking a possibility to be pressing, or taking it to be nearby in the relevant sense, is arguably not the same thing as taking it to be likely. Think of an optimist who looks on the bright side of a situation, even when they know that the good outcomes are unlikely. The optimist treats the good outcomes as nearby, forming part of their cheerful outlook. The acrophobe treats fearful scenarios as nearby, forming part of their fearful outlook. The sense in which the possibilities are taken to be nearby seem the same both times.

Even without a full analysis of what it is for a possibility to be salient, we can see some dimensions of this kind of salience in the case of fears that are unreasonable.

First, when fearful possibilities are salient to a subject, those possibilities present themselves as potential outcomes that have to be kept at bay. They are live possibilities that have to be dealt with.

Second, when possibilities are salient, they affect the subject's reasoning, by affecting how incoming information is interpreted. For instance, a creaky floorboard or cracks in a rail guard might be taken as evidence for their structural instability.[2] These inferential dispositions are a way for fear to regulate inferences. They are modes by which the fear regulates the subject's responses to incoming information.

This profile of fear suggests that fear has an outlook internal to it that consists in being confident, to some degree, that certain possibilities are pressing. This form of confidence can be epistemically appraised: one can reasonably take a possibility to be pressing, or unreasonably take it to be pressing. More generally, the idea that outlooks internal to fear can be epistemically evaluated fits with ordinary assumption that fear itself can be reasonable or unreasonable. The assumption is reflected in US self-defense law in the form of reasonable person standards, which regulate which forms of aggression count as legitimate forms of self-defense.[3]

8.1.2 Fearful outlooks and inference

We can now see how the outlook internal to fear, which is itself epistemically appraisable, can make perceptual experiences epistemically

---

[2] Railton (2014) discusses these functions of fear. For a related account of epistemic appraisability of emotion, see Vance (forthcoming).

[3] An example of self-defense law involving fear is *State vs. Bassett*, 228 P.3d (Or. Ct. App. 2010). For discussion of reasonable person standards and fear, see Lee (2003).

appraisable as well. I'll focus on cases in which the fear leads to unreasonable conclusions, starting with inferences that lead to judgments. After identifying the types of inferences that lead to these conclusions, we can see how they could lead to conclusions in the form of perceptual experiences.

Taking fearful possibilities to be more pressing than they are is one form of exaggeration found in unreasonable fear. Three other modes of exaggeration highlight inferences from fearful outlooks to judgments. Fearful subjects who exaggerate how pressing fear-congruent possibilities are prone to draw subsequent poor inferences as well. These inferences are means of exaggerating (i) the extent to which information supports fearful scenarios; (ii) how pervasive fear-congruent affordances of a situation are; and (iii) the magnitude of the fear-congruent properties.

In the first mode of exaggeration, one exaggerates how strongly information one has supports a conclusion that is congruent with a fear. For instance, one might exaggerate how much the crack in the rail guard detracts from its ability to protect someone from falling off the trail. Here, one is exaggerating the evidential support one has for thinking that the rail guard affords only partial protection. This is a way of exaggerating the extent to which one's surroundings afford fearful outcomes.

The second mode of exaggeration concerns the subject's relative focus on properties or affordances that are congruent with fear. For instance, if one focused on the cracks in the rail guard, but not on the sturdy bolts and thick metal, it would be natural to conclude that the guardrail fails to afford protection. But the conclusion is less reasonable, to the extent that other information one has about the guardrail is ignored.

If one concludes from one's fearful outlook that the situation contains mainly fear-congruent affordances, and one ignores or discounts evidence one has that it also contains protection-congruent affordances, one's conclusion about the distribution of affordances is unreasonable.[4]

Finally, the third mode of exaggeration is directed at the properties that would make the fear fitting. For instance, Proffitt and colleagues

---

[4] Another way to form conclusions about distribution of properties that are congruent with what one fears, wants, or believes involves avoiding taking in incongruent information to begin with, rather than ignoring it or discounting it. I discuss the epistemic contours of such cases in Chapter 9.

found that acrophobes overestimate the height of a balcony by greater amounts than non-acrophobes.[5] The acrophobes in the experiments have an exaggerated representation of height because of their fear.

I've argued in the bulk of this book that in addition to reaching judgments by inferences, it is also possible in principle to make inferences that result in experiences. Proffitt's experiments on their own do not settle whether height estimates occur at the level of perceptual experiences.[6] But it is possible in principle for them to have this effect. And it is possible in principle for experiences of affordances to be conclusions of inferences from other sub-experiences. In these ways, fear-induced experiences can be inferred from outlooks depicting the world as being in some respect the way that one fears. And that is how it is possible for fear to generate irrational experiences via inference.

By applying these ideas to the anger case, we can see how fear can hijack experiences. First, Jill could exaggerate the extent to which Jack's blank stare supports the conclusion that Jack is angry, and thereby ends up with an anger-experience. Here she would be failing to give the blank-stare-experience proper weight, and she'd be giving too much weight to her prior fearful outlook. Second, she might inferentially respond only to the anger-congruent features of Jack's face, registering but failing to give proper weight to the anger-incongruent features. Third, Jill's fear could make her fail to take in anger-incongruent features to begin with. In this case, Jill's epistemic situation is more complicated. This mode of hijacking is addressed in Chapter 9.

The account of fearful seeing offered here raises a question. If fear brings an outlook with it, could the outlook consist entirely in perceptual experience, without any mediating standing outlook of the kind illustrated by the acrophobia case? In a case of fearful perception with that structure, the experience could not be an inferential response to the outlook internal to fear, since the experience and the outlook would be one and the same. I am not sure whether there are compelling examples

[5] Stefanucci, J. K. (2009), Teachman et al. (2008).

[6] This experiment from collaborators with D. Proffitt, like many experiments in a similar vein, are examples of the unresolved controversy in psychology about the ways in which fears can influence perceptual experiences. Firestone and Scholl (2015) challenge some of Proffitt's results, though they seem to leave open that fears might influence perceptual experiences in ways consistent with the operation of a perceptual module.

of this kind of case. But if there are, and if they motivate the Rationality of Perception, then they cannot be analyzed by the inference model, and would mark one of its limits.[7]

8.2 Wishful Seeing

Some parts of the account of how fear can figure in inferences to experience can be applied to desire as well. Under the broad category of desire, I'll lump together motives, needs, goals, and preferences, including preferences to hold on to a belief that one already has. Any of these states can in principle influence which perceptual experience one ends up having.

To see how inferences could figure in wishful seeing, it is useful to introduce the notion of a *rationalizing property*. Suppose you are tired and walking through a big room full of beds. The beds are on a muddy floor, and all the beds you see are full of pointy nails sticking up on the place where normally a person would sleep. You want to rest, but your desire to rest does not make you want to plop down on the muddy ground, or on a bed of nails. It would not be restful to lie in those places.

Then you notice a fluffy bed. Your perception of the bed and its fluffiness gives you a reason to plop down on the bed, given that you're tired. The fact that you're tired and near a bed that is fluffy and isn't full of nails or covered in mud gives you a reason to rest on the bed. Noticing the bed gives you a new desire—the desire to lie down in the room you're in.

Relative to the desire to lie down on the fluffy bed, its fluffiness would help make it reasonable for you lie down. In general, relative to a subject S's desire to phi, F is a rationalizing property if: the fact that something has property F would give S a reason to phi, if S were appropriately related to that fact. S can be appropriately related to that fact by believing a singular proposition in a way that attributes F to an object. For instance, relative to S's desire to lie down on the fluffy bed, the bed's fluffiness is a rationalizing property. S is related to the fact that something is fluffy, by believing a proposition that attributes fluffiness to the bed.[8] When a perceptual experience represents a rationalizing property

---

[7] Thanks to Lauren Ashwell for discussion.

[8] I leave aside complications that arise when S attributes F to an object, but represents F under a mode of presentation that intuitively wouldn't give her a reason to phi. For

relative to S's desire to phi and the experience is veridical, then ceteris paribus, S would have pro tanto reason to phi.

Sometimes, one ends up with a desire because a rationalizing property figures in one's experience. For instance, one comes to want to lie down on the bed, because it looks so comfortably fluffy. Other times, having a desire helps explain why one goes on to have an experience that presents a rationalizing property for that desire. Cases like these help us see how desire can lead to irrational inferences, where the conclusions are either perceptual judgments or experiences. We can distinguish three ways this can happen. I'll focus on the cases where the conclusions are experiences.

First, desire can mediate inferences between sub-experiences, just as fear can. Often, the hungrier you are, the better something tastes. In the bed example, suppose T is a texture such that if the more T a bed's surface is (e.g., the less flat it is, or the more small soft lumps it has), the fluffier it is. A desire could exaggerate how fluffy the bed is, by exaggerating how much its T-ness supports fluffiness. For instance, the desire to lie down makes you infer that the bed you're seeing is fluffy, from your experience of its texture as having many soft lumps. Such inferences could exaggerate the extent to which a bed's having texture T supports the conclusion the bed is fluffy. In this way, a hijacked experience could be formed by a poor inference that fails to give proper weight to the texture-experience.

Second, desire can exaggerate the magnitude of desire-congruent properties through inference. For instance, a desire could exaggerate how fluffy the bed is, by exaggerating how T it is. If there is an inferential response here, it is plausibly a response to a belief that the beds that are T are fluffy. By giving too much weight to this belief, the experience is hijacked.

Finally, experiences could be inferential responses to a subject's confidence that the world is the way they want it to be. Vivek wants his audiences to approve of him, and is confident that they are as he

---

instance, if there were a microphysical property identical with fluffiness and S attributed that microphysical property to the bed, without knowing that the microphysical property is fluffiness, then attributing the property might not give her a reason to plop down on the bed. I won't try to define what makes a relation to a fact involving a rationalizing property appropriate, since it is enough to see that there is some such relation.

wants them to be. Whereas I've argued that a subject's confidence that the world is congruent with the way she fears or believes it to be is internal to fear and belief, the analogous form of confidence does not seem to be internal to desire.

We have seen in the case of fear and desire that evaluative states often operate in the mind by directing the subject's attention to aspects of the environment and possibilities of action that are congruent with the evaluative state. These modes of directing attention can shape or perpetuate an outlook, by narrowly selecting the features of the environment that the subject will experience. In Chapter 9, I examine how selection effects could give rise to hijacked experiences, and the epistemic flaws those selection effects generate.

9

Selection Effects

Your friend will soon arrive at the airport. If you want to make sure you see her the moment she exits from Customs and Immigration, you can keep your eyes on the door. Your beliefs, desires, and intentions will then influence how the airport looks to you, by influencing which objects or parts of it you see and which you don't see at all. Later on, you wade through a cluster of rose bushes. You don't take in the texture of the petals, because you are focused on avoiding its thorns. Here, features of the rose stems are selected for experience, and selected in accordance with your purposes.

Selection effects are forms of influence on the evidence or the experiences you have. Selection effects can control what you perceive by causing you to notice certain objects or features, or by causing you not to notice certain objects or features. When a mechanism causes you not to notice an object or a feature, we can say that the object or feature was anti-selected.

Since having a perceptual experience with content P is normally a way of acquiring evidence for P, or for propositions closely related to P, the selection of objects or features for experience is closely related to the selection of evidence. You can select the evidence you end up with, or anti-select evidence you don't have, in many ways. You can avoid radio programs oriented toward your political opponents. If you have already discounted a news report that you start to hear, you can turn off the radio so you won't hear the rest. You can develop a habit of forgetting information that challenges your views. In these ways, which evidence you end up with can easily depend on what you want to find out, which questions you decide to pursue, and in general what else you believe, want, or fear. The parts of the environment we focus on are often the parts of interest or importance to us.

In any of these forms, selection effects are not in the least bit extraordinary. But the unwitting influence of selection effects can pose the same epistemic problem that we find in hijacked experiences.

Here is a case that illustrates the problem at the level of evidence generally. (We'll get to the problem for experiences shortly). We met a briefer form of this example in Chapter 1.

> *Outgroup hiring*: A group of evaluators harbor implicit, ill-founded views about a group of people who constitute an "outgroup" relative to them. Due to those views, evaluators disproportionately focus (without knowing it) on the weakest parts of an outgroup candidate X's application. The negative features of X's application are not fabricated, but a fuller picture of X's candidacy would contain positive features that the evaluators did not consciously register, or did not take in at all. In response to the evidence they have about X, the evaluators conclude that X is unqualified.

On the face of it, the evaluators seem to be responding epistemically well to their evidence. They are unaware of both the prejudice and of its role in selecting their evidence, and they seem to be doing their best with the evidence they have. Yet strengthening their prejudice in response to that evidence seems epistemically inappropriate. If the anti-selection is driven by an initially unreasonable prejudice, then their prejudice does not plausibly become more rational as a result of their review of outgroup applications. The challenge is to find the epistemic culprit, or else explain away the sense that something has gone epistemically wrong.

Even though it need not involve hijacked perceptual experiences, the hiring case generates the same basic epistemological problem that we find in our other cases of perceptual hijacking. Its contours can illuminate the analogous routes to hijacked experiences. In the hiring case, ill-founded background fears, prejudice, or suspicion influence the evidence a subject ends up with in a way that is congenial to the background state. The influence extends and elaborates the background state into other parts of the subject's outlook on the world, and the subject remains unaware of the influence. And in all of these cases, a belief formed in response to this evidence seems to be epistemically compromised. Once again, the philosophical problem is to explain away the appearance of epistemic compromise, or else identify the form that it takes.

The epistemic impact of selection effects depends on the psychological mechanisms by which they occur. If one willfully or knowingly avoids taking in relevant information, then that could detract from the strength of the evidence one ends up with. In contrast, cases in which the selection or anti-selection is entirely unwitting can produce a sense that there's an epistemic flaw somewhere in the picture, but it is more challenging to identify what it is.

In this chapter I argue that at least one kind of epistemic flaw in cases like these can consist in a flawed inference. I focus on cases in which in addition to making an inference from their evidence to their ultimate conclusion, subjects also draw inferences that regulate which information they take in. These inferences shape the body of evidence from which their ultimate conclusions are drawn, and therefore influence which evidence they have. My solution locates the epistemic problem in these inferences.

After describing the broader range of problems to which the hiring case belongs and the potential alternatives to an inferential approach to the Rationality of Perception, (section 9.1), I develop my solution to the problem posed by the hiring case (sections 9.2–9.3). Finally, I apply it to a case of hijacked experience that arises from analogous selection effects (section 9.4).

9.1 Norms of Attention

Which evidence one ends up with is a function of what one pays attention to.

Can patterns of attention be appraised as better or worse? Some patterns of attention seem palpably insignificant. Strolling in a meadow, one can look at the sky or the trees. Crossing a street in traffic, it often doesn't matter whether one first looks right and then left, or vice-versa, so long as one looks both ways before crossing. If you happen to notice a spider on the sidewalk, this fact alone seems not to reflect one bit on your rational standing.

Other patterns of attention, in contrast, are regularly subject to appraisals of various kinds. Legal decisions are often based on appraisals of a subject's attention. In 1940, a Maryland court found a driver negligent for failing to notice a mule that had wandered on to a highway, leading to a car accident (thanks to Nico Cornell for identifying this case).[1] In ethics, some philosophers, including Iris Murdoch and Angela Smith, have argued that our patterns of attention reflect attitudes toward other people for which we are accountable.[2] In analytic epistemology and the philosophy of science, philosophers have discussed norms of inquiry, which bear directly on how one gathers evidence, given an aim of inquiry (such as testing a hypothesis, or answering a question), and therefore on how inquirers should direct their attention.[3] Finally, most academic disciplines operate with norms of relevance and importance. A well-designed experimental study, like a carefully researched historical narrative, can satisfy norms of accuracy and reliable methodology, without pursuing questions that matter, or without reaching conclusions that are illuminating, or both. Criticizing a body of research for "asking the wrong question," or praising it for hitting on a fruitful line of inquiry, are ways of invoking norms addressed to how attention should be directed.

So while we subject some patterns of attention to normative appraisal, we treat other patterns of attention as normative freebies which are not subject to any significant appraisal at all. This discrepancy gives rise to the first pair of questions: what makes some patterns of attention normatively appraisable and others not? And what kinds of norms govern patterns of attention?

A potential (and partial) answer to these questions says that patterns of attention are appraisable, either by moral or epistemic norms, when they inherit an outlook that is itself appraisable by those norms. Applying this answer to the hiring case, the pattern of attention that highlights negative features of the application while excluding positive features would inherit the ill-foundedness of the prejudiced outlook that gave rise to it. To develop this answer would involve explaining what the inheritance relation is. On this approach, the epistemic appraisal of the outlook would extend to the pattern of attention. Just as the constructive defense of the Rationality of Perception has to explain how experiences can be epistemically appraised, a defense of this approach

---

[1] *Dashiell vs. Moore*, 11 A.2d 640 (Md. 1940). Cornell discusses the case in (ms).

[2] Smith (2005 and ms). For discussion of Murdoch (1997) on this issue, see Katsafanas (forthcoming) and Langton (ms).

[3] Besides the literature on scientific explanation, a few among many discussions of norms of inquiry include Friedman (forthcoming and ms.), Dewey (1938). Foley and Fumerton (1982) focus on the relationship between norms of inquiry and norms of responding to evidence.

would have to explain how patterns of attention can be epistemically appraised.[4] When these patterns of attention affect the content and character of perceptual experience, an account of how such patterns can be epistemically appraised will be closely related to the Rationality of Perception. Once it's granted that the perceptual experiences can be epistemically appraised, an account of how to epistemically appraise patterns of attention that shape such experience might plausibly apply to the perceptual experiences themselves. And assuming that patterns of attention are the wrong kind of thing to be inferred from an antecedent outlook, such an account would be an alternative to the inferential approach to the Rationality of Perception.

Other patterns of attention may not arise from antecedent outlooks at all, yet may seem to be subject to normative appraisals of various kinds. For instance, Kant counsels against fixating on the faults and misfortunes of others, such as "a button missing from the coat of someone who is directly in front of us [or] on gaps between his teeth."[5] Kant says it's "the bad habit of our faculty of attention" that leads us to focus on these things. To develop this habit, one need not have an antecedent outlook according to which other people are generally faulty or unfortunate.

It is also possible to sidestep the idea that patterns of attention are in themselves normatively appraisable, and ask how it is reasonable to respond to the evidence, or the perceptual experience, that results from that pattern of attention. The hiring case brings this question into focus. It lets us examine the epistemic consequences of strengthening an outlook that led to the selection of evidence.

9.2 The Epistemic Problem in the Hiring Example

The hiring case involves prejudice. I described this prejudice as ill-founded, which implies that it can be rationally or irrationally strengthened in response to evidence. It is easy to picture cases involving well-founded prejudice, in which strengthening that prejudice is reasonable. Imagine a class of robots who want to be accountants, but who are known to be poor

---

[4] I thank Sebastian Watzl for many discussions of the structure of attention (discussed at length in Watzl 2017) and of potential norms of attention.

[5] Kant ([1798], 2006), Part 1, Book 1, section 3.

at accounting. An evaluator's prejudice against a robot application for a place in accounting school might be perfectly reasonable.

To keep things simple, I'll focus on a case in which the prejudice takes the form of a belief.[6] In this example, the prejudice plays two roles: it influences the selection of evidence, and it is doxastically strengthened in response to that evidence.

Earlier (Chapter 4), I considered and rejected several ways to explain away the impression that Jill's belief or fear that Jack is angry would be ill-founded, if it was formed or strengthened in response to her anger-experience. In the hiring case, the analogous impression is that the evaluator has an ill-founded belief, when she believes that candidate X is under-qualified. Can this impression be explained away?

Some strategies for explaining away the impression of ill-foundedness are available in the hiring case that wouldn't apply to the anger or preformationism cases. A first such strategy is to try to find a type of non-epistemic irrationality to assign to the evaluator, such as the prudential irrationality that might go with systematically overlooking some features of applications when you're trying to find the best ones. But relative to the goal of preferring to maintain the belief that outgroup applicants are unqualified, avoiding uncongenial information is prudentially *rational*.[7] And if there are conflicting goals or preferences, then the norm of prudence is harder to apply.[8] So this strategy for immunizing the epistemic status of beliefs against epistemic impropriety does not seem promising.

A second strategy for explaining the sense that the response to evidence is inappropriate tries to locate the epistemic problem in the collecting of evidence, rather than in the response to that evidence. It would be natural to look for the culprit in the exclusion of *uncongenial* evidence—evidence that's at odds with the initial prejudiced outlook. After all, the problem seems to be underway before any inferences from the specially selected evidence have been drawn.

---

[6] I argue in Chapter 10 that one of the realistic prejudices that our fictional prejudice resembles is a form of belief.

[7] I'm indebted to Shantia Rahimian for extensive discussion of this type of strategy, which he uses to argue for epistemic reasons for furthering inquiry in Rahimian (ms).

[8] Norms of prudence might be applicable to conflicting preferences, if they are arranged in a hierarchy that privileges one of them. The same point holds for goals as well. One might then propose that what appears to be an epistemic problem in the hiring case is really a practical problem: the review of applications is at odds with the preference to find good candidates. But this explanation will not work when the preference to maintain the prejudice is at the top of the hierarchy.

For this strategy to work, there must be a principled division between the exclusions of uncongenial evidence that matter epistemically for the resulting beliefs, and the exclusions that don't. The strategy relies on the assumption that epistemically poor, epistemicaly innocuous, and epistemically good exclusions of uncongenial evidence can be distinguished in a principled way. For instance, if uncongenial evidence ended up excluded via bad luck, perhaps that exclusion is epistemically innocuous. And if the initial outlook were epistemically appropriate, instead of epistemically inappropriate, then perhaps avoiding uncongenial evidence could be an epistemically good strategy for avoiding misleading evidence. Perhaps a principled distinction could be drawn that respects these observations.

Some philosophers would find the second strategy appealing, because it seems to preserve a powerful idea: however poorly one got one's evidence, once one has it, one can go on to form epistemically appropriate responses to it.[9] They would say that the conclusion in the hiring case is reached by responding properly to evidence, and that there is nothing wrong with that response.

I'll argue that a potential epistemic culprit can in principle be found in the collecting of evidence, as per the second strategy. But I'll argue that the problem extends beyond the collection of evidence. I'll highlight a type of mechanism that simultaneously determines which evidence one has, and makes the subject inferentially respond to it. This mechanism ensures that both the collection of evidence and the response to it are epistemically problematic.

9.3 How Might Uncongenial Information Get Excluded?

Let's begin with the conclusions that the evaluators draw from specially selected evidence in the hiring case. The evaluators' ultimate conclusion is that outgroup candidate X's application should be rejected. They reach this ultimate conclusion via a generalization about the distribution of features in the outgroup candidate's application ("X's qualifications are mainly mediocre"). Consider an analogous case in the selection of visual search. If one were searching a display of colored shapes for squares, one might end

---

[9] Foley and Fumerton (1982), Feldman and Conee (1985), Kelly (2008).

up believing a generalization about the distribution of redness over squares, such as "all squares in the display are red." I'll call these propositions "distribution propositions," because they are generalizations about objects or features in a domain. When a distribution proposition is the conclusion of an inference, I'll call it a distribution conclusion. Distribution propositions need not be universal generalizations. (For instance, they can involve claims about feature distribution such as "mainly mediocre," as above.)

Some distribution propositions attribute the absence of a feature or object from a domain. If you look at a photograph and discover that you're not in it, you believe that you don't appear anywhere in the photo. You believe a universal generalization, such as "none of the people in the photograph are me" or "no part of the photograph depicts me." If you're looking for Pierre in the café and find that he isn't there, you believe that he is nowhere in the café. This too is a generalization, such as "none of the people in the café are Pierre."[10] In a large class of cases, when evaluators reach their ultimate conclusion about an outgroup candidate, they reach it by inferring it from a distribution conclusion like this one:

Distribution conclusion:	X's application contains mainly mediocre features.
Ultimate conclusion:	X's application should be rejected.

(For brevity, I'll say a feature of X's application is mediocre if it suggests that X is a mediocre candidate, and that a feature of X's application is good if it suggests that X is a strong candidate.)

The question is how they got to the distribution conclusion that excludes uncongenial information. Some ways of unwittingly excluding uncongenial information mirror modes of bad inference discussed earlier. For instance, uncongenial information could be discounted or bypassed. Or the subject's cognitive access to such information could be limited, either by forgetting it or by keeping it inaccessible.[11] I'm going to focus here on a third way of anti-selecting uncongenial information: preventing its intake at the start. This mode of excluding uncongenial information from one's stock of evidence has the most interesting and challenging application to hijacked experiences. It also poses the sharpest challenge to

---

[10] For discussion of perception of absence, see Farennikova (2013) and (2015).
[11] I discuss both of these options in detail in Siegel (2013c).

the inferential approach to the Rationality of Perception, and so it is the best case for testing how far the framework of inference extends.

9.3.1 Preventing intake

If the transition from congenial information to a distribution conclusion prevents uncongenial information from being taken in to begin with, what, if anything, is the epistemic flaw with the distribution conclusion? The short answer is: too much weight is given to prior confidence that the application is going to be mediocre.

Suppose that part of the evaluator's prejudice involves having little background confidence at the outset that the application is going to turn out strong. At the first bit of information that the application is weak in one area (e.g., research plans), the background low confidence might make it seem reasonable to conclude that further inquiry into that area of the application is unlikely to turn up evidence that points in a different direction. Here, uncongenial information is avoided, by cutting off inquiry within a part of the application, before it gets very far. If inquiry was cut off in this way, each section of the application could still get examined, with inquiry cut off after congenial information comes in (or after discounting uncongenial information). Thanks to this pattern, the inquiry might seem to the examiner to be thorough.

If the selection of evidence occurs in this way, then the evaluators reach their ultimate conclusion via two sub-inferences (see Table 9.1). The first

Table 9.1. Composite inference in the hiring case

First Sub-inference	
Local bits of evidence:	X's application (/this part of it) has mediocre features F1–Fn
	....
Distribution conclusion:	X's application (/this part of it) contains mainly mediocre features

Second sub-inference	
Distribution conclusion:	X's application contains mainly mediocre features
Ultimate conclusion:	X's application should be rejected

sub-inference is from local bits of evidence (feature 1 is mediocre, feature 2 is mediocre, etc.) to the distribution conclusion. The second is from the distribution to the ultimate conclusion. We met the second part of the inference earlier.

The second sub-inference is straightforward. Its apparent acceptability is the problem: the ultimate conclusion seems epistemically bad, but the inference to it from the distribution conclusion seems fine.

If the first sub-inference is epistemically inappropriate, then the inappropriateness will be inherited by the distribution conclusion (since nothing washes out).[12] And if the belief in the distribution conclusion is ill-founded, then so is the belief in the ultimate conclusion.

Which aspects of the first sub-inference are bad? By hypothesis, the prejudice underlying the evaluators' asymmetrical responses to outgroup and ingroup candidates controls the transition from local bits of information to the distribution conclusion. We can distinguish two aspects of control of this transition.

A first type of control is control of the flow of information from the application to the evaluator. The prejudice could control the flow of information in several ways. It could control when the evaluator stops reading the application; when she finishes examining one part of the evaluation and starts examining another; or when she draws a distribution conclusion about part of the evaluation (e.g., research interests).

Stops and starts to inquiry are often guided by practical considerations. A sudden fire alarm, or your need to make a decision, might cause you to come to a conclusion from the evidence you have. In those cases, the epistemic evaluation of your belief might seem limited to which conclusion you draw, given the evidence you have. If controlling the flow of information is like the fire alarm that forces you out of inquiry, then it is not obviously epistemically appraisable. If this type of control of information flow harbors an epistemic culprit, a principled distinction is needed that sets it apart from the epistemically irrelevant causes that start or stop the flow of information, or the course of inquiry.[13]

In cases like the hiring case, where the selection effect is by hypothesis explained by an underlying outlook, the first sub-inference is not

---

[12] On washing out, see Chapter 6, section 6.1.

[13] Rinard (forthcoming) disputes whether there is such a thing as distinctively epistemic considerations for belief, and so would argue that no principled distinction here can be drawn between the two types of control over stops and starts to inquiry.

plausibly analyzed as mediated exclusively by this type of control. If the prejudice explains why uncongenial evidence is anti-selected, and the anti-selection occurs by regulating the intake of information, then stops and starts to inquiry are being guided by beliefs or other forms of confidence that further inquiry will not point in a different direction from the evidence gathered so far. These assessments are a second type of control over transitions into and out of inquiry, and inferential response to the evidence gathered by that inquiry. This second kind of assessment is clearly epistemically evaluable.

The hiring case gives us an example in which a subject makes a poor inference to a distribution conclusion. It suggests that the framework of inference helps analyze the epistemic impact of selection effects, in contexts that involve searches or other inquiries that issue in distribution conclusions. It is in drawing a conclusion about how certain properties are distributed that the distinctive bad inference is drawn.

9.4 From Selection of Evidence to Selection for Experience

The distribution conclusion in the hiring example is a belief. But the contents of distribution conclusions (such as "All x's have feature F") could also figure in the contents of perceptual experiences. This opens up the possibility that perceptual experiences with such contents could be inferred from local experiences.

Can distribution propositions be contents of experience? Yes. Consider the experience of seeing exactly three eggs lined up in an egg carton built to hold a dozen eggs. When you see the three eggs, your experience represents not only that there are three eggs in the carton, but also that there are no other eggs in the egg carton. If there were four eggs in the egg carton, but you had the same experience, then your experience would be inaccurate. Contrast this experience with the experience of seeing three pens on a cluttered table. Your experience might represent that there are three pens on the table, but not take a stand on whether there are any other pens among the clutter.[14] If there turned out to be more pens underneath the clutter, the experience would not thereby be

---

[14] The same points would hold for pen-shaped or egg-shaped volumes.

inaccurate. The compound experience is more like the egg-carton experience than the cluttered-table experience.

In the egg carton example, you see at a glance that the carton contains exactly three eggs. In other experiences, distribution conclusions might be reached only after some examination, such as when you look at a photograph that you expected to find yourself in and find that you are not pictured. In the earlier red-square example (section 9.1), you might end up with an experience that represents that all the squares in the display are red, but only after visually searching the display. Or imagine Vivek hosting a party. He wants everyone to have a good time, and feels overly confident that they are enjoying themselves. As he scans the room, his overconfidence leads him to overlook the sulky person in the corner, waiting for a ride home.[15] As he beholds the party, the room looks to be full of people enjoying themselves, with no exceptions.

Just as poor inferences to a distribution conclusion can generate a belief with that conclusion as its content, they can likewise generate a perceptual experience with that conclusion as its content. In this way, hijacked experiences can result from inferences about how certain properties are distributed.

For instance, suppose that a preference that all the squares in a display are red influenced the selection of shapes for experience by preventing intake of that information to begin with. A perceiver could end up with a perceptual experience of the display with the content "all the squares in the display are red," just as Vivek could end up with a perceptual experience with content "all the people here are happy."[16]

In closely related cases of perceptual hijacking, the distribution conclusion might be found only at a level of a judgment formed in response to an experience—not at the level of experience itself. For instance, in the red square example, if the perceptual experience represents only some of the squares in succession, the distribution conclusion that all the squares in the display are red might be reached only by inferring it from the perceptual experiences, together with the assumption that one has seen all the squares in the display.

---

[15] Thanks for Nico Silins for the example.

[16] Or "all the people here are F," where "F" stands for low-level properties of faces and bodies from which Vivek infers happiness.

The Rationality of Perception can respect the unity between these two kinds of perceptual hijacking. One kind involves hijacked experiences, the other kind does not. But according to the Rationality of Perception, the same epistemic flaw arises both times. In both cases, the epistemic problem stems from a poor inference to a distribution conclusion.

As I emphasized at the start of the chapter, selection effects bring into view the potential limits of the inferential approach to the Rationality of Perception. In the bulk of this chapter, I focused on how the inferential approach to the Rationality of Perception could explain the downgrade of experiences that are shaped by selection effects. Cases involving selection effects help bring into view the surprising extent to which the inferential approach can illuminate the epistemic contours of hijacked perception.

10

The Problem of Culturally Normal Belief

So far, I've discussed psychological influences on perception, where the influencing states range from racism to vanity to mundane familiarity with fruit. In all of these cases, we can find a route within an individual's mind from their outlook to their perception. I've argued that when the outlook reaches all the way to perceptual experiences, we can see the resulting experiences as rationally or irrationally shaped by the outlook.

My examples of hijacked experiences built in psychological precursors (such as Vivek's vanity and Jill's fear) to influence the perceptual experiences that the subjects ended up with when they saw the relevant part of the external world. Jill looks at Jack's face. Vivek looks at his audiences. The participant in Payne's experiment looks at a pair of pliers. I sidestepped the psychological controversy about what roles can be played by fear, suspicion, or other attitudes in generating visual experiences. This controversy is unlikely to be settled anytime soon. I simply assumed for the sake of discussion that perceptual experiences can be influenced in these ways. I made this assumption so that we could focus on the epistemological questions that arise in its wake.

The problem of hijacked experiences arises because there seems to be no straight answer to whether perceptual experiences provide just as much epistemic support for beliefs as those same experiences could if they were not influenced by fears, suspicions, the racial attitude that black men are dangerous, or the other psychological precursors I highlighted. Of all the hijacked experiences I've discussed, the pressure to say that the experience's epistemic role is compromised is perhaps strongest in the case of the racial attitude. These examples therefore have an especially powerful dialectical role in motivating the Rationality of Perception.

The important dialectical role played by these examples gives us reason to examine them more closely. In this chapter, I defend two assumptions that I've left implicit. I assumed that the racial attitudes my examples leaned on were epistemically appraisable, and further that they were ill-founded. These assumptions of appraisability and ill-foundedness were natural in the other cases I discussed, since I built it in to the fiction that Jill's fear or Vivek's vanity were epistemically irrational. These cases focus on the interaction between psychological states within each individual's mind. It simply did not matter how exactly the irrational fear or vanity came to be part of their minds to begin with.

The case of an individual's racial attitude is different. It operates at the interface between the mind of the individual and their cultural milieu. Unlike Jill's fear or Vivek's vanity, the racial attitudes illustrated in my examples are particular to and pervasive in a specific place and time—US society, since (at least) the end of the formal inequalities that characterized the era of Jim Crow, and it has obvious continuities with attitudes and institutions that have shaped American history from the start. The exact content, contours, and history of these attitudes are matters for empirical analysis of various kinds. So far, I have not dwelt on the nature or the exact content of the racial attitude in my examples, but I have assumed that it is epistemically appraisable, and belief-like enough to figure in inferences. Ultimately, I think this treatment of the racial attitude is correct, but that's a substantive and partly empirical claim. My first goal in this chapter is to support the dialectical role of the racial attitude in my earlier examples of hijacked experiences.

The specific racial attitude that figures in my examples of hijacked experiences presents a problem closely analogous to the problem of hijacked experiences. Whereas the problem of hijacked experiences occurs at an interface within an individual's mind between the perceptual experiences and other mental states, the analogous problem is scaled up. It occurs at the interface between individuals' minds and the cultural milieu that influences them. In both cases, subjects seem from their perspective to be taking in information from the environment, but they are instead extending a prior outlook—either their own, or one that is merely culturally entrenched. And in both cases, when we study the epistemic role of the seemingly passively formed mental state, we find a philosophical problem.

On the one hand, for one kind of subject, the racial attitude I've discussed is a socially normal response to one's social environment. It is formed and maintained in a casual way that is more like absorption than deliberation. Since many beliefs formed in this way are clearly well-founded, in certain social and psychological contexts, racial attitudes formed in the same way might seem to be their epistemic equals.

And yet, on the other hand, when one considers the patterns of obtuse reactions that racial attitudes give rise to, and the incomprehension that occurs alongside their felt normality, it seems plain that something has gone epistemically wrong. James Baldwin gives a pointed example when he describes racial beliefs held casually or as he says "helplessly" by certain whites, and alludes to their ill-founded status.[1]

And so there is a problem. I call this problem the problem of culturally normal belief. Schematically, the problem has the following structure. An individual casually absorbs a culturally entrenched presumption, and that presumption ends up operating in his or her mind as a belief.

This structure has three key ingredients: the individual, the culturally entrenched presumption, and the relationship between them whereby the individual casually, unreflectively, and seemingly naturally absorbs the presumption and comes to recapitulate it in his or her own mind.

By itself, this structure does not generate the problem. The problem arises when we ask how reasonable it is for the individual to hold the attitude that results from this absorption, and when we find opposing pressures among the plausible answers. Not every instance of the structure yields a problematic opposition, but some do.

---

[1] I thank Chris Lebron for drawing my attention to Baldwin's notion of helpless belief in a 1965 debate with William F. Buckley, Jr., where Baldwin (1965) writes:

"In the Deep South you are dealing with a sheriff or a landlord or a landlady or the girl at the Western Union desk. She doesn't know quite whom she is dealing with—by which I mean, if you are not part of a town and if you are a Northern nigger, it shows in millions of ways. She simply knows that it is an unknown quantity and she wants to have nothing to do with it. You have to wait a while to get your telegram. We have all been through it. By the time you get to be a man it is fairly easy to deal with.

"But what happens to the poor white man's, the poor white woman's, mind? It is this: they have been raised to believe, and by now they helplessly believe, that no matter how terrible some of their lives may be and no matter what disaster overtakes them, there is one consolation like a heavenly revelation—at least they are not black." I leave it to the reader to consider how similar the beliefs Baldwin describes are to the ones discussed in this chapter. I think they are very similar but I won't make the case here.

There are several possible responses to this problem. Some might deny that there is such a thing as epistemic ill-foundedness at the social level. Some might allow that there is such a thing, but hold that social-level ill-foundedness doesn't transmit to individuals' attitudes. And some might find the idea of "culturally entrenched presumptions" so murky that they neither deny nor allow that such presumptions can be epistemically appraised at a social level. Instead they struggle to make sense of the social-level phenomenon that poses the problem in the first place.

My response is that there is such a thing as social-level presumptions, they be ill-founded, and their ill-foundedness can transmit to individual attitudes.

Any defense of this response would have quite a bit to explain. My strategy is to develop an example that both illustrates a culturally entrenched presumption, and helps guide us to a plausible account of how such presumptions can be epistemically appraised, and how they can affect the epistemic situations of individuals who casually absorb those presumptions.

I develop the example in stages, starting with an exemplary culturally entrenched presumption, which is a type of racialized attitude that figures in earlier examples of hijacked experiences. After describing one of the marks that this cultural entrenchment can leave in the minds of individuals, I construct a hypothetical individual named "Whit", his social milieu, and his psychological profile. Not everyone with the attitudes Whit has comes to have them in the same way. The construction of Whit specifies how he comes to have his attitude, and that specification gives us the three ingredients needed to generate an instance of the problem: a culturally entrenched presumption that P, an individual who casually absorbs this presumption, and a conflicted sense that while such absorption often seems epistemically innocuous, the end result seems epistemically suspect.

I begin by identifying the racial attitude at issue (section 10.1) and arguing that it is not merely an association between concepts, as some psychologists have supposed (section 10.2). I introduce Whit and his background in section 10.3, and argue that his route to holding the attitude poses the problem of culturally normal belief sharply. In the rest of the chapter (sections 10.4–10.5), I consider and reject several arguments that Whit's attitude must be well-founded, given how it is formed and maintained, and finally make the case that it is ill-founded.

I conclude by highlighting my solution's broader implications and its support for the Rationality of Perception (10.6).

10.1 The Structure of Racial Attitudes Elicited in the Experiments

In one of my fictionalized cases of hijacked experiences, the fictional experience is generated by a realistic racial attitude. I identified the racial attitude in Chapter 1 by claiming that it was the cognitive state underpinning the experimental results found in Keith Payne's weapon categorization experiment. Here again is a central result of this experiment.

> *Weapon categorization*: Participants in an experiment are shown an object quickly and are asked to press a button designated for "gun" if it is a gun, and a different button if it is a hand tool—pliers, wrench, or drill. Before they see the object, they are quickly shown a man's face. The man is either black or white. Participants frequently indicate "gun" when shown a tool, but make this error more frequently following a black prime, compared with a white prime. (Payne 2001)

Payne's experiment is just one among many experiments that are designed to activate racial attitudes, and to test their prevalence in contemporary US populations. Here are highlights from four other studies.

> *The shooter task*: Participants in an experiment play a video game. They are supposed to press either a button designated for "shoot" or "don't shoot," depending on whether the person they see on the screen (the target) is holding a gun or an innocuous object—such as a cell phone or wallet. The targets are men. Sometimes the men are black, sometimes white. Participants more frequently press "shoot" when shown an unarmed black target than they do when shown an unarmed white target. (Correll et al. 2002)[2]

> *Crime-suggestive acuity*: After being shown a man's face in a subliminal prime, participants are shown a sequence of progressively less degraded

---

[2] Correll's (2002) study spawned a series of follow-up studies, designed to test whether there are differences between lay persons and police officers, often using different paradigms, as well as Correll's original paradigm (Correll et al. 2007, Plant and Peruche 2005, Glaser and Knowles 2008, James et al. 2013).

images, beginning with visual noise and ending with a clear image of an object and asked to indicate when they can recognize the object. They identify crime-relevant objects (guns or knives) at lower thresholds than crime-irrelevant objects, after being shown a black man's face, compared to crime-irrelevant objects, and compared to crime-relevant objects after being shown a white man's face. (Eberhardt et al. 2004)

Age overestimation: Participants are shown a picture of a boy aged 10–17, paired with a description of a crime that the boy is said to have committed. They are asked to estimate the boy's age. Across subjects, the pictures of boys and their names change, but the crime descriptions stay the same. Both police officers and college-age laypersons overestimate the age of black boys by at least four years when the crime is a felony, but overestimate ages of white and latino boys by only two years, for the same crime. On a scale of culpability, black boys are rated more culpable than white or latino boys for the same crime. (Goff et al. 2014)

Looking deathworthy: Defendants in capital crimes whose victims are white are more likely to be sentenced by juries to death, the more stereotypically black their faces appear. (Eberhardt et al. 2006)

One could see the experiments as recreating a fragment of a one-sided reaction. The reactions are on the part of the observer (the experimental participant) to a man or a boy, and they differ depending on whether the man or boy is black. (In the case of Looking Deathworthy, the reaction is inferred from past behavior, and in place of an experimental situation, there is just analysis of data.) The patterns of behavior elicited by the experiments do not, on their own, reveal the cognitive states underlying those patterns. But a plausible hypothesis, and indeed the hypothesis the studies were designed to test, is that the reactions occur because the participants link a concept at least as specific as blackness—and quite probably a more determinate concept—to one or more concepts in a cluster that includes 'danger' or 'crime' (I use single quotes around a word to denote a concept). These concepts are importantly different: something is a crime only relative to a legal institution, whereas what's dangerous for X depends on X's vulnerabilities. But for now we can ignore these differences.

To say that two concepts are linked leaves open how they are linked. An initial hypothesis is that they are linked in a way that attributes dangerousness, criminality, or both to people thought to belong to a racial category. This hypothesis is strengthened by the prevalence of narratives that depict reactions to black men of the sort elicited by (or depicted in) the experiments. Depicting a reaction can be a way of endorsing it, but of course it need not be—any more than a novel with a villain has to endorse or encourage villainy. Sometimes the reactions are depicted from the point of view of the recipients of the reactions. For instance, George Yancy (2008) describes a type of micro-interaction between strangers, in a narrative that is easy to recognize:

When followed by white security personnel as I walk through department stores, when a white salesperson avoids touching my hand, when a white woman looks with suspicion as I enter the elevator, I feel that in their eyes I am this indistinguishable, amorphous, black seething mass, a token of danger, a threat, a rapist, a criminal, a burden . . .

In the US, narratives resembling this one have long been found in many registers, such as memoir, fiction, film, music, poetry, ethnography, and social scientific studies, including psychological studies of stereotype threat and studies in political sciences of the effects on political attitudes of contact with the criminal justice system. Some renditions of this narrative detail what it is like to navigate public space when the possibility of being responded to as a threat or likely criminal is salient, including the often elaborate efforts and adjustments made to prevent that response, or reverse it, or negotiate it in some other way.[3] Other versions of the same narrative highlight, encourage, and enforce the point of view of the reactor, such as the high-profile Willie Horton ad in the 1988 US election, the political scientist John DiIulio introduction in the 1990s of the concept of a "superpredator" to describe black youth who were supposedly prone to crime, and around the same time, analytic philosopher Michael Levin's defense of racialized fear.[4]

---

[3] Contemporary works that focus on these negotiations include Coates (2015) in the genre of memoir, psychological research on stereotype threat (Steele 2011), sociological studies of racial profiling (Glaser 2014) and disproportionate punishment in school of black children (Smith and Harper 2016), and studies in political science on the impact of frequent contact with the criminal justice system (Lerman and Weaver 2014).

[4] For discussion of the Willie Horton ad, see Mendelberg (2001). The concept of a juvenile superpredator—a black youth supposedly prone to crime—was introduced by the political scientist J. DiIulio (1996), and its role in the development of crime policy is discussed by Hinton (2016). Levin (1992)'s explicit purpose is to argue that fear of sharing

The wealth of cultural production of narratives casting black men in this role makes it plausible that the psychology experiments are eliciting the same racial attitude. In addition, the psychological experiments provide evidence that racial attitudes can operate even in the minds of people who would explicitly disown the hypothesis that black men are dangerous.[5]

In discussing the problem of hijacked experiences, I assigned the racial attitude in my example a specific dialectical role: it was the kind of mental state that can be epistemically appraised, and furthermore, I assumed, it is ill-founded. I argue next that the racial attitude that is detected in the psychology experiments I've described can indeed play this dialectical role (for the moment I'll talk as if there is a single attitude, rather than several). Taken together, the cultural pattern and the experimental results suggest that the racial attitude operates in individual minds as a belief would, influencing how one interprets what one sees, or how one is prepared to act, or both.

10.2 Are Racial Attitudes Minimal Associations?

According to the psychologists who conducted the studies described in the previous section, the experimental tasks activate what they call a "stereotypical association" between the concepts 'black man' and 'danger' or 'crime.'[6] When the experimenters say that participants make a

public space with black men or boys is reasonable, while assuming that such fear is psychologically possible for all of his readers.

[5] For useful summary of such results, see Glaser (2014), ch. 4.

[6] As mentioned in the Preface, I purposefully focus on attitudes about black men, as do the experiments under discussion (though sometimes the experimenters describe the attitude as concerning "Blacks" or "African Americans" in general). In addition, the experimental subjects in some cases are exclusively male to control for potential gender effects (e.g. Eberhardt 2004). Eberhardt et al. (2004, 2006), Correll et al. (2002, 2007), and Payne (2006) describe their results by citing "stereotypic association between African Americans and violence," and Goff et al. (2014) described his results as eliciting a "stereotypical association with crime." Similar assumptions are made by Nosek et al, (2007) and Blair et al. (2001). For many more examples of the assumption that implicit racial bias takes the form of associations, as well as detailed argument against it, see Mandelbaum (2015).

Another possibility, explored in Haslanger (1995), is that there is a single concept that operates in the cultural milieu, and it is a concept of "threatening black male" (or perhaps an even more determinate concept). On the one-concept approach, there would be no need for an association between separate concepts 'black man' and 'crime'. My criticisms of the idea that the attitudes that explain the experimental results are minimal associations suggest "stereotypical association," they are saying that the mind moves from one concept to another. Let us consider what kind of movement of the mind this could be.

It is useful first to identify different ways to associate concepts X and Y, such as 'salt' and 'pepper.'

> *Minimal association between concepts*: transition from isolated concepts expressed by words: e.g., "drip" to "drop," "salt" to "pepper," "tic" and "tac" to "toe."

This kind of movement between concepts is a mental analog of the verbal phenomenon in which a person hears "salt" and (perhaps upon being prompted to report the word that first comes to mind) says "pepper." Associative transitions can also be made between thoughts.

> *Minimal association between thoughts*: transition from thought involving X (X-thoughts) to thoughts involving Y (Y-thoughts), with no constraints on which thoughts these are.

In a minimal association between thoughts, whenever one thinks a thought involving the concept 'salt'—such as that the chips are salty, or that the soup needs more salt, or that salt on the roads prevents skidding—one is disposed to think a thought—any thought—involving the concept 'pepper.' A minimal association between thoughts is therefore a kind of association between concepts. When it is used in a salt-thought, the concept 'salt' triggers a pepper-thought. But which thoughts are triggered is not constrained by the semantic relationships between them.

Both kinds of minimal associations leave entirely open what standing attitudes the subject has toward the things denoted by the concepts, such as salt and pepper. A subject with a minimal association may have zero further opinions about salt and pepper, if for her, the concepts are no more related than the words "tic" "tac" and "toe." If she does have further opinions, she may think that salt goes well with pepper, that salt and pepper should never be seen or tasted together, that where there is salt there tends to be pepper, that salt and pepper are exclusive seasonings, or any of an enormous variety of other thoughts. No standing outlook

---

that if the one-concept approach is correct, then activating that concept activates a belief-like representation as well.

about how the things denoted by the concepts are related belongs to a minimal association.[7]

We can also distinguish between epistemic appraisability of a transition, and epistemic appraisability of the elements of the transition. Thoughts are things that can be true or false, and can be epistemically appraised in various ways. For instance, their contents can be made more probable or less probable by other factors, and they can receive better or worse evidential support. If the thoughts are beliefs, then they can be formed epistemically well or epistemically badly. These appraisals, however, are indifferent to whether the thought happens to be an element in an associative transition.

Turning from elements of associative transition to the transition itself, we can ask: Is the movement of the mind in minimal associations ever an epistemically appraisable transition? Many writers think that epistemically appraisable transitions are limited to inferences. This limitation would exclude minimal associations. Since there are good reasons to think that prevalent racial attitudes as they operate in individual minds aren't minimal associations, we can leave this epistemological question aside. Just as a minimal association between the concepts 'salt' and 'pepper' leaves open whether salt is better than pepper, or pepper is better than salt, or pepper is salty, or salt is peppery, a minimal association would leave open many possibilities, including the possibilities that black men dissipate crime, that they are the wisest critics of crime policy, that they are the best protectors against crime, that they make more arrests than other people, and that you are unlikely to be in danger of crime when you are part of a group of black men. Minimal associations between the concepts 'black man' and 'danger' or 'crime' would leave these possibilities open, because they leave open the ways in which black men are supposedly related to danger or crime.

Of the experimental results listed earlier, at least one could be explained by a minimal association: crime-suggestive acuity, in which a black prime facilitates seeing a gun or another crime-related object at a lower threshold, compared to a white prime, or to no prime, and compared to a crime-irrelevant object. Whether it explains the weapon

---

[7] This point underlies Mandelbaum's (2013) criticism of Gendler's claim in her (2008) and (2011) that a new type of mental state, alief, is needed to explain a range of psychological phenomena, including implicit bias. For discussion of implicit bias and association, see Levy (2014), Mandelbaum (2015), and Madva and Brownstein (forthcoming).

categorization task is less clear. In contrast, a minimal association could not explain the shooter task. Minimal associations do not predict one pattern of shooting error over any other. A minimal association between 'black' (or a more specific racial concept) and 'crime' could be an artifact of a presumption that black men are especially unlikely to be holding a crime-related object, and so do not explain why people are so ready to press "shoot" when the target is black.[8] Nor do minimal associations predict the Looking Deathworthy result, or age overestimation.

Many of the experiments themselves therefore strengthen the idea that culturally prevalent attitudes sometimes operate in the minds of individuals, not as minimal associations, but in a way that recapitulates the prevalent attitudes. In the experimental circumstances described earlier, racial attitudes operate in the mind in ways that are typical of beliefs. They contribute to the interpretation of information, they lead to inferences, and they guide action.

When considering the extent to which these attitudes shape behavior beyond experimental circumstances, it is reasonable expect a lot of variation of at least four kinds: first, people in whom the attitudes are absent; second, people in whom they operate and who explicitly endorse them; third, people in whom the attitudes operate but are at odds with their explicit avowals, other behavioral dispositions, or both, leading to felt internal conflict; and finally people in whom they operate without leading to much if any felt internal conflict. People in the last group have relatively little else in their minds or lives to pull against their attitudes and the dispositions they have that are congruent with them. For an argument that individuals in these last two groups are not exceptional, see Glaser (2014), Chapter 4.

It is the last group of people—the least internally conflicted kind—who pose the problem of culturally normal belief most sharply. The problem is clearest when there is an attitude absorbed casually from one's milieu that seems ill-founded in light of one set of considerations,

---

[8] In subsequent experiments, the original results were replicated when participants wore an eye-tracker that indicated where they were foveating when they pressed the button. It was found that when the targets were black, participants tended to decide more quickly whether to shoot, compared to when targets were white, and in addition, when targets were black, participants tended to look at the targets' face more than at their hands (compared to looking at patterns with white targets), even though the task is to decide which button to press depending on what the target is holding in their hand. (Correll et al. 2015, Study 2).

but well-founded in light of another set. And an attitude can seem well-founded, if someone absorbs it from their milieu without any felt need to actively maintain their outlook in the face of potential challenges, either from within one's own mind or from their social surroundings. To make the problem vivid, I'll describe a psychological profile and social background that such a person could have. Because this person is easiest to picture as being surrounded by people who are mainly white, I'll call this person "Whit". In the end, however, how Whit is racially categorized is not essential to his epistemic situation.

10.3 Whit and his Route to the Racialized Attitude

Whit is seventeen years old. He has always lived in the same town in the early-twenty-first-century United States. He inhabits a world of a white people. All of the people that he and his parents take themselves to depend on are white. White people are his neighbors, his teachers, his schoolmates, the professionals that regularly interact with his family (accountants, teachers, doctors, lawyers, mechanics, local religious figures, and community leaders), his friends and his family's friends, his local politicians, police officers, restaurant owners, and people he sees when he goes to restaurants.

Whit knows that elsewhere, not everyone is white. He knows there are black professionals of all kinds. He knows that in other places, distant from where he lives, there are neighborhoods where people are mainly black, where they tend to be much poorer than his family is, and where many people his age have a lot of contact with the criminal justice system. He doesn't know anybody who lives there.

Whit has been a subject in all the experiments described earlier, and his responses mirror the trends in the data. His attitudes make him disposed to have interactions of the sort described by Yancy. Across a range of situations, Whit is obtuse in micro-situations like the one in the elevator. If Whit were asked to assess the productive capabilities or personal credibility of a boy or man who is black, he would tend to be disproportionally doubtful. And if he expressed or acted on his doubt, he would not face any challenges from the people within his usual social horizons. In this way, Whit has little in his mind or life to pull against his absorption of the attitude that black men are dangerous.

In the context of the prevalent narratives described earlier, Whit's racial isolation is the kind that Allport (1954) predicted would make a person more likely to absorb the presumption depicted in the narratives, rather than contesting or discounting it. Of course like any individual's outlook, Whit's cannot be entirely predicted by social context. And conversely, Whit's social situation is not the only route to the racial attitude he ends up with.

The fact that Whit's attitude is normal worsens his society. But does his attitude worsen his own epistemic standing?

From the point of view of people on the receiving end of Whit's reactions, his attitude seems clearly ill-founded. Imagine stepping into a line at an automatic teller machine where Whit and his friends are waiting, and seeing their palpable discomfort as they look uneasy and make sure their wallets are deep inside their pockets. Or imagine asking Whit for directions, and finding him ill at ease in talking to you, seemingly suspicious of whether what you want is really directions, as opposed to something else. In these situations, you'd think Whit and his friends were in the grip of a fear that they were projecting onto you. There's nothing more you could do to manifest the ordinariness of your own movements—waiting to get cash, asking for directions. Outside of Whit's world, many people would easily pick up on the ample cues that indicate innocuous everyday activity. Due to their racial attitudes, Whit and his friends are either blind to these cues, or they discount them. If Whit's attitude is ill-founded, what makes it ill-founded? Ultimately, I'll argue that the epistemically bad-making feature is that Whit has absorbed an ill-founded presumption by testimony, and by testimony the ill-foundedness has been transmitted. It is useful to distinguish this position from a distinct proposal about what makes Whit's attitude ill-founded.

Whit's epistemic situation is shaped in part by what he doesn't know. He doesn't know (we can suppose) how neighborhoods came to be racially divided, and he doesn't know what keeps them that way. He lacks books, friends, and curiosity that would lead him to know about life beyond his current social horizons. If he learned more, it might create cognitive disharmony by pulling against the attitudes he has.

The things Whit doesn't know are in some sense an epistemic cost to him.[9] But it is not obvious that his lack of knowledge makes the attitudes

---

[9] A point emphasized by Mills (2007).

he does have epistemically bad. By comparison, in many cases, we lack information that, if we had it, would complicate or fundamentally change our outlook. For instance, if you learned that your genetic background leaves you especially disposed to be struck with a certain kind of illness that your current customarily copious consumption of cheese encourages, cheese-eating could switch from being a source of pleasure for you to a locus of threat. But so long as you lack this information, your unquestioned presumption that cheese is safe to eat seems well-founded. To you, it's just plain common sense that in every way, cheese is good to eat.

10.3.1 Is Whit's racial attitude well-founded?

Some theoretical considerations would favor the view that for all I've said about Whit's social and psychological context, his attitude could be well-founded. First, some psychologists have argued that the generalizations that inform perceptual judgment overwhelmingly tend to result from statistical learning, Bayesian updating, or other forms of inductive learning.[10] And these learning patterns are supposed to be reasonable. If it's in general true that the expectations we use to help interpret what we see are by and large reasonable expectations to have, why should Whit's attitude be different? It might yield mistaken judgments once in a while, but if his prior assumptions are reasonable, then by and large one should expect inferences from them to be reasonable as well.

This consideration, however, does not support the conclusion that Whit's attitude is well-founded. Nor does it support the conclusion that attitudes like Whit's (as diagnosed by the experiments described earlier) are well-founded, when they are held by people whose social settings are not as thoroughly white as Whit's. It is implausible that racial attitudes are formed by exposure to coincidences of danger and any racial category because people who are too young to have undergone a pattern of exposure that would link those properties nonetheless have what are likely to be the same racial attitudes, or closely related precursors to them.[11] It is also improbable, because countless interactions between people whose attitudes are like Whit's and the black men they

[10] Bar (2011), Hohwy (2013), Clark (2013, 2015).

[11] Dunham et al. (2013) found preferences in children aged 4–6 for in-groups, when and only when those groups are also socially dominant. The preferences are not measured with the IAT, but they show sensitivity to culturally contingent social hierarchies.

react to are innocuous, and so an appeal to patterns of exposure cannot explain why some of these exposures coalesce into generalizations that go on to operate in the mind as beliefs while others don't.[12] Think of all the micro-interactions one has when one waits in line for the automatic teller, passes people on a sidewalk, buys stamps at a post office, congregates with others during a fire drill, buys a drink at a bar, or negotiates small spaces on an airplane. In interactions like these, rarely, if ever, is any palpable danger or threat in the picture at all. If someone operating in these contexts without the extreme racial isolation like Whit's ends up with racial attitudes like Whit's, those attitudes do not plausibly arise from any part of the cognitive system keeping accurate statistics about which people from among the ones he encountered are palpably dangerous.

A second idea that might seem to make Whit's attitude well-founded, given his social context, is that according to a US Bureau of Justice report from 2011, blacks were responsible for 52% of homicides between 1980 and 2008 in the US, despite constituting only 13% of the population.[13] This statistical generalization is accurate (let's suppose), and presumably it is possible to believe it on good grounds. So a belief in this generalization could be well-founded. Could it make Whit's racial attitude well-founded, along with the attitude that is diagnosed by the psychology experiments, even when it is held by people whose racial isolation is not as extreme as Whit's?

This question is strictly orthogonal to the problem of culturally normal belief. That problem concerns an attitude acquired by absorbing it from a situation in which having the attitude is normal—not from learning a statistic. Learning statistics like this one need not come with the trappings of social reassurance. The problem of the culturally normal belief concerns the epistemic impact of those trappings.

The orthogonal question, however, is relevant to whether Whit's attitude is *close* to being well-founded. By hypothesis, Whit doesn't

---

[12] Leslie's (2008) category of "striking property generics" can be seen as labeling the problem of identifying which generalizations one will form. According to her, in some cases, being dangerous is a striking property. For discussion of the limitations of the explanatory power of the category of strikingness, see Nickel (2016).

[13] http://www.bjs.gov/content/pub/pdf/htus8008.pdf. Munton (ms), who cites and discusses the same statistic, aims to characterize a type of epistemic flaw in beliefs in this statistical generalization and others she describes as ethically charged, such as "Men outperform women in math and science at the highest levels." According to Munton, the flaw consists in certain problematic patterns of reasoning that one is disposed to perform when one has the belief. I'm indebted to her for discussions of the issues in this section.

form his racial attitude in response to a well-founded belief in an accurate statistical generalization about homicide. But suppose someone did. Would that route to the racial attitude make it well-founded?

There's reason to think it wouldn't. For one thing, the statistical generalization does not justify the judgments reported in the Looking Deathworthy or Age Overestimation results (specifically, the culpability judgments about children). And whether other judgments in the other experiments are reasonable depends on whether the generalizations project from the circumstances of collection to the new contexts in which they are applied. They don't generalize to the kinds of micro-interactions described earlier that arise from attitudes like Whit's.

10.3.2 Normality as testimony

A much stronger route to the idea that Whit's attitude is well-founded uses testimony as a model. Here, the position that Whit's attitude is well-founded may seem to be supported by both the psychology of stereotypes and the epistemology of testimony.

According to some prominent psychologists who study stereotypes, our beliefs about social groups are by and large accurate. If in general, within a society, beliefs about social groups tend to be accurate, then why should Whit's belief be an exception? In a book that synthesizes several decades of data from social psychology about stereotypes, Lee Jussim writes, "social reality has a systematic influence on individuals' beliefs about groups." His data concern a wide range of beliefs, including many beliefs about racial groups (though he does not offer data about the accuracy of beliefs in the specific racial stereotype we have been discussing). Jussim claims that in many cases, this kind of influence produces accurate beliefs about groups.[14] The exceptions he cites are cases in which "there is some sort of organized effort (e.g., by some sort of governmental or other institution) to distort the truth about some group."

Since Jussim is interested in accuracy, rather than in well-foundedness, he does not address what might make individuals' attitudes well-founded when they are congruent with stereotypes. But a natural idea is that such attitudes would be well-founded in roughly the same way that beliefs formed by testimony can be well-founded.

---

[14] Jussim (2012). The book's subtitle is "Why Accuracy Dominates Bias and Self-Fulfilling Prophecy."

When everyone in the neighborhood drinks from the faucet without a second thought, one casually assumes that the water from faucets is safe to drink. That assumption is well-founded, as are many other beliefs acquired in the same casual way. By comparison, Whit's dispositions to be suspicious and distrustful of black men, to feel discomfort sharing public spaces, are as natural to Whit and his friends as the presumption that their water is safe to drink.

It might be objected that whereas the social level presumption that the water is safe to drink is well-founded, the social level presumption that black men are dangerous isn't. To sustain this objection, the idea that social level presumptions could be epistemically appraised as well-founded or ill-founded would have to be defended. (I offer a defense in section 10.5.) But the power of the argument from testimony for the well-foundedness of Whit's attitude lies in the idea that even if the social level presumption is ill-founded, its ill-foundedness is epistemically irrelevant to Whit. It is irrelevant to Whit, on this view, because it is plausible to think that ill-foundedness does not in general transmit via testimony.

For example, suppose your mother fears that the water is unsafe to drink, and she comes to believe that the water is as she fears it to be. Her fear is unreasonable, let's suppose, and so is her belief. When she warns you not to drink the water because it is toxic, you believe her. So now you believe that the water is unsafe to drink. Your belief may be false, but even so, it is, arguably, well-founded. It is reasonable for you to believe her—she's your mother. If your belief is well-founded, then the ill-foundedness of your mother's belief does not transmit to yours, even though you formed your belief on the basis of testimony from her.

The argument from testimony is powerful. Psychologically, one's beliefs are frequently formed on the basis of testimony. Epistemically, in many cases (such as the mother–water case) it seems intuitive that testimony does not transmit epistemically. The epistemic point might seem to scale up from testimony between individuals, to testimony inherent in social normality of practices and beliefs. Epistemically, the considerations that can make Whit's beliefs seem well-founded point to the many ways in which (speaking metaphorically) a cultural milieu seems to testify through the practices and representations that shape the milieu. So if Whit's racial attitude is ill-founded, as I have assumed it is in motivating the Rationality of Perception, then something must be wrong with the argument from testimony.

In defending my solution to the problem of culturally normal belief, I argue that ill-foundedness can transmit from the social-level testifier to individuals. My first step is to make the metaphor of a social level testifier more explicit.

10.3.3 The mind of the world

Attributing a presumption to a cultural milieu is indispensable in characterizing it, even though the metaphysical structure of such attributions is hard to articulate. Who, exactly, is the bearer of a culturally entrenched presumption? Who does the presuming? These difficult questions concerning the metaphysics of culture can be sidestepped by using a helpful metaphor: the presumptions are made by the *mind of the world*.

Sometimes it is more illuminating to unpack a metaphor than it is to leave it intact. In this case, though, it is difficult to unpack its metaphysical underpinnings in an illuminating way. What the mind of the world presumes clearly depends on the mental states of smaller individuals. But for the case we have been discussing, its entrenchment does not seem to consist exclusively of attitudes like Whit's. What other attitudes help constitute it? And in what relationship do those attitudes stand to the practices and institutional arrangements that encourage them?

The difficulty of converting the metaphor into a non-metaphorical description that would answer these questions does not detract from the metaphor's usefulness. In fact, leaving those questions unanswered may explain what makes the metaphor so apt. Here are three ways the metaphor earns its explanatory keep.

First, the metaphor of a social mind does justice to the idea that a culture traffics in representations, and in that respect a cultural world such as Whit's milieu resembles a mind. The word "the" in "the mind of the world" might suggest that there is only one locus of culturally entrenched presumptions. But hearing it that way would make the metaphor useless for describing culturally specific phenomena. It should instead be heard as the mind-of-the-world that is relevant to the cultural milieu at issue, such as Whit's milieu. Its meaning is therefore closer to "the book of the month" than "the book of the world," where the book of the world purports to be a single definitive account of the universe's foundation.[15]

---

[15] Sider (2012).

In contrast, there are many books of the month, depending on both the month, and on the community.

Second, the metaphor faces up to the difficulty of pinning down exactly who or what does the representing, and doesn't give in to this difficulty by building in to the analysis that representations pervasive in a culture must fundamentally be a collection of representations with the same content in the minds of individuals. Something like that idea may or may not in the end be correct. But it's the kind of metaphysical question that shouldn't be built in to other discussions. In addition, it seems plain that a culturally entrenched presumption involving social hierarchies, like the hierarchies that figure in our example, will leave different marks in the minds of different individuals, depending both on how they are positioned in those hierarchies, and on how they end up responding to their positions. The metaphor of the mind of the world keeps the level of social analysis in view, without assimilating a cultural mind to a group mind of a clearly defined group.

Finally, a third and perhaps most important advantage of the metaphor is that it provides a language for analyzing the epistemic relationships between a culturally entrenched presumption and its recapitulation in the mind of an individual. No matter how the metaphor of the mind of the world is unpacked, the same question arises: what epistemic impact do culturally entrenched presumptions have on the minds of individuals?

This question crystallizes the problem of culturally normal belief. My solution to the problem begins by analyzing the notion of well-foundedness more closely.

10.3.4 The social frame

Well-foundedness is an explanatory notion. A belief is well-founded only if the factors that explain why the subject has it also bestow it with epistemically good-making features.

When we ask what factors explain why Whit has his racial attitude, we can address this question using a set of contrasts. Following Garfinkel (1981), I'll call the contrasts a *frame*.[16] If we want to focus on Whit's acculturation, we can ask:

---

[16] The contrastive approach to explanation is employed by Garfinkel (1981) to highlight the differences between social and individual-level explanations.

Individual frame
Why does Whit (as opposed to someone else) absorb the presumption?
Why does Whit absorb the entrenched presumption, instead of denying it?

To answer these questions, we look to the history of Whit. According to the explanatory frames, one of the epistemically relevant processes seems to be: testimony.

We can also ask what factors explain why the racial attitudes Whit ends up with are available for him to form in the first place. Here we're asking for an explanation in what we might call a social frame, rather than an individual frame:

Social frame
Why does Whit end up with those presumptions, rather than other presumptions?

To answer this question, we look not to the history of Whit, but to the history of the world. Whit absorbs those presumptions because those presumptions, rather than other ones, are culturally entrenched. They are presumed by the mind of the world. And because they are so presumed, the mind of the world can testify to their truth. It is built in to the notion of testimony from the mind of the world that it testifies only to presumptions that are already culturally entrenched. Such testimony therefore cannot explain why any such presumptions are culturally entrenched.

The social frame helps us see the role of the mind of the world in maintaining Whit's attitude once he has it. As a thought experiment, consider someone who duplicates Whit's attitudes and dispositions, psychological and otherwise, without having been acculturated. Like Donald Davidson's Swampman, SwampWhit pops into existence as the exact duplicate of someone else.[17] Assuming that SwampWhit's lack of history wouldn't preclude him (in principle) from having contentful psychological states at all (and hence from duplicating Whit's), we can see how Whit's social surroundings would leave SwampWhit just as much at ease with his attitudes, as they leave Whit at ease with his.[18]

---

[17] Davidson (1987).

[18] This assumption puts me on the side of *internalists* about mental content, who hold that Swampman could have at least some of the same contentful mental states as the man he duplicated, as opposed to *externalists* about mental content, who hold that there are at least

Here one might object that nothing from the mind of the world is needed to reassure Whit and SwampWhit in their beliefs. Instead, all that's needed is a belief in their own minds: the belief that it is socially normal to believe that black men are dangerous. That belief is arguably well-founded, unlike the presumption in the mind of the world. So when it comes to maintaining Whit's belief, the social frame drops out, according to the objection.

In reply to this objection, there are modes of maintaining beliefs in individuals that do not operate via any mediating beliefs of theirs. Suppose that in Whit's world a series of new laws are passed that establish surveillance and extend the apparatus of punishment, and that these laws are designed to apply specifically to neighborhoods where young people live who are black and poor. In order for such laws and defenses of them to reassure Whit in holding his attitude, he need not have a mediating belief. The laws and official public defenses of them could reasonably lead Whit to strengthen his mediating belief. But for them to contribute to the ease with which Whit holds his attitude, Whit would not need to have the mediating belief already, nor would he not need to acquire it. He might, for instance, fear that the attitudes are not normal or widespread. So their role in maintaining the belief is not screened off by Whit's mediating belief.

To argue that the role of the mind of the world keeps Whit's attitude ill-founded, what's needed is a bridge principle between the maintenance and ill-founding. What might the bridge principle be, if there is one? We can formulate it as a premise of the following argument. It is premise P2 in the argument that follows.

10.4 The Argument from Maintenance

The argument from maintenance

> P1. The mind of world's presumption is the main factor that explains how Whit's attitude is maintained (rather than given up).

some contentful mental states that the man Swampman duplicated had, but that Swampman can't have.

Internalism about content is often said to fit naturally with epistemic internalism, which holds the factors that determine how rational a subject's mental state is supervene on that subject's brain. Since I am arguing that social factors beyond the brain make a difference to the epistemic status of some of those mental states, my assumption for the sake of argument only makes things easier for an opponent who holds that both Whit and SwampWhit's racial attitudes are well-founded.

P2. If mental state M1 is the main factor that explains how mental state M2 is maintained, and M1 is ill-founded, then M2 is ill-founded.

P3. The mind of the world's presumption is ill-founded.

Conclusion: Whit's attitude is ill-founded.

According to the argument from maintenance, an attitude is ill-founded if the culturally entrenched presumption that largely maintains it is formed epistemically badly.

So far, I have made a case for premise P1 by describing a scenario in which P1 is plausible. In the rest of this section I argue for the bridge principle (premise P2) and premise P3.

Premise P2 resembles a principle about epistemic basing. If M2 is based on M1, then if M1 is ill-founded, M2 will be ill-founded as well, modulo washing out. In the paradigm cases of basing within an individual's mind, basing is in part an explanatory relationship. If M2 is based on M1, then the fact that a subject S is in M1 helps explain the fact that S is in M2, and this explanatory role also affects M2's epistemic status.

As stated, the antecedent of the bridge principle P2 does not pin down the kind of explanations that would support its consequent. It is plain that there are some such explanatory relations—even if ultimately they cannot be specified without taking epistemic relevance as already understood.[19] For instance, suppose M1 is my belief that you'll cheerfully clean up any small mess I make this week, and M2 is my belief that you like to clean. It is easy to picture how M2 could control M1, due to my sensitivity to the rational relationships between my beliefs. This sensitivity would explain why, when I sadly learn that you don't like to clean anymore, I give up my original belief that you'll cheerfully clean up any small mess that I make this week. And if my belief that you like to clean was the ill-founded product of wishful thinking, then my belief that you'll cheerfully clean up my small messes this week is ill-founded, too.

The argument from maintenance assumes that an analogous kind of sensitivity applies to the relationship between the mind of the world's presumptions, and the attitudes of smaller individuals such as Whit that recapitulate those presumptions. And it is easy to find an analogy. Just as my assumption that you like to clean reassures me that you'll cheerfully

---

[19] As noted earlier (Chapter 2, section 2.4.1), useful discussions of the basing relation are Evans (2013) and Korcz (1997, 2015).

clean up, in ways that might show up to me only if I lost the assumption, the social normality of Whit's attitudes play a similarly reassuring role. If the social norms in their milieu changed, in any of the ways a political movement might endeavor to bring about, then Whit might start to see their attitudes and the behaviors that express them in a different light, and they would feel less normal.

If maintenance is a kind of testimony by the mind of the world, one might object that if the mother's testimony doesn't transmit the ill-foundedness of the mother's belief, then the mind of the world's testimony doesn't transmit its ill-foundedness to Whit. In reply, there's a range of potential epistemic good-making features that bestow well-foundedness on the beliefs that accept the mother's testimony, and none of these potential good-making features carry over to the outlook Whit absorbs from the mind of the world.

First, the mother is making an assertion whose explicit purpose is to inform her children (indeed, she is concerned that they don't drink tainted water). In contrast, the mind of the world has no special concern for Whit. And its testimony takes many forms that are not well-modeled by assertion, such as advertising and fictional narratives that are meant to be realistic. And some modes of the acculturation are better modeled by directives than assertions, such as the institutions and practices related to criminal justice mentioned two paragraphs back.

Second, lies by individuals are typically easy to detect, and going with that, truth-telling by individuals is an engine of interpersonal cooperation. These features might be thought to bestow well-foundedness on beliefs that accept other people's testimony in many interpersonal contexts. In contrast, social distortions and inaccuracies such as those found in the rationalization of hierarchies often stabilize a social order and this stabilizing role prevents them from coming out into the open.

Putting these considerations together, even if accepting the mother's testimony that the tap water is unsafe to drink yields a well-founded belief, that conclusion does not weaken the argument from maintenance. If the epistemology of interpersonal testimony prevents the mother's testimony from transmitting ill-foundedness to the beliefs her children form when they believe their mother, the factors that plausibly prevent this transmission are not found in the interface between an individual and the mind of the world.

10.5 Are Presumptions in the Mind of the World Epistemically Appraisable?

For Whit's attitude to inherit the ill-foundedness from the presumption in the mind of the world, that presumption has to be epistemically appraisable. I'm going to take it for granted that if the presumption in the mind of the world that Whit receives as testimony is epistemically appraisable, then it is ill-founded. So I won't argue that it is ill-founded from the ground up. The part of premise P3 that needs most defense is the idea that a culturally entrenched presumption could be epistemically appraisable at all. So I will focus there.

In defense of this idea, here are three types of examples of culturally entrenched presumptions, and the factors that seem to make them well-founded or ill-founded.

A first type of example involves concepts. Consider the concept of weight, according to which everything material has a weight (when it's on earth). Material things are things with mass. Because this concept of weight is the dominant concept of weight in modern cultures, there is in many places a culturally entrenched presumption that everything material has a weight. By the time one learns this fact in science class, it already rings true.

The culturally entrenched presumption that everything material has a weight seems well-founded. Arguably, what makes it well-founded includes the fact that the concept of weight formulated by Newton and Euler emerged because of discoveries that justifiably overturned previous conceptions of weight, according to which weight was an optional property of material things, and some things were too small or insignificant to have any weight.[20]

A second type of example involves rationalizations. Max Weber in his 1918 essay "Politics as a Vocation" considers a war-weary solider who becomes unable to fight anymore because of exhaustion, but rationalizes his collapse by portraying it, to himself and to others, as the product of a reasoned and reasonable decision:

[S]omebody under the frightfulness of war collapses psychologically, and instead of saying it was just too much, he feels the need of legitimizing his war weariness to himself by saying "I could not bear it because I had to fight for a morally bad cause".

---

[20] For discussion of the process by which this concept of weight emerged, see Carey (1987).

The exhausted war-weary individual ends up with a belief that the cause was morally bad, not because of a moral insight, but by a rationalization of his feeling. Whether his belief is true or false, it is formed epistemically badly.

Weber finds an analog of self-righteousness in nation-states. He describes rationalizations of defeat (on the part of the victor) in the form of beliefs that a defeated nation deserved to be defeated.

> It is no different if after a victorious war the victor in undignified righteousness claims "I won because I was right"... A nation forgives if its interests have been damaged, but no nation forgives if its honor has been offended, especially by a bigoted self-righteousness.

The attribution to a political association of a reactive attitude such as self-righteousness is a metaphor. The metaphor is apt, as the phenomenon Weber describes is easily recognizable in international politics. Even without unpacking the metaphor's metaphysical underpinning, we can make sense of the idea that a culturally entrenched presumption is ill-founded.

A third type of example involves institutional practices. In many places in the world where there are water faucets, the presumption that the water is safe to drink from the faucet is entrenched. It is entrenched in social environments in which people regularly drink from the faucet, and do not go out of their way to brush their teeth or wash their fruit with bottled water.

Usually, when water is safe to drink from faucets, it is safe to drink by design, thanks to the system of water collection and filtering that was built on the basis of knowledge about how to make water safe to drink. In these cases, the presumption that it's safe to drink water from the faucets is culturally entrenched because of the normal practices of drinking tap water. And the presumption is well-founded, because that practice was established using knowledge of how to purify water.

A different example involving institutional practices highlights an entrenched presumption that seems ill-founded, rather than well-founded. Consider one of Frederick Douglass's remarks about slavery made in 1881, during the era of Reconstruction after the US Civil War:

> the slave master had a direct interest in discrediting the personality of those he held as property. Every man who had a thousand dollars so invested had a thousand reasons for painting the black man as only fit for slavery. [...] The

holders of twenty hundred million dollars' worth of property in human chattels procured the means of influencing press, pulpit, and politician, and through these instrumentalities, they belittled our virtues and magnified our vices, and have made us odious in the eyes of the world . . . [21]

The world has eyes, according to Douglass's metaphor, which complements the metaphor of the mind of the world. The presumption that "the black man is only fit for slavery," and the human hierarchies that go with it, became entrenched, Douglass suggests, because it was congruent with slavery. Alongside this political arrangement grew presumptions that painted those arrangements as justified by the nature of the people in the hierarchy.[22] The presumption is not prevalent because it is tracking the truth about human beings, or because it is the product of discoveries made (as Newton's and Euler's were) using methods that lead to well-founded beliefs. It became socially normal to believe that water from faucets was safe to drink, and it was socially normal under slavery to believe that blacks were only fit to be slaves.[23] Social normality is a poor guide to well-foundedness.

10.6 Conclusion: The Scope of Epistemic Norms

The problem of culturally normal belief highlights one of the puzzling features of the interface between the minds of individuals and the cultures they belong to. The problem arises when a culturally entrenched presumption is ill-founded, and it leaves its mark in an individual's mind in the form of a belief (or something that operates in the mind as a belief) that is not in any obvious way ill-founded.

---

[21] Douglass (1881).

[22] Compare Stanton and Anthony (1848): "The history of mankind is a history of repeated injuries and usurpations on the part of man toward woman, having in direct object the establishment of an absolute tyranny over her . . . He has created a false public sentiment, by giving to the world a different code of morals for men and women, by which moral delinquencies which exclude women from society, are not only tolerated but deemed of little account in man."

[23] The social normality is crystallized in the remarks of Mr Shelby, a character in *Uncle Tom's Cabin* (Stowe [1852]/1951): "I have agreed to sell Tom and Harry both; and I don't know why I am to be rated as if I were a monster for doing what everyone does every day." For discussion of presumptions about blacks that impacted free as well as enslaved blacks, see Kennedy, ch. 2.

There are important differences between the problem of hijacked experiences and the problem of culturally normal belief. In the case of hijacked experiences, the seemingly passive route to a hijacked experience turns out to be an irrational mental activity. In the case of culturally normal belief, in contrast, I've argued that the epistemically bad-making features are not located in the individual's mind. Instead, those features are located where the social frame puts them: in the factors that account for the normality of what's presumed.

Another major difference concerns inference. I've argued that inference can analyze a wide range of cases of hijacked perception. Inference helps describe the epistemic impact of psychological precursors on perceptual experiences or judgments, in cases of hijacked perception. In contrast, on the face of it, inference is a poor model of the relation between Whit's attitude and the presumption in the mind of the world, if inferences occur only within a single subject's mind. Whit may constantly respond to the presumption in the mind of the world, both in forming and maintaining his attitude. But if inferring occurs only within a single subject, Whit's response is not an inferential response.

At a higher level of abstraction, however, my solutions to the two problems have something in common. They find epistemic basing relations where they haven't been studied before: in the relationship between perceptual experience and its precursors, and at the interface between the individual mind and the mind of the world. Within the subject's mind, inference is a kind of basing. When a belief is formed or strengthened by inference, it is based on what it is inferred from, so "beliefs based on inference from X" can mean the same as "beliefs based on X."

If my solutions are correct, then there are rational and irrational paths linking culturally entrenched outlooks and perception. Just as implicit attitudes may be the irrational extension of culturally entrenched distortions in how members of a society view one another, extending the distortion into perceptual experience can likewise extend its irrationality. And just as wishful, fearful, or prejudiced thinking leaves us with ill-founded beliefs, wishful, fearful, or prejudiced seeing may leave us with ill-founded experiences. *The Rationality of Perception* shows us how to stop ignoring two realms into which the scope of epistemic appraisability extends: processes within a subject leading up to perceptual experiences, and interactions between individual minds and society. In these ways, epistemic norms of ill-foundedness and well-foundedness apply beyond individuals' beliefs.

Acknowledgments

The feeling of ease one gets from discussing a problem without having to explain everything from the beginning comes in all kinds of friendships, philosophical and otherwise. A large handful of people combed over the topics in this book with me, discussing them so often and from so many angles that I felt we got to know a web of philosophical problems in the same way that one gradually finds the steady paths through a noisy, crowded, fascinating neighborhood. For their insights and acumen, for reading multiple drafts of the same material, for the detailed comments and intellectual generosity, I'm grateful to Nico Silins, Eric Mandelbaum, Matt McGrath, Ned Block, Scott Sturgeon, Zoe Jenkin, Maja Spener, Paul Boghossian, David Chalmers, Selim Berker, Susanna Rinard, Jane Friedman, Farid Masrour, John Bengson, Alex Byrne, Jim Pryor, Michael Brownstein, Jessie Munton, Lu Teng, Robert Long, Sebastian Watzl, Jonathan Vogel, and Jona Vance. In my mind, there's a neighborhood made of dialectical spaces that I saw more clearly because I could discuss them repeatedly with these people. If it seems odd to thank people for helping me discover the contours of an imaginary space, it might seem even odder to thank someone for keeping me company in it. But I won't let that stop me. In these figurative spaces, I felt I never went anywhere without Bernhard Nickel, my companion in imaginary travel and its non-imaginary foundations.

I am equally grateful for numerous chances to explain this project from the beginning, without relying on prior understanding or familiarity. When the Cornell Society for the Humanities hosted me as a visiting scholar for their project on Sensation in 2015, I had the chance to introduce this work to its fellows. I found it edifying, challenging, and delightful to combine our intellectual registers. The summer of 2016 lengthened the string of beneficial delights by giving me two more chances to explain the project as a whole from the start: first at a three-part seminar at Universidad Alberto Hurtado in Santiago, Chile, where the discussions were punctuated by helpful suggestions for translation into and out of Spanish, and then at a month-long National Endowment for the Humanities (NEH) Summer Institute on Presupposition and Perception. I'm grateful to the NEH for sponsoring our institute, to Nico Silins for directing it with me, to Zoe Jenkin for her organizational genius, and to everyone who participated in the institute discussions, which helped me understand how different modes of inquiry inspired this book.

So many people helpfully discussed the material in this book with me that hearing all their names would make even a patient person fidget. I've counted nearly ninety people whose contributions I learned from and remember vividly, and I've undoubtedly forgotten others. For exchanges that helped me write about social perception, I am grateful to many students and colleagues, and above all to Sally Haslanger and Kristie Dotson. Several reading groups and seminars read large chunks of the manuscript at various stages, and for coordinating these groups I thank Farid Masrour and John Bengson at the University of Wisconsin, Madison, Jonathan Cohen and Matt Fulkerson at UC San Diego, Maria Aarnio at the University of Michigan, and Tim Crane at the University of Cambridge. For writing extensive comments on early, middle, or late drafts in their entirety, I am very grateful to Zoe Jenkin, Matt Fulkerson, Jonathan Cohen, Craig French, Robert Audi, and Robert Long. Special forms of help and camaraderie came from the philosopher, novelist, and poet Sheridan Hough, through the buoyant magic of her creativity. Peter Railton's responses to a paper I wrote on wishful seeing in 2012 helped me clarify my views. I've been affected by his writings on belief and desire, and by his distinctive blend of honesty and craft in philosophy.

The places where versions of this material were presented are too numerous to list, but two meetings in 2015 were particularly influential: a conference in Huatulco, Oaxaca hosted by the Sociedad de Filosofía Ibero-Americano, where many sharp challenges were raised by the participants including my commentators Carlotta Pavese, Carlos Montemayor and Jack Lyons, and a reading group in Madison, where Farid Masrour and John Bengson brought several important instabilities into focus for me. At the Center for the Study of Mind and Nature at Oslo, my hosts Sebastian Watzl, Olav Gjelsvik, and Herman Cappelen provided a wonderful place for philosophy. Finally, another institution has provided me with a truly hospitable place to work: the Harvard University Philosophy Department. I thank former dean Diana Sorensen and her team of administrators in the division of Arts and Humanities for their ongoing support, as well as the Mind, Brain, and Behavior program. Together they financed the indispensable assistance I received from Sandy Diehl, Noel Dominguez, and Robert Long, whom I thank for helping me prepare the final manuscript.

I dedicate this book to Somerville, Massachusetts, and to my mothers, Sandra Siegel and Jutta Nickel, for the enclosures they have provided, including the book's cover art, which my mother created.

Bibliography

Adams, R., Ambady, N., Nakayama, K., and Shimojo, S., eds. (2010). *The Science of Social Vision*. Oxford University Press.

Alhazen, A. [ca. 1030] (1989). In A. I. Sabra, ed. and trans., *The Optics of Ibn al-Haytham*, 2 vols, Books I–III. Warburg Institute.

Allport, A. (1954). The Nature of Prejudice. Basic Books.

Armstrong, D. M. (1968). *A Materialist Theory of Mind*. Routledge.

Audi, R. (1986). "Belief, Reason, and Inference." *Philosophical Topics* 14 (1): 27–65.

Audi, R. (2001). *The Architecture of Reason: The Structure and Substance of Rationality*. Oxford University Press.

Audi, R. (2015). "The Grounds and Structure of Reasons for Action." In Audi, R., *Reasons Rights and Values*, 71–96. Cambridge University Press.

Austin, J. L. (1962). *Sense and Sensibilia*. Oxford University Press.

Ayer, A. J. (1940). *The Foundations of Empirical Knowledge*. Macmillan.

Baldwin, J. (1965). "The American Dream and the American Negro." *New York Times*, March 7.

Bar, M. (2011). "The Proactive Brain." In Bar, M., ed., *Predictions in the Brain?*, 13–26. Oxford University Press.

Bengson, J. (2013). "*Presentation and Content* A Critical Study of Susanna Siegel, *The Contents of Visual Experience* (Oxford: Oxford University Press, 2010)" *Noûs* 47 (4): 795–807.

Bergmann, M. (2006). *Justification without Awareness: A Defense of Epistemic Externalism*. Oxford University Press.

Bhalla, M. and Proffitt, D. R. (1999). "Visual-Motor Recalibration in Geographical Slant Perception." *Journal of Experimental Psychology: Human Perception & Performance* 25 (4): 1076–96.

Blair, I., Ma, J., and Lenton, A. (2001). "Imagining Stereotypes Away: The Moderation of Implicit Stereotypes through Mental Imagery." *Journal of Personality and Social Psychology* 81 (5): 828–41.

Boghossian, P. (2014). "What Is Inference?" *Philosophical Studies* 169 (1): 1–18.

Boghossian, P. (forthcoming). "Inference, Mechanism, and Normativity." In M. Balcerak-Jackson and B. Balcerak-Jackson, eds., *Reasoning: Essays on Theoretical and Practical Thinking*. Oxford University Press.

BonJour, L. (1978). "Can Empirical Knowledge Have a Foundation?" *American Philosophical Quarterly* 15 (1): 1–13.

BonJour, L. (1985). *The Structure of Empirical Knowledge*. Harvard University Press.

Bortolotti, L. (2013). "Delusion." *The Stanford Encyclopedia of Philosophy* (Summer 2015 Edition), ed. Zalta, E. N. http://plato.stanford.edu/archives/sum2015/entries/delusion/ (accessed September 25, 2016).

Briscoe, R. (2015). "Cognitive Penetration and the Reach of Phenomenal Content." In Raftopoulos, A. and Zeimbeikis, J., eds., *Cognitive Penetrability*, 174–99. Oxford University Press. (174–99).

Brogaard, B. (2013). "Phenomenal Seemings and Sensible Dogmatism." In Tucker, C. (ed.), *Seemings and Justification: New Essays on Dogmatism and Phenomenal Conservatism*. Oxford University Press.

Brogaard, B., ed. (2014). *Does Perception Have Content?* Oxford University Press.

Brogaard, B. and Gatzia, D. (forthcoming). "Is Color Experience Cognitively Penetrable?" *Topics in Cognitive Science: Special issue on cortical color.*

Broome, J. (1999). "Normative Requirements." *Ratio* 12 (3): 398–419. Reprinted in Dancy, J., ed., *Normativity* (2000), 78–99. Blackwell.

Broome, J. (2013). *Rationality through Reasoning.* Wiley Blackwell.

Broome, J. (2014). "Comments on Boghossian." *Philosophical Studies* 169 (1): 19–25.

Bruner, J. (1973). *Beyond the Information Given: Studies in the Psychology of Knowing.* Norton.

Burge, T. (2003). "Concepts, Conceptions, Reflective Understanding: Reply to Peacocke." In Hahn, M. and Ramberg, B., eds., *Reflections and Replies: Essays on the Philosophy of Tyler Burge*, 383–96. MIT Press.

Burge, T. (2010). *Origins of Objectivity.* Oxford University Press.

Byrne, A. (2009). "Experience and Content." *Philosophical Quarterly* 59 (236): 429–51.

Byrne, A. (2012). "Knowing What I See." In Stoljar, D. and Smithies, D., eds., *Introspection and Consciousness*, 183–207. Oxford University Press.

Byrne, A. (2015). "McDowell and Wright on Anti-Scepticism, etc." In Dodd, D. and Zardini, E., eds., *New Essays on Philosophical Skepticism*, 275–95. Oxford University Press.

Campbell, J. (2001). "Rationality, Meaning, and the Analysis of Delusion." *Philosophy, Psychiatry, & Psychology* 8 (2/3): 89–100.

Carey, S. (1987). *Conceptual Change in Childhood.* MIT Press.

Carey, S. (2009). *The Origin of Concepts.* Oxford University Press.

Carroll, L. (1895). "What the Tortoise Said to Achilles." *Mind* 4 (14): 278–80.

Ceci, S. J. and Williams, W. M. (2011). "Understanding Current Causes of Women's Underrepresentation in Science." *Proceedings of the National Academy of Sciences of the United States of America* 108 (8): 3157–62.

Chalmers, D. (2012). *Constructing the World.* Oxford University Press.

Chen, C. (2008). "On Having a Point of View: Belief, Action, and Egocentric States." *Journal of Philosophy* 105 (5): 240–58.

Christensen, D. (1994). "Conservatism in Epistemology." *Noûs* 28 (1): 69–89.

Chudnoff, E. (2012). "Presentational Phenomenology." In Miguens, S. & Preyer, G., eds., *Consciousness and Subjectivity*, 51–72. Ontos Verlag.

Chudnoff, E. (2013). *Intuition*. Oxford University Press.

Chudnoff, E. (2014). "The Rational Roles of Intuition." In Booth, A. and Rowbottom, D., eds., *Intuitions*, 9–35. Oxford University Press.

Clark, A. (2013). "Whatever Next? Predictive Brains, Situated Agents, and The Future of Cognitive Science." *Behavioral and Brain Sciences* 36 (3): 181–204.

Clark, A. (2015). *Surfing Uncertainty*. Oxford University Press.

Coates, T. (2015). *Between the World and Me*. Spiegel & Grau.

Coelho, C. M., Waters, A. M., Hine, T. J., and Wallis, G. (2009). "The Use of Virtual Reality in Acrophobia Research and Treatment." *Journal of Anxiety Disorders* 23: 563–74.

Cohen, S. (2002). "Basic Knowledge and the Problem of Easy Knowledge." *Philosophy and Phenomenological Research* 65 (2): 309–29.

Collins, J. A. and Olson, I. R. (2014). "Knowledge Is Power: How Conceptual Knowledge Transforms Visual Cognition." *Psychonomic Bulletin & Review* 21 (4): 843–60.

Coltheart, M. (2005). "Conscious Experience and Delusional Belief." *Philosophy, Psychiatry, & Psychology* 12 (2): 153–7.

Conee, E. and Feldman, R. (1998). "The Generality Problem for Reliabilism." *Philosophical Studies* 89 (1): 1–29. Reprinted as chapter 6 of Conee and Feldman (2004).

Conee, E. and Feldman, R. (2004). *Evidentialism: Essays in Epistemology*. Oxford University Press.

Connolly, K. (2014). "Perceptual Learning and the Contents of Perception." *Erkenntnis* 79 (6): 1407–18.

Connolly, K. (ms.). "Perceptual Learning: The Flexibility of the Senses."

Cooper, A. J. [1872]/(1998). *A Voice from the South*. Mary Helen Washington (ed.), New York: Oxford University Press.

Cornell, N. (ms.). "Inattention and Negligence."

Correll, J., Park, B., Judd, C. M., and Wittenbrink, B. (2002). "The Police Officer's Dilemma: Using Ethnicity to Disambiguate Potentially Threatening Individuals." *Journal of Personality and Social Psychology* 83 (6): 1314–29.

Correll, J., Park, B., Judd, C. M., Wittenbrink, B., Sadler, M. S., and Keesee, T. (2007). "Across the Thin Blue Line: Police Officers and Racial Bias in the Decision to Shoot." *Journal of Personality and Social Psychology* 92 (6): 1006–23.

Correll, J., Wittenbrink, B., Crawford, M. T., and Sadler, M. S. (2015). "Stereotypic Vision: How Stereotypes Disambiguate Visual Stimuli." *Journal of Personality and Social Psychology* 108 (2): 219–33.

Crenshaw, K. (2015). "Black Girls Matter: Pushed Out, Overpoliced, and Under-protected." African American Policy Forum. http://www.atlanticphilanthropies.org/app/uploads/2015/09/BlackGirlsMatter_Report.pdf (accessed September 21, 2016).

Currie, G. and Ravenscroft, I. (2002). *Recreative Minds: Imagination in Philosophy and Psychology*. Oxford: Oxford University Press.

Dancy, J. (2000). *Practical Reality*. Oxford University Press.

Davidson, D. (1982). "Two Paradoxes of Irrationality." In Wollheim, R., ed., *Philosophical Essays on Freud*, 289–305. Cambridge University Press.

Davidson, D. (1986). "A Coherence Theory of Truth and Knowledge." In Lepore, E., ed., *Truth and Interpretation. Perspectives on the Philosophy of Donald Davidson*, 307–19. Blackwell.

Davidson, D. (1987). "Knowing One's Own Mind." *Proceedings and Addresses of the American Philosophical Association* 60 (3): 441–58.

Dennett, D. C. (1969). *Content and Consciousness*. Routledge & Kegan Paul.

Deroy, O. (2013). "Object-Sensitivity versus Cognitive Penetrability of Perception." *Philosophical Studies* 162 (1): 87–107.

Dewey, J. (1938). *Logic: The Theory of Inquiry*. Henry Holt & Company.

DiIulio, J. (1996). "My Black Crime Problem, and Ours." *City Journal*. http://www.city-journal.org/html/my-black-crime-problem-and-ours-11773.html (accessed May 25, 2016).

Douglass, F. (1881). "The Color Line." *The North American Review* 132 (295): 567–77.

Dovidio, J. F. and Gaertner, S. L. (2000). "Aversive Racism and Selection Decisions: 1989 and 1999." *Psychological Science* 11 (4): 315–19.

Drayson, Z. (2012). "The Uses and Abuses of the Personal/Subpersonal Distinction." *Philosophical Perspectives* 26 (1): 1–18.

Dretske, F. (1969). *Seeing and Knowing*. University of Chicago Press.

Duncan, B. L. (1976). "Differential Social Perception and Attribution of Inter-group Violence: Testing the Lower Limits of Stereotyping of Blacks." *Journal of Personality and Social Psychology* 34 (4): 590–8.

Dunham, Y., Chen, E. E., and Banaji, M. R. (2013). "Two Signatures of Implicit Intergroup Attitudes: Developmental Invariance and Early Enculturation." *Psychological Science* 24 (6): 860–8.

Durgin, F. H., Baird, J. A., Greenburg, M., Russell, R., Shaughnessy, K., and Waymouth, S. (2009). "Who Is Being Deceived? The Experimental Demands of Wearing a Backpack." *Psychonomic Bulletin & Review* 16 (5): 964–9.

Eberhardt, J. L., Davies, P. G., Purdie-Vaughns, V., and Johnson, S. L. (2006). "Looking Deathworthy: Perceived Stereotypicality of Black Defendants Predicts Capital-Sentencing Outcomes." *Psychological Science* 17(5): 383–8.

Eberhardt, J. L., Goff, P. A., Purdie, V. J., and Davies, P. G. (2004). "Seeing Black: Race, Crime, and Visual Processing." *Journal of Personality and Social Psychology* 87 (6): 876–93.

Emerson, R. W. (1844). "Experience." In *Essays: Second Series*. James Munroe & Co.

Evans, I. (2013). "The Problem of The Basing Relation." *Synthese* 190 (14): 2943–57.

Farennikova, A. (2013). "Seeing Absence." *Philosophical Studies* 166 (3): 429–54.

Farennikova, A. (2015). "Perception of Absence and Penetration from Expectation." *Review of Philosophy and Psychology* 6 (4): 621–40.

Farennikova, A. (ms.). Experience and Probability.

Feldman, R. & Conee, E. (1985). "Evidentialism." *Philosophical Studies* 48 (1): 15–34. Reprinted as chapter 4 of Conee and Feldman (2004).

Fields, B. (1982). "Ideology, Race, and American History." In Kousser, J. M. and McPherson, J. M., eds., *Region, Race, and Reconstruction: Essays in Honor of C. Vann Woodward*, 143–77. Oxford University Press.

Firestone, C. and Scholl, B. J. (2015). "Cognition Does Not Affect Perception: Evaluating The Evidence for 'Top-Down' Effects." *Behavioral and Brain Sciences*, 1–72.

Fodor, J. (1984). "Observation Reconsidered." *Philosophy of Science* 51 (1): 23–43.

Fodor, J. (1988). "A Reply to Churchland's 'Perceptual Plasticity and Theoretical Neutrality.'" *Philosophy of Science* 55 (2): 188–98.

Foley, R. and Fumerton, R. (1982). "Epistemic Indolence." *Mind* 91 (361): 38–56.

Frege, G. (1979). "Logic." In Hermes, H., Kambartel, F., and Kaulbach, F., eds., Long, P., and White, R., trans., *Posthumous Writings*. University of Chicago Press.

Friedman, J. (2015). "Why Suspend Judging?" *Noûs*. Published online 24 Dec. 2015.

Friedman, J. (ms.). "Inquiry and Belief."

Frith, C. and Johnstone, E. (2003). *Schizophrenia: A Very Short Introduction*. Oxford University Press.

Fumerton, R. (1995). *Metaepistemology and Skepticism*. Rowman & Littlefield.

Fumerton, R. (2013). "Siegel on the Epistemic Impact of 'Checkered' Experience." *Philosophical Studies* 162 (3): 733–9.

Garfinkel, A. (1981). *Forms of Explanation: Rethinking the Questions in Social Theory*. Yale University Press.

Gendler, T. S. (2008). "Alief in Action (and Reaction)." *Mind & Language* 23 (5): 552–85.

Gendler, T. S. (2011). "On the Epistemic Costs of Implicit Bias." *Philosophical Studies* 156 (1): 33–63.

Ghijsen, H. (2016). "The Real Epistemic Problem of Cognitive Penetration." *Philosophical Studies* 173 (6): 1457–75.

Gibson, J. J. (1977). "The Theory of Affordances." In Shaw, R. and Bransford, J., eds., *Perceiving, Acting, and Knowing: Toward an Ecological Psychology*, 67–82. Lawrence Erlbaum.

Ginsborg, H. (2006). "Reasons for Belief." *Philosophy and Phenomenological Research* 72 (2): 286–318.

Glaser, J. (2014). *Suspect Race: Causes and Consequences of Racial Profiling.* Oxford University Press.

Glaser, J. and Knowles, E. (2008). "Implicit Motivation to Control Prejudice." *Journal of Experimental Social Psychology* 44 (1): 164–72.

Glüer, K. (2009). "In Defence of a Doxastic Account of Experience." *Mind & Language* 24 (3): 297–327.

Goff, P. A., Jackson, M. C., Di Leone, B. L., Culotta, C. M., & DiTomasso, N. A. (2014). "The Essence of Innocence: Consequences of Dehumanizing Black Children." *Journal of Personality and Social Psychology* 106 (4): 526–45.

Goldin, C., & Rouse, C. (2000). "Orchestrating Impartiality: The Impact of 'Blind' Auditions on Female Musicians." *The American Economic Review* 90 (4): 715–41.

Goldman, A. (2008). "Immediate Justification and Process Reliabilism." In Smith, Q., ed., *Epistemology: New Essays*, 63–82. Oxford University Press.

Goldman, A. and McGrath, M. (2014). *Epistemology: A Contemporary Introduction.* Oxford University Press.

Goldstone, R. (1995). "Effects of Categorization on Color Perception." *Psychological Science* 6 (5): 298–304.

Goldstone, R. and Byrge, L. (2015). "Perceptual Learning." In Matthen, M., ed., *The Oxford Handbook of the Philosophy of Perception*, 812–32. Oxford University Press.

Greco, J. (1999). "Agent Reliabilism." *Noûs* 33: 273–96.

Gupta, A. (2006). *Empiricism and Experience.* Oxford University Press.

Gupta, A. (2011). "Appearances and their role in cognition." In *Experience, Truth, and Meaning.* Oxford University Press.

Hansen, T., Olkkonen, M., Walter, S., and Gegenfurtner, K. R. (2006). "Memory Modulates Color Appearance." *Nature Neuroscience* 9 (11): 1367–8.

Harman, G. (1986). *Change in View: Principles of Reasoning.* MIT Press.

Haslanger, S. (1995). "Ontology and Social Construction." *Philosophical Topics* 23 (2): 95–125.

Hatfield, G. (2002). "Perception as Unconscious Inference." In Heyer, D. and Mausfeld, R., eds., *Perception and the Physical World: Psychological and Philosophical Issues in Perception*, 113–43. Wiley.

Heck, R. (2000). "Nonconceptual Content and the 'Space of Reasons.'" *Philosophical Review* 109 (4): 483–523.

Helmholtz, H. von (1867/1910). *Handbuch der physiologischen Optik* [Handbook of physiological vision]. L. Voss.

Hinton, E. (2016). *From the War on Poverty to the War on Crime: The Making of Mass Incarceration in America.* Harvard University Press.

Hlobil, U. (2014). "Against Boghossian, Wright and Broome on Inference." *Philosophical Studies* 167 (2): 419–29.

Hohwy, J. (2013). *The Predictive Mind.* Oxford University Press.

Hornsby, J. (2001). *Simple Mindedness: In Defense of Naive Naturalism in the Philosophy of Mind.* Harvard University Press.

Huemer, M. (2007). "Compassionate Phenomenal Conservatism." *Philosophy and Phenomenological Research* 74 (1): 30–55.

Huemer, M. (2013). "Epistemological Asymmetries between Belief and Experience." *Philosophical Studies* 162 (3): 741–8.

Jackson, A. (2011). "Appearances, Rationality, and Justified Belief." *Philosophy and Phenomenological Research* 82 (3): 564–93.

Jackson, F. (1977). *Perception: A Representative Theory.* Cambridge University Press.

James, L., Vila, B., and Daratha, K. (2013). "Results from Experimental Trials Testing Participant Responses to White, Hispanic and Black Suspects in High-fidelity Deadly Force Judgment and Decision-making Simulations." *Journal of Experimental Criminology* 9 (2): 189–212.

Jenkin, Z. (ms. 1). "Core Cognition and Epistemic Evaluability."

Jenkin, Z. (ms. 2). "Perceptual Expectations and Epistemic Accountability."

Jenkin, Z. and Siegel, S. (2015). "Cognitive Penetrability: Modularity, Epistemology, and Ethics." *Review of Philosophy and Psychology* 6 (4): 531–45.

Jiang, Y. V., Costello, P., Fang, F., Huang, M., & He, S. (2006). "A Gender- and Sexual Orientation-dependent Spatial Attentional Effect of Invisible Images." *Proceedings of the National Academy of Sciences* 103 (45), 17048–52.

Johnston, M. (2001). "The Authority of Affect." *Philosophy and Phenomenological Research* 63 (1): 181–214.

Jussim, L. (2012). *Social Perception and Social Reality: Why Accuracy Dominates Bias and Self-Fulfilling Prophecy.* Oxford University Press.

Kant, I. [1798] (2006). *Anthropology from a Pragmatic Point of View*, trans. Louden, R.B. Cambridge University Press.

Katsafanas, P. (forthcoming). "Nietzsche and Murdoch on the Moral Significance of Perceptual Experience." *European Journal of Philosophy.*

Kelly, T. (2008). "Disagreement, Dogmatism, and Belief Polarization." *Journal of Philosophy* 105 (10): 611–33.

Kennedy, R. (1997). *Race, Crime and the Law.* Vintage Books.

Klauer, K., Eder, A., Greenwald, A., and Abrams, R. (2007). "Priming of Semantic Classifications by Novel Subliminal Prime Words." *Consciousness and Cognition, 16*, 63–83.

Korcz, K. (1997). "Recent Work on the Basing Relation." *American Philosophical Quarterly* 34 (2): 171–92.

Korcz, K. (2015). "The Epistemic Basing Relation." *The Stanford Encyclopedia of Philosophy* (Fall 2015 Edition), Edward N. Zalta (ed.), http://plato.stanford.edu/archives/fall2015/entries/basing-epistemic/ (accessed September 25, 2016).

Kriegel, U. (2009). *Subjective Consciousness: A Self-Representational Theory.* Oxford University Press.

Kriegel, U. (2012). "Personal-Level Representation." In Miguens, S. and Preyer, G., eds., *Consciousness and Subjectivity*, 109–46. Ontos Verlag.

Kvanvig, J. (2003). "Propositionalism and the Perspectival Character of Justification." *American Philosophical Quarterly* 40 (1): 3–18.

Kvanvig, J. and Menzel, C. (1990). "The Basic Notion of Justification." *Philosophical Studies* 59 (3): 235–61.

Kvanvig, J. and Riggs, W. (1992). "Can a Coherence Theory Appeal to Appearance States?" *Philosophical Studies* 67 (3):197–217.

Langton, R. (ms.). "Moral Realism and the Plasticity of Mind."

Laplace, P. S. [1814] (1995). *Philosophical Essay on Probabilities*, trans. Dale, A. I. Springer.

Lee, C. (2003). *Murder and the Reasonable Man: Passion and Fear in the Criminal.* NYU Press.

Lehrer, K. (1990). *Theory of Knowledge.* Westview Press.

Lerman, A. and Weaver, V. (2014). *Arresting Citizenship: The Democratic Consequences of American Crime Control.* University of Chicago Press.

Leslie, S. J. (2008). "Generics: Cognition and Acquisition." *Philosophical Review* 117 (1): 1–47.

Levin, D. T. and Banaji, M. R. (2006). "Distortions in the Perceived Lightness of Faces: The Role of Race Categories." *Journal of Experimental Psychology: General* 135 (4): 501–12.

Levin, M. (1992). "Responses to Race Differences in Crime." *Journal of Social Philosophy* 23 (1): 5–29.

Levy, N. (2014). "Neither Fish nor Fowl: Implicit Attitudes as Patchy Endorsements." *Noûs* 49 (4): 800–23.

Logue, H. (2014). "Experiential Content and Naïve Realism: A Reconciliation." In Brogaard, ed. (2014), 220–41.

Lowe, J. (2015). "Perceptual Content, Cognitive Penetrability, and Realism." In Zeimbekis, J. and Raftopoulos, A., eds. (2015), 361–77.

Lycan, W. (2013). "Phenomenal Conservatism and the Principle of Credulity." In Tucker, C., ed., *Seemings and Justification: New Essays on Dogmatism and Phenomenal Conservatism*, 293–305. Oxford University Press.

Lyons, J. (2011a). "Circularity, Reliability, and the Cognitive Penetrability of Perception." *Philosophical Issues* 21 (1): 289–311.

Lyons, J. (2011b). *Perception and Basic Beliefs: Zombies, Modules, and the Problem of the External World.* Oxford University Press.

Lyons, J. (2016). "Inferentialism and Cognitive Penetration of Perception." *Episteme* 13 (1): 1–28.

Machery, E. (2009). *Doing without Concepts*. Oxford University Press.

Macpherson, F. (2012). "Cognitive Penetration of Color experience: Rethinking the Issue in Light of an Indirect Mechanism." *Philosophy and Phenomenological Research*. Vol 84(1), 24–62.

Macpherson, F. (2015). "Cognitive Penetration and Predictive Coding: A Commentary on Lupyan." *Review of Philosophy and Psychology* 6(4): 571–84.

Macpherson, F. (2016). "The Relationship between Cognitive Penetration and Predictive Coding." *Consciousness and Cognition* Published online April 2016.

Madva, A. and Brownstein, M. (forthcoming.). "Stereotypes, Prejudice, and the taxonomy of the Implicit Social Mind." *Nous*.

Mandelbaum, E. (2013). "Against Alief." *Philosophical Studies* 165 (1): 197–211.

Mandelbaum, E. (2015). "Attitude, Inference, Association: On the Propositional Structure of Implicit Bias." *Noûs* 50(3), 629–58.

Markie, P. (2006). "Epistemically Appropriate Perceptual Belief." *Noûs* 40 (1): 118–42.

Martin, M. G. F. (2004). "The Limits of Self-Awareness." *Philosophical Studies* 120 (1): 37–89.

McDowell, J. (1994). *Mind and World*. Harvard University Press.

McGrath, M. (2013a). "Phenomenal Conservatism and Cognitive Penetration: the 'Bad Basis' Counterexamples." In Tucker, C., ed., *Seemings and Justification: New Essays on Dogmatism and Phenomenal Conservatism*, 225–47. Oxford University Press.

McGrath, M. (2013b). "Siegel and the Impact for Epistemological Internalism." *Philosophical Studies* 162 (3): 723–32.

McGrath, M. (forthcoming). "Looks and Perceptual Justification." *Philosophy and Phenomenological Research*. Published online 1 April 2016.

Mendelberg, T. (2001). *The Race Card: Campaign Strategy, Implicit Messages, and the Norm of Equality*. Princeton University Press.

Mills, C. (2007). "White Ignorance." In Sullivan, S., and Tuana, N., eds., Race and Epistemologies of Ignorance. SUNY Press.

Morris, M. (2016). Pushout. The New Press.

Morrison, J. (2016). "Perceptual Confidence." *Analytic Philosophy* 57 (1): 15–48.

Moss, S. (forthcoming). *Probabilistic Knowledge*. Oxford University Press.

Mudrik, L., Breska, A., Lamy, D., & Deouell, L. (2011). "Integration without Awareness: Expanding the Limits of Unconscious Processing." *Psychological Science, 22*(6), 764–70.

Munton, J. (forthcoming). "Visual Confidences and Direct Perceptual Justification." *Philosophical Topics* 44 (2).

Munton, J. (ms.). *On Believing Our Eyes*. Doctoral dissertation, Yale University.

Murdoch, I. (1997). *Existentialists and Mystics: Writings on Philosophy and Literature*, ed. Conradi, P. Penguin.

Nickel, B. (2016). *Between Logic and the World: An Integrated Theory of Generics*. Oxford University Press.

Nosek, B., Smyth, F., Hansen, J., Devos, T., Lindner, N., Ratliff, K., Smith, C., Olson, K., Chugh, D., Greenwald, A., and Banaji, M. (2007). "Pervasiveness and Correlates of Implicit Attitudes and Stereotypes." *European Review of Social Psychology* 18: 36–88.

Olkkonen, M., Hansen, T., and Gegenfurtner, K. R. (2008). "Colour Appearance of Familiar Objects: Effects of Object Shape, Texture and Illumination Changes." *Journal of Vision* 8 (5): 13, 1–16.

Pagondiotis, C. (2015). "Cognitive (Im)Penetrebility of Vision: Restriction Vision versus Restricting Cognition." In Zeimbekis, J. and Raftopoulos, A., eds. (2015), 378–404.

Pascal, B. [1670] (1966). *Pensées*. Trans. Krailsheimer, A. J. Penguin.

Pautz, A. (2010). "Do Theories of Consciousness Rest on a Mistake?" *Philosophical Issues* 20 (1): 333–67.

Payne, B. K. (2001). "Prejudice and Perception: The Role of Automatic and Controlled Processes in Misperceiving a Weapon." *Journal of Personality and Social Psychology* 81 (2): 181–92.

Payne, B. K. (2006). "Weapon Bias: Split-Second Decisions and Unintended Stereotyping." *Current Directions in Psychological Science* 15 (6): 287–91.

Payne, B. K. (2008). "What Mistakes Disclose: A Process Dissociation Approach to Automatic and Controlled Processes in Social Psychology." *Social and Personality Psychology Compass* 2 (2): 1073–92.

Peacocke, C. (1995). *A Study of Concepts*. MIT Press.

Peacocke, C. (2004). *The Realm of Reason*. Oxford University Press.

Phillips, I. (2015). "Consciousness and Criterion: On Block's Case for Unconscious Seeing." *Philosophy and Phenomenological Research* 92 (3).

Phillips, I. and Block, N. (2016). "Debate on Unconscious Perception" in *Current Controversies in Philosophy of Perception*. Ed. B. Nanay. Routledge.

Pinto-Correia, C. (1997). *The Ovary of Eve*. University of Chicago Press.

Pitcher, G. (1971). *A Theory of Perception*. Princeton University Press.

Plant, E. A. and Peruche, B. M. (2005). "The Consequences of Race for Police Officers' Responses to Criminal Suspects." *Psychological Science* 16 (3): 180–3.

Pollak, S. D. and Sinha, P. (2002). "Effects of Early Experience on Children's Recognition of Facial Displays of Emotion." *Developmental Psychology* 38 (5): 784–91.

Pollock, J. (1970). *Knowledge and Justification*. Princeton University Press.

Pollock, J. (1986). *Contemporary Theories of Knowledge*. Hutchinson.

Pollock, J. & Oved, I. (2005). "Vision, Knowledge, and the Mystery Link." *Noûs* 39 (1): 309–51.

Price, H. H. (1932). *Perception*. Methuen and Co.

Proffitt, D. R., Stefanucci, J., Banton, T., & Epstein, W. (2003). "The Role of Effort in Perceiving Distance." *Psychological Science* 14 (2): 106–12.

Pryor, J. (2000). "The Skeptic and the Dogmatist." *Noûs* 34 (4): 517–49.

Pylyshyn, Z. (1999). "Is Vision Continuous with Cognition? The Case for Cognitive Impenetrability of Visual Perception." *Behavioral and Brain Sciences* 22 (3): 341–423.

Quine, W.V.O. (1951). "Two Dogmas of Empiricism." *Philosophical Review* 60 (1): 20–43.

Quine, W.V.O. (1960). *Word and Object*. MIT Press.

Rahimian, S. (ms.). "Epistemic Reasons for Action."

Railton, P. (2012). "That Obscure Object, Desire." *Proceedings and Addresses of the American Philosophical Association* 86 (2): 22–46.

Railton, P. (2013). "Reliance, Trust, and Belief." *Inquiry* 57 (1): 122–50.

Railton, P. (2014). "The Affective Dog and Its Rational Tale: Intuition and Attunement." *Ethics* 124 (4): 813–59.

Rescorla, M. (2015). "Bayesian Perceptual Psychology." In Matthen, M., ed., *The Oxford Handbook of the Philosophy of Perception*, 694–716. Oxford University Press.

Richard, M. (forthcoming). "On Inference." In M. Balcerak-Jackson and B. Balcerak-Jackson, eds., *Reasoning: Essays on Theoretical and Practical Thinking*. Oxford University Press.

Rinard, S. (forthcoming). "No Exception for Belief." *Philosophy and Phenomenological Research*. Published online 7 Sep. 2015.

Rock, I. (1975). *An Introduction to Perception*. Macmillan.

Rowlands, M. (2006). *Body Language: Representation in Action*. MIT Press.

Russell, R. and Durgin, F. H. (2008). "Demand Characteristics, Not Effort: The Role of Backpacks in Judging Distance." *Journal of Vision* 8(6): 755a.

Sagar, H. A. and Schofield, J. W. (1980). "Racial and Behavioral Cues in Black and White Children's Perceptions of Ambiguously Aggressive Acts." *Journal of Personality and Social Psychology* 39 (4): 590–8.

Schellenberg, S. (2010). "The Particularity and Phenomenology of Perceptual Experience." *Philosophical Studies* 149 (1): 19–48.

Schnall, S., Harber, K. D., Stefanucci, J., and Proffitt, D. R. (2008). "Social Support and the Perception of Geographical Slant." *Journal of Experimental Social Psychology* 44 (5): 1246–55.

Sellars, W. (1956). "Empiricism and the Philosophy of Mind." *Minnesota Studies in the Philosophy of Science* 1: 253–329.

Setiya, K. (2012). *Knowing Right From Wrong*. Oxford University Press.

Shelby, T. (2003). "Ideology, Racism, and Critical Social Theory." *Philosophical Forum* 34: 153–88.

Sider, T. (2012). *Writing the Book of the Word*. Oxford University Press.

Siegel, S. (2010). *The Contents of Visual Experience*. Oxford University Press.

Siegel, S. (2013a). "The Epistemic Impact of the Etiology of Experience." *Philosophical Studies* 162 (3): 697–722.

Siegel, S. (2013b). "Reply to Fumerton, Huemer, and McGrath." *Philosophical Studies* 162 (3): 749–57.

Siegel, S. (2013c). "Can Selection Effects on Experience Influence its Rational Role?" In Gender, T. S. and Hawthorne, J., eds., *Oxford Studies in Epistemology*, vol. 4, 240–70. Oxford University Press.

Siegel, S. (2015). "Epistemic Evaluability and Perceptual Farce." In Zeimbekis, J. and Raftopoulos, A., eds. (2015), 405–24.

Siegel, S. (2016). "Rich or Thin?" In Nanay, B., ed., *Current Controversies in Philosophy of Perception*. Routledge.

Siegel, S. and Silins, N. (2014). "Consciousness, Attention, and Justification." In Dodd, D. and Zardini, E., eds., *Scepticism and Perceptual Justification*, 149–69. Oxford University Press.

Siegel, S. and Silins, N. (2015). "The Epistemology of Perception." In Matthen, M. ed., *The Oxford Handbook of Philosophy of Perception*, 781–811. Oxford University Press.

Silins, N. (2008). "Basic Justification and the Moorean Response to the Skeptic." In Gendler, T. S. and Hawthorne, J. (eds.), *Oxford Studies in Epistemology*, vol. 2. Oxford University Press.

Silins, N. (2011). "Seeing through the 'Veil of Perception.'" *Mind* 120 (478): 329–67.

Silva Jr., P. (2013). "How to Be Conservative: A Partial Defense of Epistemic Conservatism." *Australasian Journal of Philosophy* 91 (3): 501–14.

Sklar, L. (1975). "Methodological Conservatism." *Philosophical Review* 84 (3): 374–400.

Smith, A. (2005). "Responsibility for Attitudes: Activity and Passivity in Mental Life." *Ethics* 115 (2): 236–71.

Smith, A. (ms.). "Implicit Bias, Moral Agency, and Moral Responsibility."

Smith, A. D. (2001). "Perception and Belief." *Philosophy and Phenomenological Research* 62 (2): 283–309.

Smith, A. D. (2002). *The Problem of Perception*. Harvard University Press.

Smith, E. and Harper, S. (2016). "Disproportionate Impact of K-12 School Suspension and Expulsion on Black Students in Southern States." https://www.gse.upenn.edu/equity/sites/gse.upenn.edu.equity/files/publications/Smith_Harper_Report.pdf (accessed September 25, 2016).

Smithies, D. (2014). "The Phenomenal Basis of Epistemic Justification." In Kallestrup, J. and Sprevak, M., eds., *New Waves in Philosophy of Mind*, 98–124. Palgrave MacMillan.

Smithies, D. (2015). "Why Justification Matters." In Henderson, D. & Greco, J., eds., *Epistemic Evaluation: Point and Purpose in Epistemology*, 224–44. Oxford University Press.

Smithies, D. (2016). "Perception and the External World." *Philosophical Studies* 173 (4): 1119–45.

Sosa, E. (2007). *A Virtue Epistemology: Apt Belief and Reflective Knowledge, Volume I*. Oxford University Press.

Stanton, E. C. and Anthony, S. B. [1848] (1881). "Declaration of Sentiments." In *History of Woman Suffrage*, ed. Stanton, E. C., Anthony, S. B., and Gage, M. J., vol. 1, 70–1. Fowler and Wells.

Steele, C. (2011). *Whistling Vivaldi: And Other Clues to How Stereotypes Affect Us*. Norton.

Stefanucci, J. K. and Proffitt, D. R. (2009). "The Roles of Altitude and Fear in the Perception of Height." *Journal of Experimental Psychology, Human Perception & Performance* 35 (2): 424–38.

Steinpreis, R. E., Anders, K. A., and Ritzke, D. (1999). "The Impact of Gender on the Review of the Curricula Vitae of Job Applicants and Tenure Candidates: A National Empirical Study." *Sex Roles* 41 (7–8): 509–28.

Stokes, M. B. and Payne, B. K. (2010). "Mental Control and Visual Illusions: Errors of Action and Construal in Race-Based Weapon Misidentification." In Adams, R., Ambady, N., Nakayama, K., and Shimojo, S., eds. (2010), 295–305.

Stowe, H. B. [1852] (1981). *Uncle Tom's Cabin*. Penguin.

Sylvan, K. (2015). "What Apparent Reasons Appear to Be." *Philosophical Studies* 172 (3): 587–606.

Sylvan, K. (ms.). "On Divorcing the Rational from the Justified in Epistemology."

Tamir, D. and Mitchell, J. (2013). "Anchoring and Adjustment during Social Inferences." *Journal of Experimental Psychology: General* 142 (1): 151–62.

Teachman, B. A., Stefanucci, J. K., Clerkin, E. M., Cody, M. W., and Proffitt, D. R. (2008). "A New Mode of Fear Expression: Perceptual Bias in Height Fear." *Emotion* 8 (2): 296–301.

Teng, L. (forthcoming). "Cognitive Penetration, Imagination, and the Downgrade Thesis." *Philosophical Topics* 44 (2).

Teng, L. (ms.). "Cognitive Penetration, Inferentialism, and Bayesian Perception."

Teng, L. (2016). *Cognitive Penetrability and the Epistemological Significance of Etiology*. Doctoral dissertation, Cornell University.

Travis, C. (2013a). "Susanna Siegel, *The Contents of Visual Experience*." *Philosophical Studies* 163 (3): 837–46.

Travis, C. (2013b). *Perception: Essays after Frege*. Oxford University Press.

Triesch, J., Ballard, D., Hayhoe, M., and Sullivan, B. (2003). "What You See Is What You Need." *Journal of Vision* 3 (1): 86–94.

Tucker, C. (2010a). "When Transmission Fails." *Philosophical Review* 119 (4): 497–529.

Tucker, C. (2010b). "Why Open-Minded People Should Endorse Dogmatism." *Philosophical Perspectives* 24 (1): 529–45.

Tucker, C. (2011). "Phenomenal Conservatism and Evidentialism in Religious Epistemology." In Clark, K. J. and VanArragon, R. J., eds., *Evidence and Religious Belief*, 52–73. Oxford University Press.

Tucker, C. (2012). "Movin' On Up: Higher-Level Requirements and Inferential Justification." *Philosophical Studies* 157 (3): 323–40.

Tucker, C. (2013). "Seemings and Justification: An Introduction." In Tucker, C., ed., *Seemings and Justification: New Essays on Dogmatism and Phenomenal Conservatism*, 1–29. Oxford University Press.

Turri, J. (2010). "On the Relationship between Propositional and Doxastic Justification." *Philosophy and Phenomenological Research* 80 (2): 312–26.

Vahid, H. (2014). "Cognitive Penetration, the Downgrade Principle, and Extended Cognition." *Philosophical Issues* 24 (1): 439–59.

Vance, J. (2014). "Emotion and the New Epistemic Challenge from Cognitive Penetrability." *Philosophical Studies* 169 (2): 257–83.

Vance, J. (2015). "Cognitive Penetration and the Tribunal of Experience." *Review of Psychology and Philosophy* 6 (4): 641–63.

Vance, J. (forthcoming). "Phenomenal Commitments: A Puzzle for Experiential Theories of Emotion." In Teroni, F., and Naar, H., eds., The Ontology of Emotion. Cambridge University Press.

Vogel, J. (2000). "Reliabilism Leveled." *Journal of Philosophy* 97 (11): 602–23.

Watzl, S. (2017). *Structuring Mind: The Nature of Attention and How it Shapes Consciousness*. Oxford University Press.

Weber, M. [1918] (1946). "Politics as a Vocation." In Gerth, H. H. and Mills, C. W., ed and trans., *From Max Weber: Essays on Sociology*. Oxford University Press.

Williamson, T. (2000). *Knowledge and its Limits*. Oxford University Press.

Witt, J. K. and Proffitt, D. R. (2005). "See the Ball, Hit the Ball." *Psychological Science* 16 (12): 937–8.

Witt, J. K., Proffitt, D. R., and Epstein, W. (2005). "Tool Use Affects Perceived Distance, But Only When You Intend to Use It." *Journal of Experimental Psychology: Human Perception and Performance* 31 (5): 880–8.

Witzel, C., Valkova, H., Hansen, T., and Gegenfurtner, K. R. (2011). "Object Knowledge Modulates Colour Appearance." *iPerception* 2 (1): 13–49.

Wright, C. (1991). "Skepticism and Dreaming: Imploding the Demon." *Mind* 100 (397): 87–115.

Wright, C. (2004). "Warrant for Nothing (and Foundations for Free)?" *Aristotelian Society Supplementary Volume* 78 (1): 167–212.

Wright, C. (2007). "The Perils of Dogmatism." In Nucatelli, S. and Seay, G., eds., *Themes from G. E. Moore: New Essays in Epistemology and Ethics*, 25–48. Oxford University Press.

Wright, C. (2014). "Comment on Paul Boghossian, 'What is Inference.'" *Philosophical Studies* 169 (1): 1–11.

Yancy, G. (2008). "Elevators, Social Spaces, and Racism: A Philosophical Analysis." *Philosophy & Social Criticism* 34 (8): 843–76.

Yang, E., Zald, D., and Blake, R. (2007). "Fearful Expressions Gain Preferential Access to Awareness during Continuous Flash Suppression." *Emotion*, 7, 882–6.

Zagzebski, L. (2009). *On Epistemology*. Wadsworth.

Zeimbekis, J. (2013). "Color and Cognitive Penetrability." *Philosophical Studies* 165 (1): 167–75.

Zeimbekis, J. (2015). "Seeing, Visualizing, Believing: Pictures and Cognitive Penetration." In Zeimbekis, J. and Raftopoulos, A., eds. (2015), 298–328.

Zeimbekis, J. and Raftopoulos, A., eds. (2015). *The Cognitive Penetrability of Perception: New Philosophical Perspectives*. Oxford University Press.

Index of Names

Index of Subjects

Index of Examples